Issues in Business Ethics

Volume 49

The Issues in Business Ethics series aims to showcase the work of scholars who critically assess the state of contemporary business ethics theory and practice by means of rigorous philosophical analyses and/ or normative evaluation. The series wants to be an outlet for authors who bring the wealth of philosophical literature to bear on contemporary issues in the global business ethics realm.The series especially welcomes work that addresses the interrelations between the agent, organization and society, thus exploiting the differences and connections between the micro, meso and macro levels of moral and political analysis. The series aims to establish and further the conversation between scholars, experts and practitioners who do not typically have the benefit of each others' company and as such, it welcomes contributions from various philosophical paradigms, and from a wide array of scholars who are active within in the international business context. Its audience includes scholars and practitioners, as well as senior students, and its subject matter will be relevant to various sectors that have an interest and stake in international business ethics. The scope of the series is therefore broad, but preference will be given to studies that draw on a thorough literature review and other theoretical methodologies, rather than empirical work. Authors from all continents are welcome to submit proposals, though the series does seek to encourage a global discourse of a critical and normative nature. The series insists on rigor from a scholarly perspective, but authors are encouraged to write in a style accessible to a broader audience and to seek out subject matter of practical relevance.

More information about this series at http://www.springer.com/series/6077

Rosa Slegers

Adam Smith's Moral Sentiments in Vanity Fair

Lessons in Business Ethics from Becky Sharp

Springer

Rosa Slegers
Babson College
Wellesley, MA, USA

ISSN 0925-6733 ISSN 2215-1680 (electronic)
Issues in Business Ethics
ISBN 978-3-030-07525-5 ISBN 978-3-319-98731-6 (eBook)
https://doi.org/10.1007/978-3-319-98731-6

Softcover re-print of the Hardcover 1st edition 2018

This Springer imprint is published by the registered company Springer Nature Switzerland AG
The registered company address is: Gewerbestrasse 11, 6330 Cham, Switzerland

Contents

Chapter 1
Introduction

Abstract This introduction offers an outline of Adam Smith's thoughts on vanity and sets up a framework for the literary case study at the heart of this book. Smith holds that our desire to obtain the regard of others often encourages us to fixate on wealth, power and status. Because of this preoccupation with the way others see us, the relationships that most interest Smith in his *Theory of Moral Sentiments* are essentially theatrical: those between spectator and actor. Smith invites us to regard our own behavior the way we would regard the behavior of others and to become our own spectators. One way in which we can acquire more experience as a spectator is through literature. As readers of novels we learn to see through the eyes of (imagined) others and are in a position to develop our moral imagination. The fictional 19th Century heroines central to this book share Smith's interest in spectatorship and offer a decidedly female perspective that helps to both complement and critique Smith's theory of vanity in TMS.

Adam Smith: Not a Whining and Melancholy Moralist

Adam Smith believes that it is natural for us to be happy when we are doing well economically. He is irritated by authors who blame us for experiencing what Smith calls "the natural joy of our prosperity" (TMS 168). These "whining and melancholy moralists" are apt to emphasize the pain of distant others and hold that we have no right to be happy while there is so much suffering in the world.[1] Smith rejects the "artificial commiseration" these moralists propose as both absurd and "altogether unattainable." The "affected and sentimental sadness" that marks the writings of whining moralists makes them disagreeable and renders their theories

[1] The editors of TMS suggest that Smith is referring to Pascal's *Pensées* and James Thomson's *The Seasons*, "Winter:" "Ah! little think the gay licentious proud / Whom pleasure, power, and affluence surround— / They, who their thoughtless hours in giddy mirth, / And wanton, often cruel, riot waste— / Ah! little think they, while they dance along, / How many feel, this very moment, death/ And all the sad variety of pain" (Cited in TMS, 379). James Thomson was a popular eighteenth century playwright and poet-moralist. He will make another appearance in Chap. 2 in the context of eighteenth century conduct literature.

R. Slegers, *Adam Smith's Moral Sentiments in Vanity Fair*, Issues in Business Ethics 49, https://doi.org/10.1007/978-3-319-98731-6_1

"perfectly useless." Ethical theories that would have us feel guilty about our own happiness are artificial because "Nature" has "wisely ordered" it so that we do not feel much for people "remote from us" (TMS 168) – our sympathy is first and foremost extended to ourselves and the ones near and dear to us.

Smith's dig at whining and melancholy moralists is appealing not only to those who relish philosophical squabbles. Writing in the second half of the eighteenth century, Smith puts into words an objection to business ethics not uncommon today: ethical theory, as commonly understood, puts a damper on business pursuits. This is not Smith's perspective, however. He takes issue with the moralists described above not because they apply moral judgments to economic phenomena but because they do so incorrectly. They disregard the complexity of moral sentiments and the role they play in both our personal and public lives. Smith's appeal to twenty-first century people interested in business ethics lies exactly in this complexity: instead of a cut and dry theory neatly separating right from wrong, Smith's *Theory of Moral Sentiments* seeks to do justice to our experience of a morally messy world full of imperfect actors often at odds with both each other and themselves. Smith recognizes the tension between our desire to better our condition and the sympathy we should - and often do - feel for others standing in the way of this desire. The theories proposed by the whining moralists are "perfectly useless" both because they presuppose a simplified version of the world we live in and because they go against our natural sentiments. Even so, Smith agrees that we often have too little fellow feeling and that "the favour which we bear to prosperity is rather apt to be too great" (TMS 168). Yet the solution does not lie in sentimental and unsustainable self-denial. Rather than blaming us for our excessive worship of the "fortunate, the powerful and the great" and our contempt for the poor, Smith proposes to study these tendencies in detail. This descriptive, down to earth approach is one of the reasons why it serves to read Smith today: his acute observations about our flawed moral psychology and the character traits and emotions underlying our behavior together constitute a moral perspective that places us right in the thick of lived experience.

Smith is an applied philosopher *avant la lettre* and his *Theory of Moral Sentiments* is concerned with themes that preoccupy people interested in business ethics today. Smith's notion of vanity is at the heart of this book and though it has the ring of an old fashioned vice, one of the goals of the following chapters will be to show that vanity is a driving force behind many of our personal and economic pursuits. One of the ideas underpinning the analysis offered in this work is that vanity is an interesting vice in part *because* it is minor. Smith is one of the few authors in the Western philosophical tradition to write about it extensively and to argue that though there are much worse character traits, vanity plays a major role in both our personal lives and society at large.[2] Furthermore, vanity is not an altogether unwelcome character

[2] Other authors paid less attention to vanity and did not regard it as a particularly dangerous (or interesting) vice. Benjamin Franklin notes that "Vanity is often productive of good to the possessor, and to others that are within his sphere of action" (Franklin 2005, 8). David Hume, Smith's friend and correspondent, considered vanity a mere "social passion" without much "pernicious consequence" (Hume 1978, 491). Apart from the scholarship on Smith's treatment of the topic,

trait. As we will see, vain people can make for pleasant company and may make great flatters. But more importantly, vanity contains a promise: the vain person is much more likely than the person with low self-esteem to accomplish great things. Twentieth and twenty-first century studies about the (economically) advantageous side-effects of overconfidence and narcissism suggest something similar to what Smith observed in the eighteenth century: character traits that register as problematic from a moral perspective may make one more likely to succeed in business, politics and other public pursuits.[3] This is yet another way in which Smith distinguishes himself and his theory from more ideological strands of thought: he recognizes ambiguities in our moral landscape and is unafraid to discuss the resulting tensions in our motivations and behaviors, even when a straightforward resolution appears unattainable. Central to Smith's TMS is the idea that our moral sentiments and the actions and judgments they inspire are pulling us in different directions.

Reading Smith is refreshing because he does not attempt to resolve the many ambiguities of our moral situation. He does, however, offer many insights that help us look critically at moral character and its implications for our personal and professional lives. Smith's TMS is a tapestry of anecdotes, observations and examples – so much so that it at times reads more like a work of literature than a traditional work of philosophy. This book picks up on Smith's own literary inclinations and draws on a number of nineteenth century novels to offer a critical reading of Smith's thoughts on vanity and its related traits. First among these novels is William Makepeace Thackeray's *Vanity Fair: A Novel Without a Hero,* featuring the fearless Becky Sharp (not a hero, though perhaps a heroine), who understands the workings of vanity and uses her insights to exploit it in everyone she meets. Drawing on the cultural trope of society as a Vanity Fair, the chapters comprising this volume explore Smith's notion of vanity with the help of a literary sisterhood drawn from the novels of Austen, Thackeray, Brontë and Eliot.[4] By bringing Smith into conversation with nineteenth century literature, this book also seeks to do justice to the evocative and

---

vanity as a subject of philosophical study has not received a lot of attention recently. A late twentieth century exception is the excellent short article simply called "Vanity" by A.T. Nuyen in which he discusses the importance of vanity in the context of the rising interest in virtue ethics at the time. Nuyen does not mention Smith but offers an interesting overview of traits close to and overlapping with vanity. He uses *Vanity Fair's* Joseph Sedley as his "paradigm" of vanity and argues that he is what Immanuel Kant calls a "snob" (Nuyen 618).

[3] Sigmund Freud comments on the link between narcissism and leadership in his 1931 essay "Libidinal Types." Narcissists tend to attract admiration and attention and often emerge as leaders because of their highly active and confident attitudes (Freud 1950). Smith does not mention "narcissism" (a term coined long after Smith's death) but writes at length about the character traits commonly linked to it and central to this book (vanity, ambition, pride, self-esteem, etc.). For contemporary studies examining the (dis)advantages of narcissistic leadership see Brunell et al. (2008) and Lubit (2002). For an overview of the closely related notion of hubristic leadership see Sadler-Smith et al. (2017).

[4] For an analysis of the history of the Vanity Fair trope from Bunyan's *The Pilgrim's Progress* to the 21st Century, see Kirsty Milne, *At Vanity Fair. From Bunyan to Thackeray.* Her aim is to recover the origins of a cultural trope and explain how VF developed from a dystopian puritan fantasy into an image for modernity and modern consumerism (Milne 2015).

even poetic nature of TMS. Smith not only writes about sympathy but triggers fellow feeling in his readers through his style and examples. Form and content are interwoven in TMS and this book continues this interweaving by introducing characters from a genre that would only come into itself after Smith's death. Smith shares with the female protagonists featured in this volume an astuteness of observation that makes large parts of TMS as relevant today as are the timeless novels that inspire the reading of Smith's work proposed here.

Due to its hybrid nature, this book will be of interest to an interdisciplinary audience of people with an interest in nineteenth century English literature and business ethics broadly construed. An overarching theme of this book is the power of narrative to enrich and deepen our understanding of philosophy and to disclose parts of experience in a fresh way (cf. Gosling and Villiers 2013). The story and character of Becky Sharp as described in Thackeray's *Vanity Fair* serves as a literary case study which will appeal to those interested in vanity in its many permutations, be it in our business or personal lives.[5] Adding to the appeal of the dialogue between Smith and the nineteenth century English novel is the wit common to both parties of the conversation. From Thackeray's acerbic humor to Austen's subtle sense of irony to Smith's often unexpected sarcastic asides, the various styles of the authors informing the story told in this book help reveal the absurd and even ridiculous aspects of life in Vanity Fair, today as in the past.[6] The sense of humor inherent in the philosophical and literary works discussed here not only makes these texts agreeable (as opposed to the theories proposed by the whining moralists), it also makes them decidedly modern. Form and content work together to help us understand the role of vanity in the most frivolous and the darkest aspects of our lives alike.

Preliminary Notes on Vanity and Spectatorship

The moralists Smith derides are whiny because they are sentimental. Sentimentality, a morally deplorable and "affected" attitude, is in stark opposition to sympathy, the virtue central to Smith's *Theory of Moral Sentiments*. Sentimental people do not experience sympathy the way they should, that is to say, towards the right people, in the right way, and under the right circumstances. Rather, they are apt to exaggerate like the whining moralists who tell us to feel bad about our own joy when distant others are suffering. Instead of adopting the unnatural rules and principles set forth by these moralists, we should cultivate our minds to learn how to judge and how to

[5] See the Introduction to *Good Novels*, Better *Management* for a compelling account of the role of novels in the case study tradition. Czarniawska-Joerges and Guillet de Monthoux even refer to nineteenth century novelists in particular, comparing them to today's business case writers (Czarniawska-Joerges and Guillet de Monthoux 1994).

[6] Czarniawska-Joerges and Guillet de Monthoux observe: "Fiction offers at least two methods of rebellion unauthorized within the traditional research: irony and wit"(Czarniawska-Joerges and Guillet de Monthoux 1994, 11–12).

feel. This requires training of the moral imagination (Griswold 212). Over time, we accumulate the experience necessary for our moral education and learn to regard the emotions as essential parts of our selves and necessary ingredients to our moral decision making processes. When we fall prey to sentimentality, we have lost sight of the propriety and proportion of our emotions.

Yet how can we distinguish between sentimentality and proper sentiments? We can easily conceive of situations in which the melancholy moralists are justified in judging us for being preoccupied with our own well-being while others suffer. Elsewhere in TMS, Smith mocks the "man of humanity" who is more concerned about losing his little finger than he is about "the great empire of China" being "swallowed up by an earthquake" (TMS 166). This man has lost all sense of proportion and Smith paints him as both ridiculous and lacking in moral judgment. But how does Smith propose to strike a balance between our preoccupation with our own well-being and what he calls our fellow feeling with others near and far? There are no hard and fast rules the way the whining moralists would have it. All we have, according to Smith, are experience and habit, and the goal of moral education is to develop in us a particular kind of impartiality that allows us to correctly judge others and ourselves. Over time, we come to identify with what Smith calls "the impartial spectator," an entity representing an imagined third person perspective on the situation or action at hand. This process of identification is quite natural: from a young age, we feel the need for approval from those around us. Even as children we learn to look at ourselves through the eyes of others. Over time, and with much practice, we acquire moral judgment as we develop our capacity to regard ourselves as it were from a distance. For this reason, the relationships that most interest Smith in his *Theory of Moral Sentiments* are essentially theatrical: those between spectator and actor (Griswold, Marshall, Barish). Smith invites us to regard our own behavior the way we would regard the behavior of others and so become our own spectators.

Ideally, we learn to distance ourselves from our own passions and biases enough to judge our own behavior as impartially as we might the behavior of anyone else. In doing so we will achieve a "harmony of sentiments" with the people around us, a state which, according to Smith, has an inherent beauty (TMS 70, 75). But though we are naturally drawn to this state of harmony with others, we rarely achieve it. Because we realize that others are looking at us and judging us, we are concerned with how we come across and are tempted to play a role that we hope will make others sympathize with us. Preoccupied with gaining praise, we fixate on wealth, power, and status. As Smith observes, "The vain man sees the respect which is paid to rank and fortune, and wishes to usurp this respect, as well as that for talents and virtues" (TMS 261). What matters most to the vain man is esteem, and he is willing to lie and pretend in order to get it. Even if he is not in fact rich, nor virtuous, he wants you to think that he is so you will respect him accordingly. "His dress, his equipage, his way of living, accordingly, all announce both a higher rank and a greater fortune than really belong to him." This "foolish imposition" means many a young person's ruination as people will go to great expense to gain respect. "As long as he can continue his expence, however, his vanity is delighted with viewing himself, *not in the light in which you would view him if you knew all that he knows*; but in that in which, he imagines, he has, by his own address, induced you actually to view him. Of all the illusions of vanity this is, perhaps, the most common" (TMS 261, emphasis added). The vain person takes advantage of the fact that his spectator does not know "all that he knows." He plays a part, stages a performance, and delights in the effect it has on his spectators – even if, deep down, he knows that he is not truly worthy of the praise he receives.

Smith argues that the best way to resist the temptation to put on a show is to regard ourselves through the eyes of an impartial spectator, someone who is willing to sympathetically enter into our situation but who is not inclined to go along with our excessive self-love (or, in rare cases, lack thereof). The vain person ignores the impartial spectator and is subject to self-delusion, incapable of judging situations impartially. Vanity at its most extreme, when the desire for praise eclipses our capacity for impartial judgment, results in fanaticism and a lust to enslave others – a theme central to Chaps. 4 and 8 in this volume. And yet, vanity would not exist if it were not for our capacity for sympathy. It is because we want to be loved, and to feel love for others in return, that we value praise and like to bestow it on others as well. The desire for the harmony of feelings that results from mutual sympathy makes us vulnerable to vanity. Conversely, we can regard vanity as "sympathy gone wrong" and try to correct it, recognizing that underlying our vain behavior is the desire to be acknowledged, heeded, and sympathized with. This is one of the great insights presented in TMS, and much of this book is devoted to a proper understanding of this part of Smith's theory.

Smith and the Heroines of Romance

Given the importance Smith assigns to the role of the spectator in our moral lives, it is not surprising that he draws heavily on historical accounts and narrative fiction for examples. As readers of novels and history books and as spectators of plays, we are in a position to enrich our moral imagination and learn to see through the eyes of (imagined) others.[7] Furthermore, our experience as readers of books and spectators of plays bears out Smith's criticism of the moralists from the previous section:

> When we read in history or romance, the account of actions either of generosity or of baseness, the admiration which we conceive for the one, and the contempt which we feel for the other, neither of them arise from reflecting that there are certain general rules which declare all actions of the one kind admirable, and all actions of the other contemptible. (TMS 183)

[7] Marshall (1984) observes: "It is no coincidence that Smith illustrates a discussion of how we enter into the sentiments and actions of others with a description of reading: whether we are confronted with a person or a text, we must face a fiction. We must imagine that we are persons who, in reality, can be only representations to us; through imagination we transport ourselves to a distant place, try to place ourselves in someone else's situation. We take their part by trying to play their part" (Marshall 1984, 595).

General rules do not come ready-made but flow from our experience and are established over time. Our moral judgments are formed as it were organically and are not the result of the simple application of abstract rules to concrete situations, fictional or otherwise. General rules emerge from our natural responses to particular scenarios, not the other way round. Moral education aims to guide these natural responses so they will not run amuck - as they are apt to do when we are not taught to regard our behaviors and motivations with impartiality.

One way in which we can acquire more experience and develop our moral range is through literature. Throughout TMS, Smith is interested in the emotions of bystanders, those not directly involved in the action. The readers of a book or spectators of a play are therefore in an interesting moral position from Smith's point of view. The "heroes of tragedy and romance" and our reaction as readers/spectators to their plight play a crucial role in Smith's understanding of sympathy.[8] The following chapters will build on this interdisciplinary approach and bring Smith into conversation not with the heroes but the heroines of a number of nineteenth century English novels. Women are largely absent from Smith's work: their presence and work in the household is taken for granted but, on Smith's account, they rarely enter the public space and they do not take part in the economy. They are the unmentioned, unnoticed bystanders and spectators in Smith's work. The fictional nineteenth century heroines central to this book share Smith's interest in third party perspectives though for them this bystander point of view is decidedly female.

Jane Austen, who had clearly read Smith and even has one of the characters in *Pride and Prejudice* summarize part of TMS (Austen 2004, 13), is a master of observation and her novels abound with women who are keenly aware of what it means to be first and foremost a spectator, not an actor.[9] Jane Austen's heroines are subtle, insightful, intelligent and usually very proper and polite. Their integrity is important to them and when they compromise it they feel remorse and shame. They are keenly aware of the patriarchal system of which they are a part and though they rebel against it in their way, refusing to marry if not for love, they do not actively seek to "better their condition" in Smith's sense.[10] It is a different story for Becky Sharp, protagonist of Thackeray's *Vanity Fair*. Outwardly she shares many traits with Austen's heroines but Becky's explicit goal is to rise up in the world and claim the position that she feels is rightfully hers. She, too, is an experienced spectator, but the information she gathers from her observations serves first and foremost to make her a more effective actor in the double sense of the word: Becky is an active agent in both the personal and the public sphere and she is also a highly skilled actress.

---

[8]Among the plays that Smith particularly admired were Jean Racine's *Phèdre* (which allows us to "enter into" the feeling of remorse) and Voltaire's *Mahomet* (which shows the dangers of religious fanaticism) and *L'Orphelin de la Chine* (offering the spectator insights into ambition, love, and character). See TMS 83, 198, 238.

[9]The relevant passage from *Pride and Prejudice* will be discussed in Chap. 6.

[10]Austen's heroines do in fact usually end up marrying rich men of rank but not because they schemed and plotted to reach this goal. Their gain in social status is more of a happy side effect of true love - or at least the heroines themselves appear to regard it as such.

Becky Sharp is this book's main (anti-) heroine because of her double part as spectator and actor. Other fictional heroines will help develop and enrich aspects of the literary case study presented to us by *Vanity Fair* in general and Becky in particular. These heroines include Austen's Elizabeth Bennet (*Pride and Prejudice)* and Emma (*Emma*), Brontë's Jane Eyre (*Jane Eyre*), and Eliot's Dorothea Brook and Rosamond Vincy (*Middlemarch*). Lesser characters from the same novels also make an appearance, like Charlotte Lucas (*Pride and Prejudice*) who marries the ridiculous Mr. Collins and Laure (*Middlemarch*) who killed her husband because he bored her. Their combined narratives inform our reading of Smith's account of vanity in TMS. The value of this strategy is hence twofold: it builds on Smith's own appreciation of literature as a source of moral insight and it takes seriously his emphasis on spectatorship. Not only are the women we read about in nineteenth century English literature of necessity spectators in a male-dominated world, we, as readers, are spectators in turn.

Of course the nineteenth century novels listed above are full of interesting male characters as well, and they, like Becky Sharp, are both actors and spectators. Less constrained than the women around them they can move about freely and take on active roles in society if they feel so inclined. But they too are spectators, judges of behavior: their female counterparts are often forced to look at themselves through the eyes of the men looking at them.[11] Gentlewomen are forced to be passive, to sit about in drawing rooms engaging in quiet "female" pursuits, and to give a lot of thought to what is proper and how they might come across to a casual observer. Vanity has everything to do with the way we imagine others see us and women are thus in a position that would make them seem especially susceptible to this vice. Yet it is the male characters in the novels under consideration here who are consistently painted as the most vain. The opening sentences of Austen's *Persuasion* read as follows:

> Vanity was the beginning and the end of Sir Walter Elliot's character; vanity of person and of situation. He had been remarkably handsome in his youth; and, at fifty-four, was still a very fine man. Few women could think more of their personal appearance than he did, nor could the valet of any new made lord be more delighted with the place he held in society. He considered the blessing of beauty as inferior only to the blessing of a baronetcy; and the Sir Walter Elliot, who united these gifts, was the constant object of his warmest respect and devotion. (Austen, *Persuasion* 2)

Several themes illustrated in this passage will be central to this book. Vanity is a character trait, one that usually invites gentle mockery rather than righteous condemnation. Yet it can come to determine the whole of one's character as it does in the case of Sir Walter Elliot, and reading *Persuasion* we find that his vanity is so extreme that it warps his perspective on the world and his place in it. His vanity concerns both his personal beauty and his rank as a baronet; two characteristics that Sir Walter believes make one stand out and noticed in a positive way. Importantly, he is described as more preoccupied and pleased with his beauty than are most

[11] Mr. Darcy in *Pride and Prejudice* is a good example of this kind of male spectator. See in particular Austen 2004, 76.

women. In the novels considered in this volume, this will be a recurring trope: a man's vanity so great it is unparalleled even by women. As we will see, Smith regards vanity as an "effeminate" vice characteristic of a society gone soft with prosperity and luxury. This is another reason to bring Smith in conversation with the fictional heroines featured in this book: they, on the whole, will turn out to be far less effeminate (as Smith uses the term) than their male counterparts.

Together, the fictional heroines of the nineteenth century English novels discussed here form an affective community that helps to both supplement and critique Smith's theory of vanity in TMS. "Affective" because their affects and sentiments link them together, especially "negative" ones like resentment, scorn, contempt, shame, mortification, envy, and remorse. Becky Sharp is singled out as our main (anti-) heroine because she, more than any of her literary sisters, uses the vanity of others for her own gain. It is hard to imagine anyone further removed from the "whining melancholy moralists" mocked in Smith's TMS. Free not only of sentimentality but also of what she regards as (economically) unproductive sentiments like remorse and shame, Becky provides a case study to both test Smith's theory and help us understand Becky's appeal as a deeply ambiguous role model.

Calling a Vice by its Proper Name

Vanity does not seem to be a particularly lovable trait, nor a virtuous one. And yet Smith claims: "the great secret of education is to direct vanity to proper objects" (TMS 263). While Becky engages the vanity of others in order to direct it to her own ends, Smith believes that vanity is a malleable vice that with proper care can be turned into something more like a virtue. At the very least, vanity can be made to serve the greater good by inspiring ambition in the individual and order in society.[12] But how do vain people become (more) virtuous? What is the connection between vanity and ambition? What is the reach of sympathy and impartiality in Vanity Fair? And how does gender factor into an analysis of the role of vanity, traditionally construed as a "feminine" or at least an "effeminate" vice?

Thackeray's narrator observes that "the moral world … has perhaps no particular objection to vice, but an insuperable repugnance to hearing vice called by its proper name" (VF 812). Vanity is therefore often disguised as something else, as when Old Osborne believes himself to be a loving father, George Osborne thinks of himself as a gentleman and Pitt Crawley regards himself as a misunderstood political genius. In his *Theory of Moral Sentiments,* Smith shows a keen awareness of the many ways in which vanity factors into everyday life, the actions of "the great," and the workings of society and industry. Smith was committed to preserve both common experience and language in his discussion of ethics and as a result, his *Theory of Moral Sentiments* is almost entirely jargon-free and full of anecdotes and examples meant

[12] Smith's position was not unusual at the time. The similarity between his position and Bernard Mandeville's in *The Fable of the Bees* will be discussed in Chap. 5.

to bridge the gap between theoretical ethics and everyday moral experience.[13] He provides a detailed and multi-faceted description of moral spectatorship, engaging his readers' imagination with his many literary and real life examples (Griswold 85). Smith regards this approach as a conscious departure from philosophical tradition.

Smith remarks on the "propensity, which is natural to all men, but which philosophers in particular are apt to cultivate with a peculiar fondness, as the great means of displaying their ingenuity, the propensity to account for all appearances from as few principles as possible" (TMS 294). To arrive at a neat, coherent theory, philosophers tend to reduce a multitude of phenomena to a few abstract rules that, though aesthetically pleasing, fail to do justice to the complexity of lived experience. It is otherwise with the tragedies Smith admired: they engage the imagination with their thick and subtle narratives, evoking insights rather than explaining them.[14] *Vanity Fair,* with its many characters, tensions, and unresolved disputes, is even more "messy" than the tragedies referred to in TMS. It is satirical and sarcastic in its description of the ills of commercial society but rarely pedantic; when the narrator addresses his reader directly, he never claims to have a cure or solution for the events he is describing but rather passes judgment as an involved and jaded spectator aware of his own bias. The narrator of *Vanity Fair* describes himself as a puppeteer and calls himself "the Manager of the Performance,"[15] emphasizing as does Smith the theatrical nature of the public sphere, i.e., the "fair." He engages and addresses his readers, both male and female, never allowing them to forget that they, too, live in Vanity Fair.[16] As readers of *Vanity Fair* we are forced both to keep our distance and to be active, sympathetic interpreters at a level with the characters we encounter.[17] There are no reliable, static standards for moral judgment in *Vanity Fair*

[13] As Ryan Patrick Hanley points out, "When we consider virtue and vice in an abstract and general manner, the qualities by which they excite these several sentiments seem in great measure to disappear, and the sentiments themselves become less obvious and discernable" (Hanley 79).

[14] As Gosling and Villiers put it in their introduction to *Fictional Leaders*: "Fiction is … well suited to giving us a rounded view…. Writers of fiction are able to present the inner musings and unconscious drives of their characters, as if they were observed events. These are insights that we can never obtain through the surveys and personality typologies of social scientific method" (Gosling and Villiers 2013, 1).

[15] Lisa Jadwin points out that the narrator bears a distinct resemblance to Becky Sharp: "Both narrator and protagonist are seducers, shape-shifters, mimetists" (1992, 682).

[16] As Harriet Blodgett puts it: "The reader himself is a performer in the larger Vanity Fair of which the story gives but a sample; he must never be permitted smugly to distance himself from the tale" (1976, 213).

[17] Kate Flint's article "Women, Men and the Reading of Vanity Fair" argues that "the mode of reading which Thackeray most admires and wishes to promote is one which does not deny readerly pleasure, but which goes hand in hand with a capacity to stand back from too close, too emotional an involvement with fictional characters and situations" (262). Flint does not refer to Adam Smith but her description of Thackeray's preferred mode of reading shows the complementarity of the two authors on the issue of readership and spectatorship. Julia Bninski highlights another feature of Thackeray's writing that balances closeness and detachment. She argues that the narrator evokes "emotion without relying on represented sincerity … to guarantee the ethical status of emotional

and this makes the novel particularly suited as a complement to Smith's *Theory* in general and as a case study of vanity in particular.

Smith places subjective experience front and center and refuses to discuss moral phenomena from a supposedly "objective" point of view. He is convinced that to be an effective and praiseworthy moral agent, one needs to be engaged. This means that theoretical reason alone cannot constitute moral excellence (Griswold 202). To judge and evaluate moral behavior we need to sympathetically "enter into" the situation of the agent the way we would when watching a play or reading a novel. Sympathizing with the actors, on stage, in a novel, or in real life, we "go along with" their passions yet remain aware of the distance between us and the (fictional) personages under consideration. If we strike the right balance between sympathy and distance, regarding the actor's actions with the mix of detachment and fellow-feeling that Smith calls "impartiality," we are in a position to judge and act appropriately. In the following chapters, Thackeray's Fair serves as a messy, complicated situation we are invited to "bring home to ourselves" and to judge "impartially." At the center of the fair is Becky, the "assertive, upwardly mobile female consumer who sells herself as coolly as she sells her horses" (Milne 2015, 104).

Structure and Themes

Directly following this introduction is a profile of Becky Sharp meant to introduce the heroine of our literary case study and to anchor the conversation in the chapters to follow. To do justice to both VF's rich and complex narrative and Adam Smith's many voices in TMS,[18] the themes central to this book's argument are interwoven and crop up in different chapters and contexts so their various aspects can receive due attention.

First and foremost there is the theme of vanity. Becky understands vain people like no other in VF, and knows exactly who she needs to be and how she needs to appear in order to use other people's vanity to her advantage. Becky uses people's vanity to satisfy her ambition to move up in society. Vanity, according to Smith, is the reason why there exists a social hierarchy in the first place. It is a corruption of our natural desire for acknowledgment, esteem and approbation. We know from experience that status will get us approbation and this is why much of our behavior

identification or transference between text and reader" (121) When, for example, Osborne Senior learns of his son George's death, the narrator turns to address the reader directly and positions the reader and himself within "the same ethical space" as Osborne (121). Osborne Senior's pride will further discussed in Chap. 6.

[18]Vivienne Brown convincingly shows that WN has a mostly "uniform, detached, and didactic voice that carries the argument forward and brooks no opposition" while TMS has many voices. As a result, "In TMS truly moral outcomes are open; they are not rule-bound or obligatory, but are the result of an open process of debate between the moral agent and the impartial spectator, in which the final outcome is neither predetermined nor legislated upon by a theological determinism" (Brown 1992, 248).

is geared at moving up in the world or, as Smith calls it, "bettering our condition." Becky wants to better her condition and uses other people as means to this end. She is hardly a moral heroine, but then by the Manager's own admission VF is not a moral or a happy place, just a noisy one (VF 1). To understand the nature of vanity we need to understand the workings of sympathy, a sentiment almost entirely absent from VF. Vanity, for Smith, is sympathy gone wrong, and Chap. 3 therefore starts with an introduction to Smith's famous account of sympathy. Our capacity for sympathy is central to the development of a strong impartial spectator and so sympathy is also a central theme of Chap. 7 which discusses this entity and the dangers of partiality.

Second is Smith's understanding of status as a positional good, a theme central to Chap. 5. Our desire for sympathy easily devolves into vanity and in our vanity we seek "wealth, power, and preheminence." We value status for the respect (we think) it brings us but status can only exist in a hierarchy. In seeking status we of necessity strive to be above others and so for us to rise, others must fall. In contrast with the parts of Smith's legacy which emphasize the beneficial effects of the "invisible hand" and extoll the virtues of free-market capitalism, he laments what he regards as a near universal lust to dominate and enslave. Becky shares in what Smith pessimistically calls the "love of domination" (Lectures 179), the common drive to gain power over others even when it goes against our economic interests to do so. Becky realizes that praise is worthless if it is extended to everyone equally. Space is limited in the higher strata of society, which is exactly why she strives to occupy a position among the aristocracy. She recognizes that rank is sought after because it makes one visible, and only when one is visible can one have spectators. The prospect of visibility does not make Becky bashful, as would become a young woman of her lowly station. On the contrary, Becky enjoys nothing more than the "toil and bustle" over rank.

Smith pessimistically observes that virtue and wisdom, being less visible than wealth and rank, often go unnoticed. Ignoring a person's moral worth, we tend to judge him on his appearance. The rich person delights in his riches because he knows he deserves to be seen while the poor person has learned to regard poverty as in itself shameful. The solution enacted by Becky is to play whatever part will make her be noticed and regarded. Most often this means acting as if she has money when in fact she does not; other times she plays up her poverty to win the sympathy of rich gentlemen. Though money is almost always central to her motivations, it is not what drives her: most of all, Becky delights in working the complicated machinery of society. She wants to "better her condition," as Smith puts it, but it is the process itself that is most enjoyable to her. When at a certain point Becky has "won" and is eating off golden plates in the company of royal personages, she is bored.

Closely related to Smith's understanding of status as a positional good is the importance he assigns to order and hierarchy. Smith holds that order is inherently beneficial because it preserves peace, but he also believes it to be the result of the often unfounded admiration of the great described above. Class and rank are not based on merit but on chance of birth and fortune, but for all Smith's praise of virtue and wisdom as superior standards for judgment, he does not believe that we will ever move beyond a hierarchical system based on conspicuous wealth and power. Chapters 5 and 6 connect the order of society to the theme of ambition and Chaps. 4 and 8 explore Smith's pessimistic views on the universal desire to dominate over others.

Third are the themes of ambition and the gendered nature of Smith's ambitious subject. Becky's ambition is best defined in what for Smith are primarily masculine traits: Chap. 4 features her as a prime example of what he calls the "martial spirit" in contrast with the "effeminate" behavior of many of her male foils. Becky's ambition is a complex sentiment best understood in relation to her other character traits. While for Smith ambition is an extreme form of vanity, Becky does not appear vain according to the definition Smith provides. Her self-esteem, higher than the vain person's though perhaps not excessive, appears to rank her among the proud. Yet she lacks both the sincerity and the surliness that accompany pride according to Smith. Becky succeeds in her ambitious pursuits because of her iron self-command, enabling her to resist temptations and hide her anger until she finds a suitable opportunity to take revenge. This makes Becky dangerous – much like the "great conquerors" in history whose reputation today, Smith remarks, depends more on the success or failure of their pursuits than on their virtue. Ambition is the topic of Chap. 5 and the "martial spirit" essential to the successful pursuit of ambition is so much part of Becky's character that it factors into every chapter of this book. Chapter 6 links the martial spirit to self-command and also makes explicit the danger of ambitious people like Becky.

Outwardly Becky appears as the perfectly amiable, innocent and modest woman – at least when she so chooses. Becky's ambition is an undercurrent visible only to the people she has not ensnared with her mostly very convincing act. A fourth theme therefore is the performance, mimicry, and playacting required of ambitious women who, like Becky, want to better their condition while remaining (or becoming) part of "proper" society. Unlike other women in VF, Becky delights in her act both for its own sake as for the advantages it brings her. The necessity to play a role may be imposed on her by the contingencies of history and society, but rather than submitting to resentment she takes pleasure in her mastery of the part. Chapters 3 and 4 discuss the particular performance required of middle class women in the late 18th and early to mid nineteenth century. This discussion returns in Chap. 8, which describes Becky's downfall and the enmity between women.

A fifth theme is the effect of the four previous themes on moral judgment. Though Becky feels resentment and anger at people who thwart her, she never judges them morally. They are nuisances and obstacles to her project. She takes pleasure in the perfectly executed roles she plays both on and off stage and delights in learning new skills that allow her to better "work" the machinery of society. An actress by nature, she understands that the gaze of the spectator is everything. And yet for all the attention Becky pays to the way other people regard her, her internal spectator's judgments are nothing like Smith's. This raises questions about the gendered nature of Smith's "impartial judge" and these are addressed in Chaps. 7 and 8. The book concludes with an analysis of Becky as an uncomfortable, ambiguous role model for us who read about her – and sympathize with her – against the backdrop of our own Vanity Fair.

References

Austen, Jane. 2004. *Pride and Prejudice*. Oxford: Oxford University Press.

Barish, J. 1981. *The Antitheatrical prejudice*. Berkely: California UP.

Blodgett, Harriet. 1967. Necessary presence: The rhetoric of the narrator in vanity fair. *Nineteenth-Century Fiction* 22 (3): 211–223.

Bninski, Julia. 2011. *Vanity Fair's* ethic of readerly emotion. *Victorians Journal*: 118–128.

Brown, Vivienne. 1992. The dialogic experience of conscience: Adam smith and the voices of stoicism. *Eighteenth-Century Studies* 26 (2): 233–260.

Brunell, A.B., W.A. Gentry, W.K. Campbell, et al. 2008. Leader emergence: The case of the narcissistic leader. *Personality and Social Psychology Bulletin* 34 (12): 1663–1676.

Czarniawska-Joerges, B., and P. Guillet de Monthoux, eds. 1994. *Good Novels, better management: Reading organizational realities in fiction*. Switzerland: Harwood Academic Publishers.

Flint, Kate. 1996. Women, men and the reading of vanity fair. In *The practice and representation of reading in England*, ed. James Raven et al., 246–262. Cambridge: Cambridge UP.

Franklin, Benjamin. 2005. *Autobiography*. Philadelphia: Philadelphia UP.

Freud, Sigmund. 1950(1931). Libidial Types. In *The standard edition of the complete psychological works of Sigmund Freud*, ed. J. Strachey, vol. 21, 217–220. London: Hogarth.

Gosling, J., and P. Villiers, eds. 2013. *Fictional leaders: Heroes, villains and absent friends*. New York: Palgrave.

Griswold, Charles. 1999. *Adam Smith and the virtues of enlightenment*. Cambridge: Cambridge University Press.

Hanley, Ryan Patrick. 2011. *Adam Smith and the character of virtue*. Cambridge: Cambridge UP.

Hume, David. 1978. *A treatise of human nature*. Oxford: Oxford UP.

Jadwin, Lisa. 1992. The seductiveness of female duplicity in vanity fair. *Studies in English Literature, 1500–1900* 32 (4): 663–687.

Lubit, R. 2002. The long-term organizational impact of destructively narcissistic managers. *Academy of Management Executive* 16 (1): 127–138.

Milne, Kirsty. 2015. *At vanity fair: From Bunyan to Thackeray*. Cambridge: Cambridge UP.

Nuyen, A.T. 1999. Vanity. *The Southern Journal of Philosophy* 37: 613–627.

Sadler-Smith, Eugene, Vita Akstinaite, and Graham Robinson. 2017. Hubristic leadership: A review. *Leadership* 13 (5): 525–548.

Smith, Adam. 1982a. The theory of moral sentiments. In *Vol. I of the Glasgow Edition of the Works and Correspondence of Adam Smith*, ed. D.D. Raphael and A.L. Macfie. Indianapolis: Liberty Fund.

———. 1982b. Lectures on Jurisprudence. In *Vol. 5 of the Glasgow Edition of the Works and Correspondence of Adam Smith*, ed. R.L. Meek, D.D. Raphael, and P.G. Stein. Indianapolis: Liberty Fund.

Thackeray, William Makepeace. 1983. In *Vanity fair: A novel without a hero*, ed. John Sutherland. New York: Oxford UP.

Chapter 2
A Profile of Becky Sharp

Abstract The story of Becky Sharp is at the heart of the literary case study presented in this book. Becky's exploits are no mere fictional examples illustrating Smith's theory; rather, the complex and rich narrative of VF deepens our understanding of some parts of TMS while helping us question others. The profile of Becky offered here contains a first sketch of her character and anchors the conversation about the many vices, virtues, and moral sentiments in the chapters to follow. It also introduces the societal system within which Becky operates and her relationship to this system. Becky is well aware of the existence of social inequalities and she resents people for what she perceives as their unfair superiority over her. But she is not outraged by the existence of inequality as such; on the contrary, she welcomes it – just as long as she sees opportunities to be upwardly mobile. Her concerns and interests are egocentric through and through: Becky cares for herself and all her calculations are geared toward her own success. She does not empathize or feel solidarity with those who share her plight, be they fellow governesses, fellow wives, or fellow mothers. People are means, not ends in themselves (Nuyen does not discuss Becky Sharp but focuses on Jos Sedley as a "paradigm" of vanity and a snob. He refers to Kant's notion of snobbery to explain that the vain person values everything (including other people) as means to an end. Even when the vain person desires something that is inherently valuable (like a virtuous character trait), he or she values it not for its inherent worth but its instrumental nature (Nuyen, Vanity, The Southern Journal of Philosophy 37: 613–627, 1999)). Becky is undaunted in the face of uncertainty and takes risks when she expects high rewards; she has an eye for opportunity and reinvents herself whenever circumstances call for an innovative approach. She is, as the narrator of VF suggests, is a skilled and effective manager, using all tools at her disposal to realize her goals. Implicit in Becky's story is a sharp critique of the gender ideology that marks Thackeray's time (For a thorough analysis of Thackeray and early Victorian feminism, see Micael M. Clarke, *Thackeray and Women* Dekalb: Northern Illinois University Press, 1995). Elements of this ideology are introduced here and explored in later chapters.

The story of Becky Sharp is at the heart of the literary case study presented in this book. Becky's exploits are no mere fictional examples illustrating Smith's theory;

R. Slegers, *Adam Smith's Moral Sentiments in Vanity Fair*, Issues in Business Ethics 49, https://doi.org/10.1007/978-3-319-98731-6_2

rather, the complex and rich narrative of VF deepens our understanding of some parts of TMS while helping us question others. The profile of Becky offered here contains a first sketch of her character and anchors the conversation about the many vices, virtues, and moral sentiments in the chapters to follow. It also introduces the societal system within which Becky operates and her relationship to this system. Becky is well aware of the existence of social inequalities and she resents people for what she perceives as their unfair superiority over her. But she is not outraged by the existence of inequality as such; on the contrary, she welcomes it – just as long as she sees opportunities to be upwardly mobile. Her concerns and interests are egocentric through and through: Becky cares for herself and all her calculations are geared toward her own success. She does not empathize or feel solidarity with those who share her plight, be they fellow governesses, fellow wives, or fellow mothers. People are means, not ends in themselves.[1] Becky is undaunted in the face of uncertainty and takes risks when she expects high rewards; she has an eye for opportunity and reinvents herself whenever circumstances call for an innovative approach. She is, as the narrator of VF suggests, is a skilled and effective manager, using all tools at her disposal to realize her goals. Implicit in Becky's story is a sharp critique of the gender ideology that marks Thackeray's time.[2] Elements of this ideology are introduced here and explored in later chapters.

Wealth and Marriage

"People in Vanity Fair fasten on to rich folks quite naturally," the narrator and self-proclaimed "Manager of the Performance" states in *Vanity Fair.* "The notion of Wealth" is pleasant to even "the simplest people," he continues, and more so to "old worldlings" like Mr. Osborne. His "affections rush out to meet and welcome money" and his "kind sentiments awaken spontaneously towards the interesting possessors of it" (VF 284). Addressing his readers directly and blurring the line between spectator and actor as he does throughout VF, the narrator add in parentheses: "(for I defy any member of the British public to say that the notion of Wealth has not something awful and pleasing to him; and you, if you are told that the man next you at dinner has got half a million, not to look at him with a certain interest)" (VF 284).

Like Smith, the Manager of VF's Performance is aware of the attraction of wealth and its connection to vanity. When Mr. Osborne hears of the arrival of Miss Schwartz, a wealthy heiress from the West Indies, he decides his son George should

[1] Nuyen does not discuss Becky Sharp but focuses on Jos Sedley as a "paradigm" of vanity and a snob. He refers to Kant's notion of snobbery to explain that the vain person values everything (including other people) as means to an end. Even when the vain person desires something that is inherently valuable (like a virtuous character trait), he or she values it not for its inherent worth but its instrumental nature (Nuyen 1999).

[2] For a thorough analysis of Thackeray and early Victorian feminism, see Micael M. Clarke, *Thackeray and Women* (Dekalb: Northern Illinois Univ. Press. 1995).

marry her. "Young Fred Bullock," one of the people dispatched by Mr. Osborne to gather information about Miss Schwartz, "would have liked to make a bid for her himself (it was so the young banker expressed it), only he was booked to Maria Osborne. But not being able to secure her as a wife, the disinterested Fred quite approved of her as a sister-in-law" (VF 284). When George Osborne defies his father's wishes and is cut off from his inheritance, Fred Bullock realizes that his fiancée, George's sister, stands to inherit a much greater fortune than he had foreseen when he started wooing her.

> Mr. Bullock was a man of the world, and a junior partner of a wealthy firm. He knew what money was, and the value of it: and a delightful throb of expectation lighted up his little eyes, and caused him to smile on his Maria, as he thought that by this piece of folly of Mr. George's she might be worth thirty thousand pounds more than he had ever hoped to get with her. "Gad! Jane," said he, surveying even the elder sister with some interest, "Eels will be sorry he cried off. You may be a fifty thousand pounder yet." (VF 275)

Old Osborne and Fred Bullock do not hide their economic self-interest and their intention to satisfy it in Vanity Fair where a large segment of the market deals in sexual wares (Barickman et al. 1982, 173). Their open pursuit of wealth through marriage contrasts with the more subtle approach practiced by Becky Sharp. She, too, seeks to gain fortune through her relationships but knows that marriage is only the most obvious of the many financial instruments at her disposal. Furthermore, Becky, like Adam Smith, knows that the accumulation of wealth is merely the most common way to gain social esteem and that power and status can be obtained without it as well. Becky understands that what ultimately drives Old Osborne and Fred Bullock is vanity: the desire to be approved of and praised in a society that values (the appearance of) wealth and luxury above all else. Maria Osborne, the "fifty thousand pounder," is as pragmatic about her married future as is her husband-to-be. The narrator describes Miss Maria Osborne's engagement as "a most respectable attachment," noting that "she would have taken Bullock Senior just the same, her mind being fixed— as that of a well-bred young woman should be— upon a house in Park Lane, a country house at Wimbledon, a handsome chariot, and two prodigious tall horses and footmen, and a fourth of the annual profits of the eminent firm of Hulker & Bullock" (VF 138).[3] Maria could have gained all these advantages by marrying "gouty, old, bald-headed, bottle-nosed Bullock Senior" as well, "only the old gentleman was married already; so she bestowed her young affections on the junior partner" (VF 138). Husbands with the similar fortunes are interchangeable because what matters in Vanity Fair is not a husband's character or personality but the esteem he confers upon his spouse and her relations. Vanity, in short, is the driving force behind most marriages.

[3] Chapter 8 discusses Becky Sharp's desire for "respectability" which, though more complex than Maria Osborne's, also has wealth as one of its primary objectives.

Gauging a Gentleman's Vanity

While most of the characters in Thackeray's novel are vain in one way or another, Becky stands alone in her ability to unscrupulously use other people's vanity to her advantage. Smith explains that vanity springs from our desire to have other people think highly of us. The vain person constantly seeks the "approbation" and "esteem" of others because it is only through their recognition that the vain person can feel good about him- or herself. Vanity comes in different degrees and can attach itself to very different objects though as we have seen already, wealth is its most common object. Becky senses what kind of esteem and approbation the people around her desire and manipulates them accordingly. Pitt Crawley, for example, enjoys reading agricultural pamphlets and his vanity is flattered by Becky's interest in hearing him talk about the Corn Laws. Years later, while her husband Rawdon Crawley is dining out out, Becky receives his brother Pitt and modestly offers him salmi, saying "a poor man's wife must make herself useful, you know!" The poor man's wife's salmi is made of her secret benefactor Lord Steyne's pheasants, but Pitt does not need to know this. "Sir Pitt thought, with something like mortification, of Lady Jane at home, and of a certain pie which she had insisted on making, and serving to him at dinner—a most abominable pie" (VF 557). With the salmi she serves him a white wine which, she says, Rawdon "picked up for nothing" in France but which in truth is a White Hermitage from Lord Steyne's cellars. After dinner, Becky "let [Sir Pitt] talk as she listened with the tenderest kindly interest, sitting by him, and hemming a shirt for her dear little boy. Whenever Mrs. Rawdon wished to be particularly humble and virtuous, this little shirt used to come out of her work-box. It had got to be too small for Rawdon [Jr.] long before it was finished" (VF 557). On his way back home to his Lady Jane, Sir Pitt "thought to himself how she respected him and how he deserved it, and how Rawdon was a foolish dull fellow who didn't half-appreciate his wife; and how mum and stupid his own wife was compared to that brilliant little Becky" (VF 557).

George Osborne, one of several husbands tempted by Becky to stray from his wife, is vain about his appearance and his reputation as an honorable military man. His father made his fortune as a merchant and bought rather than inherited the family's coat of arms, which is why both Osborne Junior and Senior are keen to pass as gentlemen. For George this involves wining and dining members of the true aristocracy, being well dressed, and cultivating a spectacular mustache. Looks, of course, are important to any account of vanity, both because good looks are attractive in their own right and because appearance can connote wealth and status. George Osborne disparages his friend Dobbin's looks: "'There's not a finer fellow in the service,' Osborne said, 'nor a better officer, though he is not an Adonis, certainly.' And he looked towards the glass himself with much *naïveté*" (VF 57). As he looked in the mirror, he "caught Miss Sharp's eye fixed keenly upon him, at which he blushed a little, and Rebecca thought in her heart, '*Ah, mon beau monsieur!* I think I have *your* gauge'—the little artful minx!" (VF 57)

The narrator of *Vanity Fair* reminds the reader time and again that beauty will fade while vanity remains.[4] Becky is aware of her own beauty and coolly uses it as a tool in her pursuit of power, wealth, and status. She is interested in personal appearance only insofar as it is relevant to her schemes. She is as pragmatic as Maria Osborne, the "fifty-thousand pounder," but forced to be much more clever because she has no fortune of her own. Her ambition makes it impossible for her to be content with her lowly station and so she makes it her business to climb up through the ranks. Becky understands that vanity drives much of the behavior in Vanity Fair and ensures the continued existence of hierarchical society. She therefore engages and exploits this common trait wherever she encounters it.

Becky Beyond Morality: A Good Woman on Five Thousand a Year

Visiting her husband's rich relatives in the country, Becky reflects on the relationship between wealth and moral behavior: "It isn't difficult to be a country gentleman's wife," Rebecca thought. "I think I could be a good woman if I had five thousand a year" (VF 532). For Becky, being a "good woman" consists in living a simple life: "I could dawdle about in the nursery and count the apricots on the wall. I could water plants in a green-house and pick off dead leaves from the geraniums." She would even perform good offices: "I could ask old women about their rheumatisms and order half-a-crown's worth of soup for the poor. I shouldn't miss it much, out of five thousand a year." And she would bring sacrifices, too: "I could even drive out ten miles to dine at a neighbour's, and dress in the fashions of the year before last." She could practice going to sleep at church "behind the curtains, with my veil down." As an afterthought, she adds: "I could pay everybody, if I had but the money." Becky resents the wealthy "conjurers" out in the country who "think themselves generous if they give our children a five-pound note, and us contemptible if we are without one." The narrator remarks:

> And who knows but Rebecca was right in her speculations— and that it was only a question of money and fortune which made the difference between her and an honest woman? If you take temptations into account, who is to say that he is better than his neighbour? A comfortable career of prosperity, if it does not make people honest, at least keeps them so. An alderman coming from a turtle feast will not step out of his carnage to steal a leg of mutton; but put him to starve, and see if he will not purloin a loaf. Becky consoled herself by so balancing the chances and equalizing the distribution of good and evil in the world. (VF 533)

[4]VF's narrator is ruthless in his mockery of faded beauties: "A stout countess of sixty, *décolletée*, painted, wrinkled with rouge up to her drooping eyelids, and diamonds twinkling in her wig, is a wholesome and edifying, but not a pleasant sight." Stout countesses of sixty should not be asked to make their appearance by bright daylight but "drawing-rooms should be announced for November, or the first foggy day, or the elderly sultanas of our Vanity Fair should drive up in closed litters, descend in a covered way, and make their curtsey to the Sovereign under the protection of lamplight" (VF 601).

Becky resents comfortably prosperous people for their superior attitude but she also wants to be like them. Her story in VF shows that moral propriety is not her goal but rather a possible and not very important side effect. As is clear from her reflections on the subject cited above, she regards a life of prosperity in the country as placid and likely boring. It would be an easy life, but not a very interesting one. Becky's sights are set much higher and the picture she conjures of herself counting apricots on the wall should be taken to represent not her personal aspiration but her contempt for the insipid women who do not deserve their place above her in the social hierarchy. The reader knows Becky would never be content as a country gentleman's wife as she enjoys the "toil and bustle" of the world too much. Becky is ambitious, and (in her case at least) ambition and moral probity do not go hand in hand. More precisely, morality appears to be a non-issue for Becky who seems impervious to remorse. She experiences regret when she fails to take advantage of an opportunity to further her career, but she never experiences feelings of guilt when she has hurt someone or used them for personal gain. Condemned by many as immoral, it might be more accurate to say that Becky operates beyond good and evil. All that matters to her is her ambition and the projects it spurs her to undertake.[5] Becky resents those who stand in her way but she does not for that reason condemn them as morally bad people. It is just not a mode of judgment that appears to matter to her.

Becky's general unconcern about morality is less exceptional than it may at first appear. In TMS, Smith points out that "to superficial minds, the vices of the great seem at all times agreeable" (TMS 216–217) People who have not given the matter much thought are apt to overlook and even admire the vices of their social superiors because they do not separate them from "the splendor of fortune." It is not hard to see why these superficial minds would ascribe to the rich and powerful a "spirit of freedom and independency:" they seem to move around in a world that, unlike our own, appears to be free of constraints. But the admiring masses do not stop there: they see the vices of the great as part of a web containing also "many superior virtues" like "frankness, generosity, humanity, and politeness" (TMS 217). While vices appear less serious to the masses when they belong to the great, they appear more contemptible when they belong to "the inferior ranks of people." People in the inferior ranks are supposed to have an "abject, cowardly, ill-natured, lying, pilfering disposition" and even their virtues ("their parsimonious frugality, their painful industry, and rigid adherence to rules") are disagreeable to the observer (TMS 217). We are, Smith observes, extremely prejudiced in matters of class and rank, unfairly admiring our superiors and despising our inferiors.

Becky is aware of this double standard. Her social superiors in the country consider themselves "generous" when they give poor children a five-pound note while

[5]As Richard C. Stevenson points out, "Thackeray joins our necessarily harsh moral judgment with an artistic judgment" (2). He explains: "The text provides us with a "double" yet coherent way of viewing Becky: on the one hand we are given a firm basis on which to judge her severely, and on the other we are encouraged to see the limitations of that judgment and to feel a guarded admiration for the way in which she comports herself in *Vanity Fair*" (4). In line with Stevenson's comments, the following chapters aim to highlight the limitations of our moral judgments on Becky and to investigate why our admiration for her makes us uncomfortable.

they look down on these children's parents. Becky imagines that if she were a country gentleman's wife, she, too, would be "generous," giving "half-a-crown's worth of soup" to the poor. But unlike the superficial minds Smith mentions, Becky is not fooled by the "virtues" of the rich and powerful and sees their vices for what they are – especially their vanity. To Becky, a person's character traits, be they moral or immoral by commonly accepted standards, provide information about the ways in which someone may be useful to her. Like the Manager of the Performance, she understands that it is easy to be friendly, generous, and polite if you are secure in the superiority granted by money and status. She knows that the "humanity" praised in the rich is usually just disguised condescension and she resents being the object of it. But these insights do not make Becky any less interested in rising to more elevated ranks herself. Furthermore, she intends to one day act exactly like the great people she resents in her current position. Becky wants there to be ranks, clearly distinguished by outside markings so everyone knows who fits in where in the hierarchy of society. She is convinced of her ability to climb to the position that suits her ambition so she herself can become an object of admiration to the inferior masses. Becky does not regret the existence of inequality in the least; she merely finds that due to unfortunate circumstances she has started out on the wrong end of the social spectrum. As noted above, this mistake must be corrected by "balancing the chances and equalizing the distribution of good and evil in the world."

When Becky and her husband Rawdon Crawley settle in Curzon Street in London, they gather about them all the trappings of a respectable household. They do this, however, without paying anyone, causing the Manager of the Performance to wonder: "how many families are driven to roguery and to ruin by great practitioners" like the Crawleys (VF 466). Like "the great" Smith mentions, and quite contrary to the splendid reputation that "superficial minds" commonly assign to them, noblemen are apt to "rob their petty tradesmen, condescend to swindle their poor retainers out of wretched little sums and cheat for a few shillings." Consistent with Smith's observations, we tend to forgive these people their vices and even admire them for actions we would condemn in a poor person. Hence "when we read that a noble nobleman has left for the Continent, or that another noble nobleman has an execution in his house— and that one or other owes six or seven millions, the defeat seems glorious even, and we respect the victim in the vastness of his ruin" (VF 466). Because the noble nobleman's losses are "vast," they only confirm his greatness. "But who pities a poor barber who can't get his money for powdering the footmen's heads; or a poor carpenter who has ruined himself by fixing up ornaments and pavilions for my lady's *déjeuner*"? (VF 466) Becky adopts the attitude befitting a gentle- or even a noblewoman without ever having the fortune or title to support her claim to the corresponding social status. She convincingly proves that playacting and careful management gets one a long way in the attempt to emulate the "great" so admired by the masses. She pays neither "the blacksmith who opened the lock; nor the glazier who mended the pane; nor the jobber who let the carriage; nor the groom who drove it; nor the butcher who provided the leg of mutton; nor the coals which roasted it; nor the cook who basted it; nor the servants who ate it." The narrator adds: "this I am given to understand is not unfrequently the way in which people live elegantly on nothing a year" (VF 467).

Becky rarely shows any concern about the morality of her actions, only about the way in which they may be perceived by people who matter (i.e. people who can help her get closer to her goal of social superiority). If she ever thinks about the less than virtuous nature of her actions, she knows that her past conduct will not matter once she has achieved a higher status. She is like "the ambitious man" who, Smith states in TMS, "flatters himself that, in the splendid situation to which he advances, he will have so many means of commanding the respect and admiration of mankind, and will be enabled to act with such superior propriety and grace, that the lustre of his future conduct will entirely cover, or efface, the foulness of the steps by which he arrived at that elevation" (TMS 109). Becky over time becomes ever more adept at acting "with superior propriety and grace" and eventually gains all the "lustre" she desires. But her calculations and cleverness can not prevent her eventual downfall when at the height of her career her plans are disrupted by one of the many women she offended along the way.

When she finally loses her place in society, all the people who worked for her and never got paid are dragged down with her, "especially the poor ones." As the narrator observes "When the great house tumbles down, these miserable wretches fall under it unnoticed: as they say in the old legends, before a man goes to the devil himself, he sends plenty of other souls thither" (VF 467). Thackeray does not critique the economic system that is the context (as well as perhaps the cause) of this common phenomenon but rather takes aim at the social behaviors found within it (Milne 2015, 117). Smith explicitly addresses the ills of commercial society and warns against vanity as a driving force of industry. Becky Sharp regards the rise and fall of other people in society with detached interest, never lamenting the existence of hierarchy and inequality but always preoccupied with the bettering her own condition. The narrator of VF describes her as a proficient manager, effective in large part because she is unhindered by the restraints of what conventionally would be called a conscience.

Devil, Actress, Manager

There are few people in Vanity Fair who can fully appreciate Becky's outlook on the world and her place in it. Of all the people she meets, the dissipated Lord Steyne of the House of Gaunt is the one who comes closest to seeing Becky for the ambitious and cunning woman she really is. Lord Steyne habitually dines with the King and ranks among the most prestigious of Becky's conquests. Her mentor and admirer (and, the reader suspects, lover), he ushers Becky into high society, advises her on the realism of her expectations and ambitions, and bestows upon her monetary and other material gifts. At one point Becky addresses a tearful plea to Lord Steyne for more money to pay off her debts but after making some inquiries Lord Steyne finds out that she kept to herself an earlier sum he had given her for the same purpose:

> "What an accomplished little devil it is!" thought he. "What a splendid actress and manager! She had almost got a second supply out of me the other day; with her coaxing ways. She beats all the women I have ever seen in the course of all my well-spent life. They are babies compared to her. I am a greenhorn myself, and a fool in her hands— an old fool. She is unsurpassable in lies." His lordship's admiration for Becky rose immeasurably at this proof of her cleverness. Getting the money was nothing— but getting double the sum she wanted, and paying nobody— it was a magnificent stroke. (VF 663)

Where one might expect moral outrage, Lord Steyne feels admiration for Becky's clever deceit. Becky is a devil, an actress, and a manager – three important descriptors in the context of VF. VF's narrator calls himself the Manager of the Performance in the brief section "Before the Curtain" that prefaces the first Chapter of the book: "As the manager of the Performance sits before the curtain on the boards and looks into the Fair, a feeling of profound melancholy comes over him in his survey of the bustling place" (VF 1). And he adds: "Yes, this is VANITY FAIR; not a moral place certainly; nor a merry one, though very noisy (VF 1). The Manager tells us that he hopes his puppets will give satisfaction, noting that "the famous little Becky Puppet has been pronounced to be uncommonly flexible in the joints, and lively on the wire" (VF 1). Then, with "a profound bow to his patrons, the Manager retires, and the curtain rises" (VF 2). Despite his claim that he will be stepping back from the action, Vanity Fair's "patrons" are never allowed to forget that someone is managing the performance and pulling the strings.

Yet one of his puppets is a manager in her own right, as we soon learn. When Becky, just out of boarding school, is in the old Sir Pitt's employ as a governess, one of the household staff reports on her to Mrs. Bute Crawley, Sir Pitt's meddling sister in law who lives nearby: "the new governess be a rare manager – Sir Pitt be very sweet on her – Mr. Crawley too – He be reading tracts to her –." (VF 115) To Mrs. Bute's dismay, Becky the intruder quickly becomes much more than just a governess: she starts managing the entire household. Further reports confirm that "the governess had "come round" everybody, wrote Sir Pitt's letters, did his business, managed his accounts – had the upper hand of the whole house, my lady, Mr. Crawley, the girls and all" (VF 116). In a move that she will repeat many times throughout the narrative, Becky makes people her puppets and manages them at will. But her management style is subtler and more effective than, for example, Mrs. Bute's. The latter heavy-handedly manages her husband's finances and his lifestyle. Remarking that he would be in jail if it were not for her, he responds: "'I know I would, my dear,' said the Rector, good-naturedly. 'You *are* a clever woman, but you manage too well, you know': and the pious man consoled himself with a big glass of port" (VF 422).[6]

Part of what makes Becky an effective manager is her great skill as an actress and performer. She is the picture of innocent, active servitude when showing interest in Mr. Pitt Crawley's tracts on the Corn Laws, correcting the spelling of Sir Pitt's

[6] Mr. Bute Crawley's remark is born out by his wife's management of their rich relative Miss Crawley. When the latter is ill, Mrs. Bute moves in with her and "manages" her almost to death with her rules and medications.

letters, and generally making every member of the household do her bidding. She appears modest and humble but meanwhile runs the Crawley estate. "Little, eager, active, black-faced Mrs. Bute Crawley," clumsy in her own management style but sharp enough to see what is going on in her brother-in-law's household, calls Becky "an abandoned wretch" and rightly perceives her as a threat (VF 115): realizing that Becky has become indispensable to him, old Sir Pitt throws all regard for rank and birth to the wind and proposes marriage to her. Becky's acting skills are essential to the efficacy of her management style but they are also "devilish" because of the deceit involved in her performance. Lord Steyne admires Becky's accomplishments as a crafty manager-actress but he is also one of the few men fully aware of her special skill set. Most of the people who know that Becky's innocent, likeable persona is a clever act are women, and most of them can only stand by helplessly as the "artful minx" (VF 58, 638) manages and manipulates everyone around her.

Becky is ambitious and always looks for opportunities to further her own interests, like when she informs herself about malt pamphlets to be of use to Mr. Crawley. She is clear on what her interests are: she wants to rise in society and acquire greater status, primarily through accumulating wealth or at least the appearance of wealth. Though Mr. Crawley (who becomes Sir Pitt after the old Sir Pitt dies) never gives her any money, her early flattery of him never loses its effect and he remains of use to her throughout her career, as when for example he introduces Becky at Court. In her pursuit of riches Becky is not afraid to take risks and she is prepared to deal with a great amount of uncertainty. In fact, Becky appears to relish risk, often taking on more than is necessary or prudent. This means that she sometimes meets with failure, like when she marries prematurely and loses the chance of a better match. Other times the high risks she takes yield high rewards, eventually propelling Becky to the highest rungs of London society. Yet even when she moves in the best circles, Becky has no ready money and she creatively uses her modest means to great effect. Knowing that appearance goes a long way, Becky comports herself with the air of a lady and always wears the latest fashions, even if that means that her creditors go unpaid and she has to pilfer the closets of Sir Pitt's estate for the expensive lace that once belonged to the now deceased Ladies Crawley.

Becky recognizes and evaluates the obstacles in her way, deftly maneuvering around them or clearing them out of the way. She does not get stuck but is always on the move, planning and strategizing. When the obstacle blocking her way is a person who cannot be moved, she gets him or her (but usually him) on her side, as in the case of George Osborne who first obstructs Becky's plans to marry Jos Sedley but later becomes one of her most fervent admirers. Becky shows relentless energy in the pursuit of her goals and appears to only gain momentum as she moves forward: her joy in taking on ever new initiatives buoys her up. When she fails, she does not feel defeated but looks to the future for new and better opportunities.

Realizing at a young age that she has a talent for playacting and mimicry, Becky perfects these skills and tries them out on different audiences. She invests in herself. She educates herself to master the appropriately female skills of the time (like playing the piano and singing), the unwritten rules of polite society, and whatever other skills she needs in any particular situation (like accounting and business correspondence when she is in Sir Pitt's employ). Becky is self-confident and self-aware, and she always measures others' reactions to her so she may adjust her course to accord with the opinions of the people she values. She monitors herself closely, playing to her strengths in both her appearance and her conduct to achieve the greatest possible effect.

As the following chapters will suggest, Becky acts the part of a moral woman of her time in order to get what she wants. Morality, for Becky, is a performance. To achieve success, Becky does not rely on other people's goodness but on their vanity. She praises them, knowing full well that they are no better than her, just less smart and more easily manipulated through flattery. Becky gets angry when things do not go her way, but she never blames other people for their dishonesty, breach of trust, or other behavior that could be construed as morally blameworthy. More importantly, Becky is driven by a pleasure that is almost aesthetic in nature: she enjoys using social expectations and constraints to her advantage, operating the complex machinery of society. She delights in the mastery she acquires through her practice and becomes a consummate actress and manager, as Lord Steyne observes.

References

Barickman, Richard, Susan McDonald, and Myra Stark. 1982. *Corrupt relations: Dickens, Thackeray, Trollope, Collins, and the Victorian sexual system*. New York: Columbia UP.

Clarke, Micael M. 1995. *Thackeray and women*. Dekalb: Northern Illinois UP.

Milne, Kirsty. 2015. *At vanity fair: From Bunyan to Thackeray*. Cambridge: Cambridge UP.

Nuyen, A.T. 1999. Vanity. *The Southern Journal of Philosophy* 37: 613–627.

Smith, Adam. 1982a. The theory of moral sentiments. In *Vol. I of the Glasgow Edition of the Works and Correspondence of Adam Smith*, ed. D.D. Raphael and A.L. Macfie. Indianapolis: Liberty Fund.

———. 1982b. Lectures on Jurisprudence. In *Vol. 5 of the Glasgow Edition of the Works and Correspondence of Adam Smith*, ed. R.L. Meek, D.D. Raphael, and P.G. Stein. Indianapolis: Liberty Fund.

Stevenson, Richard C. 2006. The problem of judging Becky sharp: Scene and narrative commentary in *Vanity Fair*. In *Nineteenth-Century literature criticism*, vol. 169.

Thackeray, William Makepeace. 1983. In *Vanity fair: A novel without a hero*, ed. John Sutherland. New York: Oxford UP.

Chapter 3
To Be Quiet and Very Much Interested

Abstract In *Vanity Fair,* Becky Sharp is described as a Siren: half sweet and compliant angel and, hidden below the waterline, half monster. Becky's performance as a proper lady is effective because it relies on the universal human desire to be loved and, if love is not forthcoming, flattered. Like Adam Smith, Becky Sharp understands the power of vanity, the corrupted cousin of sympathy. To explain how sympathy works, Adam Smith refers to the heroes in tragedy and romance. We enter into their situation and experience feelings analogous to theirs. In real life as in the theater, we enjoy the harmony of sentiments that exists between actor and spectator. We like to be able to bring someone else's case home to ourselves just as we expect others to experience fellow-feeling with us in both our sorrow and our joy. This desire for sympathy can lead us to play a part in hopes that our spectators may like us better or admire us more. For the vain, outward praise and recognition are more important than an inner sense of praiseworthiness. Becky Sharp knows, as does Smith, that most people are vain and therefore easily manipulated through flattery. But unlike Smith, Becky seeks to exploit the vanity of others for her own gain. Men in particular make for willing victims as they are less used to playing a part the way women are and fail to see through the "arts" Becky and other women employ to use men to better their own condition.

Sympathy and Spectatorship

Smith opens TMS with a chapter entitled "of Sympathy" in which he makes his readers aware of what we already know about sympathy from our own experience. All of us have experienced sympathy at one point or another, Smith holds, and hence it is a good starting point for his *Theory*. We find ourselves on familiar territory, discussing "a matter of fact too obvious to require" any proof. After all, even "the greatest ruffian, the most hardened violator of the laws of society" sometimes derives "sorrow from the sorrow of others." Sympathy is not a virtue but an "original passion of human nature," a sentiment which some of us feel more acutely than others but nobody is entirely without (TMS 60).

R. Slegers, *Adam Smith's Moral Sentiments in Vanity Fair*, Issues in Business Ethics 49, https://doi.org/10.1007/978-3-319-98731-6_3

But having just stated that sympathy is so common a phenomenon that we do not need proof or examples, Smith gives us a few anyway, carefully broadening the scope of sympathy as he goes along. When we see a dancer on the slack rope we "twist and balance" our bodies as we imagine he must do to keep himself from falling. When we see the "sores and ulcers" which beggars expose to us on the street, we feel our arms itching as if we were similarly afflicted. We change "places in fancy with the sufferer," and "enter as it were into" the other person's body, imagining that we endure "the same torments." What we feel may be weaker in degree, but is not "altogether unlike" the original pain we are witnessing. Not only "persons of delicate fibres," but also "men of the most robust make" are subject to this kind of sympathy, demonstrated by the fact they feel soreness in their own eyes when they observe soreness in the eyes of other people (the eyes being the most delicate part of the body and hence most vulnerable to this sensation) (TMS 61).

Building on this first set of examples, Smith then shows that our "fellow-feeling" is called forth not just by sorrow, but by other passions as well. In fact, any passion a person experiences can cause "an analogous emotion … in the breast of every attentive spectator." With this, Smith turns to a very different set of examples from the ones he has just employed:

> Our joy for the deliverance of those heroes of tragedy or romance who interest us, is as sincere as our grief for their distress, and our fellow-feeling with their misery is not more real than that with their happiness. We enter into their gratitude towards those faithful friends who did not desert them in their difficulties; and we heartily go along with their resentment against those perfidious traitors who injured, abandoned, or deceived them. In every passion of which the mind of man is susceptible, the emotions of the by-stander always correspond to what, by bringing the case home to himself, he imagines should be the sentiments of the sufferer. (TMS 61)

Smith wishes to make the point that though the word sympathy was perhaps originally used "to signify our fellow-feeling with the sorrow of others," it "may now, however, without much impropriety, be made use of to denote our fellow-feeling with any passion whatever" (TMS 61). But his choice of examples in this step of his argument reveals something else as well: while Smith called on his readers to consider a slack rope dancer and beggars to evoke our own experience of a particular kind of "bodily" sympathy, he here asks us to imagine ourselves as spectators of a tragedy or readers of a romance. We are spectators watching a performance both when we look at the slack rope dancer and when we watch a tragedy being performed on the stage. But when we see the sores and ulcers "which are exposed by beggars in the streets" the situation is less straightforward. The sores are real and if the beggars appeal to us for money they make it difficult for us to remain mere "spectators" or "by-standers." What connects Smith's example of the beggars to that of the slack rope dancer is the bodily sympathy we cannot help but feel with other bodies, just like when we cringe when she see somebody about to be hit by another person. But even these simple examples raise questions that threaten to complicate Smith's account of sympathy in its early stages.

"When we see a stroke aimed and just ready to fall upon the leg or arm of another person, we naturally shrink and draw back our own leg or our own arm; and when it does fall, we feel it in some measure, and are hurt by it as well as the sufferer" (TMS 61). Do we rush to help the victim or to interfere before the stroke falls? Do the beggars' sores and the itching they cause us to feel on our own arms repel and disgust us and/or does our sympathy cause us to give them money or first aid? These questions would distract from the issue that interests Smith at this early stage of the argument. He wants to explain what sympathy is, and how this almost reflexive "bodily" sympathy is on a spectrum with the sympathy we feel when confronted with complex situations involving both sorrowful and joyful emotions. Nevertheless, Smith's focus on theatrical performance sets the tone for a theory of moral sentiments which takes as its starting point the perspective of the spectator or bystander: someone who witnesses the action but is not him- or herself directly affected.

Smith's approach also shows that fiction is as important and legitimate a source of examples illustrating moral theory as is real life experience. In the passage cited above, Smith uses the language of "entering into" someone else's feelings and "bringing home" to ourselves their situation. This sympathetic imaginative exercise is easiest when the object of our attention is a character in a play or a novel because we can both allow ourselves to be drawn into the action and know that we are merely spectators. But we rarely find ourselves mere spectators in real life, as the example of the beggars made clear. Or rather, in reducing ourselves to mere spectators we distance ourselves, moving in the opposite direction from the natural human tendency to sympathize and hence identify with the people around us. Though as spectators we find ourselves observing from what may appear as a safe distance from the action, pure spectatorship cuts us off from the source of our greatest happiness: to be on the receiving end of sympathy: "whatever may be the cause of sympathy, or however it may be excited, nothing pleases us more than to observe in other men a fellow-feeling with all the emotions of our own breast; nor are we ever so much shocked as by the appearance of the contrary" (TMS 64). As spectators we sympathize with actors, be they on stage or in real life; as actors we hope and expect to receive sympathy from our own spectators in both our sorrow and our joy. Furthermore, because we have all been on both sides, we have the ability to look at our own suffering and pleasure through the eyes of our spectators, real and imagined. This fundamental principle opens up the way to both moral development (resulting in wisdom and virtue) and moral corruption (resulting in vanity).

This chapter provides a first sketch of vanity and explains why Smith believes it to be a form of moral corruption. Our eagerness to receive sympathy and feel like other people esteem us can lead us to focus on our appearance and outward conduct alone, neglecting our character and virtue. To those aware of our craving for sympathy, this provides an opportunity: targeting the people most desperate to be esteemed, a keen observer may take advantage of their "folly" and flatter them for (financial) gain. Smith regards vanity as a sign of "effeminacy" and it is male vanity in particular which will be of interest in this chapter. Vanity is not only a driving force behind industry commerce, a topic explored in Chap. 5, but also provides women with the opportunity to "better their condition" in a society that provides them with very few options to make a career. To advance in this world, women need to perfect the "art" of being what their spectators expect them to be, playing their appropriately feminine roles. The result is a complicated performance of femininity that flatters male vanity but also subverts the system that necessitated the performance in the first place.

Effeminacy and the Vanity of Bearded Creatures

The most obviously vain character in *Vanity Fair* is Joseph (Jos) Sedley. Joseph is Amelia's brother and appears on the scene having just returned from Boggley Wollah where he spent some years as a collector in the East India Company's Civil Service. A large man, "his bulk caused Joseph much anxious thought and alarm." He occasionally goes on a diet but never persists and uses stays and waistbands to "give himself a waist." "He never was well dressed; but he took the hugest pains to adorn his big person" (VF 28). Living like a "gay young bachelor" in London, he "would issue forth to take a drive with nobody in the Park; and then he would come back in order to dress again and go and dine with nobody at the Piazza Coffee-House. He was as vain as a girl; and perhaps his extreme shyness was one of the results of his extreme vanity" (VF 29). Joseph is sensitive to his father's jokes about his appearance, from his weight to his Hessian boots in which he takes great pride. In London he is as "lonely as in his jungle at Boggley Wollah. He scarcely knew a single soul in the metropolis: and were it not for his doctor, and the society of his blue-pill, and his liver complaint, he must have died of loneliness. He was lazy, peevish, and a bon-vivant; the appearance of a lady frightened him beyond measure" (VF 29).[1]

According to Smith, a vain person seeks more praise and admiration than is his due. In other words, the praise the vain person seeks exceeds his actual praiseworthiness. Jos, for example, enjoys talking about his adventures in India, in particular those relating to his experience as a tiger hunter – even though Jos went tiger hunting only once, when he was "half-killed," "not by the tiger, but by the fright" (VF 40). Since we are inclined to look at ourselves as we imagine others might see us, we base our self-estimation on what others might think of us. Our sense of self-worth therefore depends on the (apparent or imagined) opinion of others. Smith argues that we will go to great lengths to make others think well of us: to acknowledge, respect and admire us. Our desire for sympathy is natural and hence this need to be "seen" by others and gain their praise is not in itself vicious. But Smith condemns this natural tendency when it goes too far, as it does in Jos. When our need for praise trumps our desire to be praiseworthy, and we are more concerned with the

[1] Nikole King argues that Thackeray offers "multiple, often conflicting ideals associated with what it meant to be a middle-class Victorian man" and "challenges the assumption, and literary convention, that outer beauty reflects inner beauty." More importantly for the purpose of this chapter's argument, "Jos's corpulent body and overeating suggest he lacks manly self-restraint and discipline" (107). His "slavish devotion to fashion… raises questions about his masculinity." Vanity marks both Jos Sedley and George Osborne as ungentlemanly men not because they are well dressed but because they too obviously took great pains to look good (King 2011, 110).

way we appear than with the person we ought to be, we can rightly be called vain. Though by no means the worst of the vices, "the words *vain* and *vanity* are never taken in a good sense," even when we use them good-humoredly or teasingly. Vanity is always "a foible and a ridicule in [one's] character," as it clearly is in Jos's case (TMS 262).

Though it is a foible and the target of (lighthearted) ridicule, vanity as a character trait performs a complicated and important role in both the functioning of the economy and the corruption of our moral sentiments. According to Smith, we have a tendency to admire the rich and powerful and want to be like them: "To deserve, acquire, and to enjoy the respect and admiration of mankind, are the great objects of ambition and emulation" (TMS 107). To attain this respect, we may choose to devote ourselves to "the study of wisdom and the practice of virtue" or try to acquire "wealth and greatness" like the rich and powerful at the center of public attention (TMS 107). These two roads, Smith explains, may lead to the same goal of gaining respect, but moral evaluation shows them to be very different. And yet "inattentive observers" easily mistake one for the other and admire the rich as much as (or more than) the wise and virtuous. Our prejudice in favor of the rich is so strong that we accept a great degree of "vice and folly" in the "man of fashion" while we would judge it severely in someone "of meaner condition." In the "drawing rooms of the great," "flattery and falsehood too often prevail over merit and abilities" (TMS 108). Especially during peacetime, a prince will surround himself with "buffoons" and "the external graces, the frivolous accomplishments of that impertinent and foolish thing called a man of fashion." In this corrupt society, frivolity is "commonly more admired than the solid and masculine virtues of a warrior, a statesman, a philosopher, or a legislator" (TMS 108). Jos, *Vanity Fair's* main "man of fashion" is vain, shy, and lonely. Moreover, he is what Smith calls "effeminate:"

> We have talked of Joseph Sedley being as vain as a girl. Heaven help us! the girls have only to turn the tables, and say of one of their own sex, "She is as vain as a man," and they will have perfect reason. The bearded creatures are quite as eager for praise, quite as finikin over their toilettes, quite as proud of their personal advantages, quite as conscious of their powers of fascination, as any coquette in the world (VF 29).

Jos does not have any of the "masculine virtues" marking the warrior, statesman, philosopher or legislator. On the contrary, he exemplifies what Smith describes as the "unwarlike" nature of commercial society. Luxury, Smith holds, results in effeminacy and a decline in the "martial spirit." The masculine character, shaped by war to be prudent, active, resolute and sober, is overcome by effeminacy, defined as rash, insolent, slothful, and voluptuous. While the masculine, martial spirit ensures prosperity, the rise of effeminacy spells society's ruin. This presents Smith with a problem: the masculine approach brings the prosperity that leads to luxury and hence the decline of masculinity.[2] Enter Becky, the most ambitious, warlike, active, and resolute (if not always the most prudent) of all of Vanity Fair's inhabitants.

[2] Mark Neocleous describes and compares the work of various Scottish Enlightenment thinkers on the connection between effeminacy, war, luxury, and (masculine) virtue. He argues that thinkers like Ferguson and Smith hold that "martial virtue is somehow *threatened* by new forms of

Rebecca in Presence of the Enemy

Almost the moment she enters the Sedleys' house, Becky sets her sights on Jos. He is not her first romantic target in life: while at boarding school she made a conquest of Mr. Crisp, a young curate "fresh from Oxford" who was "shot dead by a glance of her eyes which was fired all the way across Chiswick Church from the school-pew to the reading-desk" (VF 16). After head mistress Miss Pinkerton intercepts a note in which Mr. Crisp "proposed something like marriage," she realizes there is "an eagle in the Chiswick dovecot," "a dangerous bird" (VF 17). Miss Pinkerton is one of the first people to realize that Becky presents a threat to order, decency, and most importantly, to pompous people like herself.

Chapter III, in which Becky first meets Jos, is titled "Rebecca Is in Presence of the Enemy" (VF 24). The narrator describes Becky's "romantic" endeavors in violent, war-like terms. After she has practiced her shot on Mr. Crisp, Becky sets her sights on Jos. Caught in a nervous fit of laughter, Joseph, "encountering the eye of Miss Sharp, … stopped all of a sudden, as if he had been shot" (VF 25). Forestalling his readers' criticism of Becky's aggressive tactics, the narrator asks us to bear in mind that while most girls can rely on their mothers to do their "husband-hunting" for them, Becky has to look out for herself (VF 25). Continuing the trope of the hunt, we are asked to consider all the trouble parents and their daughters put themselves through in order to "bring down some 'desirable' young man with those killing bows and arrows of theirs" (VF 25). Becky fails to "bring down" Jos during her stay at the Sedleys' because George Osborne, future husband to Amelia Sedley, intervenes. However, Jos will fall prey to Becky many years later when, after marrying her, he dies under mysterious circumstances, leaving his widow to collect the life insurance money.

After their first dinner together at the Sedleys', Jos thinks about the "nice, gay, merry young creature" he just met (VF 31). Before dinner, he heard Becky whisper to Amelia "he's very handsome," whereupon Becky "started back timid as a fawn" at Amelia's suggestion that she tell her brother about the compliment. Becky "had previously made a respectful virgin-like curtsey to the gentleman, and her modest eyes gazed so perseveringly on the carpet that it was a wonder how she should have found an opportunity to see him" (VF 24). Becky carefully chooses when to deploy her weaponized gaze and makes sure her eyes (described by the narrator as "very large, odd, and attractive" (VF 16)) are modestly cast down whenever she means to convey shyness. Her apparent bashfulness complements her dress on the occasion of the Sedley dinner: "She was dressed in white, with bare shoulders as white as snow—the picture of youth, unprotected innocence, and humble virgin simplicity." Preparing to seduce Jos, she thinks to herself: "I must be very quiet, … and very much interested about India" (VF 29).

---

accumulation" and the resultant "rise of effeminacy." Like Smith's "man of fashion," the "dandy" and the "fop" are "emblematic of the crisis of masculinity" (Neocleous 2014, 92–93).

Clearly, the warlike language used to describe Becky's "campaign" is in stark contrast to her modest and unassuming appearance.[3] But her appearance (including both her looks and her conduct) is also her most formidable weapon in a society where marriage is the only means of economic mobility open to women. Becky is not subject to the sentimentality she detects in her friend Amelia, who marries for what she believes to be love. Becky knows that if her campaign is to be successful, she must appear to embody the angelic ideal of femininity popular at the time and described in the conduct books and novels of the late 18th and early nineteenth century.[4] This idealized female plays a role in Smith's work as well, all be it a subtle one: because the best kind of woman knows her place is in the home (first as a daughter and later as a wife), she barely enters the public arena of Smith's economy. If she performs her role correctly, she is absent from public life, supporting and making possible the activities of the men who venture out of the home to labor, socialize, philosophize, wage war, and engage in politics. For Becky to both appear in public and build and maintain a reputation of respectability is therefore a complicated balancing act. She disguises her martial spirit and acts ladylike, but her conduct is more than a diversionary tactic: it also is the main instrument at her disposal to make a career.[5]

On the Conduct of Proper Ladies

Women are largely absent from Smith's work and only make the occasional appearance in TMS and WN. They belong to the private sphere, performing the kind of "unproductive" household labor that does not result in sellable goods but only in goods and services consumed within the household.[6] Furthermore, women's labor, according to Smith, for the most part proceeds not from "rational calculation" (governing the economic activities of men) but from altruistic motives. Women, in short, are not part of the economic sphere (Rendall 1987 and Pujol 1998). And yet: in

[3] Chapter II of *Vanity Fair* bears the title "In which Miss Sharp and Miss Sedley prepare to open the campaign" (VF 13).

[4] These texts not only had a profound influence on the history of the novel but also fill in the cultural backdrop against which Smith wrote about effeminacy and, just as importantly, did *not* write about women. For a thorough discussion of eighteenth and nineteenth century conduct literature and the way it helped shape society, see Nancy Armstrong's *Desire and Domestic Fiction: A Political History of the Novel* (1990). The conduct book authors Armstrong discusses include Timothy Rogers, Thomas Gisborne, T.S. Arthur, Rev. Thomas Broadhurst, Dr. Fordyce, and Dr. Gregory. Female authors of conduct books include Sarah Tyler, Miss Catherine E. Beecher, and the Countess Dowager of Carlisle, Hester Chapone, Hannah More, and Mafia Edgeworth.

[5] As Ann Jones observes, "If marriage is a woman's only career, it might as well be her profession" (Jones 1981, 129).

[6] Robert W. Dimand, Evelyn L. Forget, and Chris Nyland provide a helpful overview of the work women did for pay in Smith's Scotland and elsewhere in Europe. Women worked as ironmongers, plumbers and glaziers, buttonmakers and brass manufacturers. They were often widows who had taken over their husbands' businesses (Dimand et al. 2004).

Vanity Fair it is Becky who has the most "masculine" economic drive, while Jos (and many of the other "bearded creatures" in VF) is "vain as a girl" and, as a man of fashion, the effeminate and lamentable result of an overly luxurious commercial society. In one of his rare published comments on the role of women in society, Smith observes the following:

> There are no publick institutions for the education of women ... They are taught what their parents and guardians judge it necessary or useful for them to learn; and they are taught nothing else. Every part of their education tends evidently to some useful purpose; either to improve the natural attractions of their person, or to form their mind to reserve, to modesty, to chastity, to oeconomy; to render them both likely to become the mistresses of a family, and to behave properly when they have become such (WN ii 168).

It is to "improve the natural attractions of their person" and, as the narrator of VF would add, to "bring down" the desirable young men mentioned in the previous section, that young women "labour at pianoforte sonatas, ... learn four songs from a fashionable master at a guinea a lesson, and ... play the harp if they have handsome arms and neat elbows" (VF 26). The ideal young lady is angelic in her appearance and submissive, selfless and modest in her behavior. A representative description of this female specimen can be found in Erasmus Darwin's *A Plan for the Conduct of Female Education in Boarding Schools* (1798), one of the more famous conduct books popular at the turn of the century:

> The female character should possess the mild and retiring virtues rather than the bold and dazzling ones; great eminence in almost anything is sometimes injurious to a young lady; whose temper and disposition should appear to be pliant rather than robust; to be ready to take impressions rather than to be decidedly marked; as great apparent strength of character, however excellent, is liable to alarm both her own and the other sex; and to create admiration rather than affection. (Darwin 1798, 3)

Darwin aimed to institutionalize proper female conduct by prescribing a curriculum for boarding schools like Miss Pinkerton's, where Becky's friend Amelia Sedley has learned to become the ideal young lady while Becky has learned to appear like one. As Nancy Armstrong argues in *Desire and Domestic Fiction*, the conduct literature from the eighteenth century represents "the household as a world with its own form of social relations, a distinctively feminine discourse," and the ideas and ideals prevalent in this discourse have passed into "the domain of common sense" by the start of the nineteenth century. As such, conduct literature like Darwin's "provided the frame of reference for other kinds of writing, among them the novel" (Armstrong 1990, 71).

Jane Austen, writing her "novels of manners" in the early nineteenth century, frequently mocks and exaggerates proper ladylike conduct and in doing so draws on what she could suppose to be common knowledge among her readership. Especially at the time of her mature work, conduct literature like Erasmus Darwin's has become part of the culture and no longer needs to be read to be discovered: the ideal has become part of middle class culture.[7] The character of Mary Bennet, one of

[7] "The novel, together with all manner of printed material, helped to redefine what men were supposed to desire in women and what women, in turn, were supposed to desire to be" (Armstrong 1990, 258). This common knowledge is the subject of much of Austen's signature irony.

Elizabeth's younger sisters in *Pride and Prejudice* reads like a caricature of one version of this female ideal while the much more nuanced and complex Elizabeth, just like most of Austen's heroines, is trapped in a domestic sphere determined by the values elaborately described in eighteenth century conduct literature (Austen 2004). Running through all of Austen's work is an awareness of the economic foundations of the patriarchy within which her heroines operate: entails, succession rights, and wills, all drawn up by and favoring men, ensure woman's complete dependence.[8] "Single women have a dreadful propensity for being poor," writes Austen in a letter to her niece (Gilbert and Gubar 1980, 62). As Gilbert and Gubar point out in their seminal work *The Madwoman in the Attic*, Austen examines the relation between "female powerlessness" and "the monetary pressure to marry, … the injustice of inheritance laws, the ignorance of women denied formal education, the psychological vulnerability of the heiress or widow, the exploited dependency of the spinster, the boredom of the lady provided with no vocation" (Gilbert and Gubar 1980, 136).[9] Austen's subtle criticism, invisible to readers who cannot or do not want to engage the deeper, less accessible meanings of her text, needs to be understood against the backdrop of the conduct literature that, as Armstrong puts it, demands that a woman "fulfills her role by disappearing into the woodwork to watch over the household" (Armstrong 1990, 88). In Erasmus Darwin's words:

> Hence if to softness of manners, complacency of countenance, gentle unhurried motion, with a voice clear and yet tender, the charms which enchant all hearts can be superadded internal strength and activity of mind, capable to transact the business or combat the evils of life, with a due sense of moral and religious obligation, all is attained which education can supply; the female character becomes compleat, excites our love and commands our admiration. (Darwin 1798, 4)

The standard of perfection for the female character resides in the love it will excite in men. A lady therefore should not aim to gratify herself or to be admired but because she is ""the least engaged of any member of the household," she should devote herself to the good of others."[10] And she should do this silently, without calling attention to her exertions because "all that would tend to draw away her thoughts from others and fix them on herself, ought to be avoided as an evil to her" (Gilbert and Gubar 1980, 52).[11] As Gilbert and Gubar put it: "Plainly, both writers meant

---

[8] As Gilbert and Gubar observe: "Austen does characteristically explore the specific ways in which patriarchal control of women depends on women being denied the right to earn or even inherit their own money" (Gilbert and Gubar 1980, 136).

[9] Jane Austen's novels can be read as a lighthearted discourse about romance and domesticity, but fundamentally her works deal with "the failure of the father, the emptiness of the patriarchal hierarchy, and, as Mary Burgan has shown, the inadequacy of the family as the basic psychological and economic unit of society" (Gilbert and Gubar 1980, 137).

[10] Mrs. Sarah Ellis, "Victorian England's foremost preceptress of female morals and manners," 1844, cited in Gilbert and Gubar (1980, 24).

[11] Similarly, John Ruskin stated in 1865 that the woman's "power is not for rule, not for battle, and her intellect is not for invention or creation, but for sweet orderings" of domesticity (Gilbert and Gubar 1980, 52).

that, enshrined within her home, a Victorian angel-woman should become her husband's holy refuge from the blood and sweat that inevitably accompanies a "life of significant action," as well as, in her "contemplative purity," a living memento of the otherness of the divine" (Gilbert and Gubar 24).

Vanity Fair's Amelia Sedley comes very close to this model of feminine purity and passivity. She can "sing like a lark," dance, embroider, and "spell as well as a Dixonary itself." She has a "kindly, smiling, tender, gentle, generous heart" and "won the love of everybody who came near her" (VF 6). This last trait especially is emphasized in the conduct literature, which requires a woman to be "all things to all people": a loving daughter, wife, mother (Armstrong 1990, 116). VF's narrator tells us "at the outset of our acquaintance" that Amelia is "a dear little creature; and a great mercy it is, both in life and in novels, which (and the latter especially) abound in villains of the most sombre sort, that we are to have for a constant companion so guileless and good-natured a person." The narrator continues: "As she is not a heroine, there is no need to describe her person" but he goes on to describe her nonetheless:

> Her face blushed with rosy health, and her lips with the freshest of smiles, and she had a pair of eyes which sparkled with the brightest and honestest good-humour, except indeed when they filled with tears, and that was a great deal too often; for the silly thing would cry over a dead canary-bird; or over a mouse, that the cat haply had seized upon; or over the end of a novel, were it ever so stupid. (VF 7)

Amelia clearly is a reader of exactly the sentimental novels that rose in popularity in the eighteenth century hand in hand with conduct books. She is the living exemplar of the ideal ladies that populate these novels, yet, according to the narrator, she is not herself a heroine. She is self-less in the sense that she has no self; a pretty but blank canvas onto which people can project their wishes and desires. Twelve out of the twenty-four fellow boarders at Chiswick Hall are her "bosom friends," further proof that Amelia can indeed be "all things to all people" (VF 7). It is no coincidence that George Osborne, one of the most self-satisfied and selfish men in *Vanity Fair,* is attracted to Amelia: she never asserts herself, is never "disagreeable," because she is not a heroine, and appears to have very little substance. She is frail and needs to be treated "with the utmost gentleness, as harsh treatment was injurious to her" (VF 8). She is at her most lovely when she cries – though as the narrator points out her tears flow even at the most trivial occasions.[12] She is sentimental and most of all feminine, lacking all the assertive and active qualities that Smith so emphatically defines as masculine.

Tertius Lydgate, the ambitious young doctor in George Eliot's *Middlemarch,* expects to bring home someone very much like Amelia when he marries Rosamond Vincy, daughter of the town mayor and the image of female perfection. "She is grace itself," he thinks to himself when he first meets her, "she is perfectly lovely and accomplished. That is what a woman ought to be: she ought to produce the

[12] Julia Bninski points out that Amelia is a victim of the sentimental literature popular at the time. She cries at the drop of a hat and persists in a romantic but completely misplaced love for George (Bninski 2011).

effect of exquisite music" (Eliot 1996, 88). Rosamond has "true melodic charm," and Lydgate closely observes her graceful behavior, noting that she is careful not to show "her dimples on the wrong occasion." He sees how she treats plain Mary Garth "with so much good-natured interest, that Lydgate, after quickly examining Mary more fully than he had done before, saw an adorable kindness in Rosamond's eyes" (Eliot 1996, 108). Lydgate thinks even more highly of Rosamond because of her kindness to a woman so clearly her inferior in looks. As for himself, "plain women he regarded as he did the other severe facts of life, to be faced with philosophy and investigated by science" (Eliot 1996, 88).

Just like Miss Pinkerton praises Amelia in *Vanity Fair*, Mrs. Lemon, head of school in Middlemarch, regards Rosamond as a model of ladylike perfection: "Mrs. Lemon herself had always held up Miss Vincy as an example: no pupil, she said, exceeded that young lady for mental acquisition and propriety of speech, while her musical execution was quite exceptional" (Eliot 89). Miss Pinkerton and Mrs. Lemon, guardians of female conduct, hold up their protégées as ideals of femininity: Amelia excels most of all in the "virtues" of frailty and passivity, Rosamond in propriety and angelic prettiness. Rosamond has "hair of infantine fairness," "eyes of heavenly blue," and it is no wonder that "some called her an angel" (Eliot 104). But unlike Amelia, Rosamond is not a blank space or empty canvas. Contrary to Lydgate's first impressions, she is far from pliable and selfless. When Lydgate is troubled by the debts the couple incurred when they were just married, she is unhappy about "his moodiness - a name which to her covered his thoughtful preoccupation with other subjects than herself" (Eliot 550). Trying to share with her the burden of their debt, Lydgate finds that Rosamond does not intend to cooperate with any course of action that will result in her having to live beneath her station. As the narrator puts it, "Rosamond was particularly forcible by means of that mild persistence which, as we know, enables a white soft living substance to make its way in spite of opposing rock" (Eliot 324). Similarly, when Lydgate tries to use his authority as medical doctor and husband to forbid Rosamond from horseback riding while she is pregnant, Rosamond seems to comply but then goes out riding anyway and has a miscarriage.

> Lydgate could only say, "Poor, poor darling!"— but he secretly wondered over the terrible tenacity of this mild creature. There was gathering within him an amazed sense of his powerlessness over Rosamond. His superior knowledge and mental force, instead of being, as he had imagined, a shrine to consult on all occasions, was simply set aside on every practical question. He had regarded Rosamond's cleverness as precisely of the receptive kind which became a woman. He was now beginning to find out what that cleverness was—what was the shape into which it had run as into a close network aloof and independent. No one quicker than Rosamond to see causes and effects which lay within the track of her own tastes and interests (Eliot 549).

Rosamond has the appearance and manner of the Victorian angel but in conforming perfectly to the standards of female beauty and propriety she asserts herself like a "white soft living substance" in the patriarchal context of matrimony. She is obstinate but never inappropriate, she never raises her voice or shows anything besides perfect propriety, and she has a strong disdain for anyone who gets angry with her.

She thinks to herself that she would not have married Lydgate had she known about his "moodiness." After Lydgate dies many years later, Rosamond marries "an elderly and kindly physician" and lives in luxury. She often spoke of her happiness as "a reward"— she did not say for what, but probably she meant that it was a reward for her patience with Tertius, whose temper never became faultless" (Eliot 782).

Husbands, Necessary but Wearisome

Before coming to Middlemarch, Lydgate lived in Paris where he fell in love with an actress, Laure. At the time, she was married to a fellow actor who played her husband on stage. One night she stabbed her husband, in the play and in real life, presumably because her foot slipped. Talking to Lydgate after she has been cleared of all charges, Laure says:

> "I meant to do it."
>
> Lydgate, strong man as he was, turned pale and trembled: moments seemed to pass before he rose and stood at a distance from her.
>
> "There was a secret, then," he said at last, even vehemently. "He was brutal to you: you hated him."
>
> "No! he wearied me; he was too fond: he would live in Paris, and not in my country; that was not agreeable to me." (Eliot 142)

Knowing that Lydgate is in love with her, she adds: "You are a good young man. But I do not like husbands. I will never have another" (Eliot 142). Boredom and ennui are serious threats to the middle class ladies raised according to conduct book rules. They are not supposed to work outside the home, let alone for money, nor is it proper for them to "make a display of themselves" like the members of the aristocracy. Laure is not a proper lady: she is an actress, unaristocratic yet very much on display and therefore deemed improper. There is an almost negligible difference between appearing on stage for money and prostituting oneself: in both cases a woman uses her body for financial gain.[13] Given her subversive profession, it is no surprise that Laure delivers a shock to Lydgate's patriarchal outlook on the world: she murdered her husband not because she hated him or because he hurt her, but because she was bored.

Boredom threatens the heroines of many Victorian novels. To pass the time, they are supposed to embroider, sign, play the piano, gossip (within the bounds of propriety) and think about escaping their parents' house through marriage. In Jane Austen's *Emma,* Harriet Smith is surprised that her friend Emma Woodhouse,

---

[13] Women publicly selling goods (like Becky in the bazaar at the end of *Vanity Fair*) are similarly suspect (Womick 2011).

charming as she is, is not yet married. Emma responds that she has "very little intention of ever marrying at all." She explains: "I cannot really change for the better. If I were to marry, I must expect to repent it." It shocks the naïve Miss Smith "to hear a woman talk so," and Emma continues:

> I have none of the usual inducements of women to marry. Were I to fall in love, indeed, it would be a different thing! but I never have been in love; it is not my way, or my nature; and I do not think I ever shall. And, without love, I am sure I should be a fool to change such a situation as mine. Fortune I do not want; employment I do not want; consequence I do not want: I believe few married women are half as much mistress of their husband's house as I am of Hartfield; and never, never could I expect to be so truly beloved and important; so always first and always right in any man's eyes as I am in my father's. (Austen 2003, 68)

Emma's father, Mr. Woodhouse, is a mild old hypochondriac who can find no fault with his daughter and happily leaves the running of the household to her. Why would she exchange this situation for another, necessarily inferior one which would include a husband who would expect her to be a "proper wife"? That economic motives play a large role in Emma's considerations is emphasized in Emma's response to Harriet's exclamation that her friend will be "an old maid" if she remains unmarried:

> Never mind, Harriet, I shall not be a poor old maid; and it is poverty only which makes celibacy contemptible to a generous public! A single woman, with a very narrow income, must be a ridiculous, disagreeable old maid! the proper sport of boys and girls, but a single woman, of good fortune, is always respectable, and may be as sensible and pleasant as anybody else. (Austen 2003, 69)

Since she has a large fortune, she will be free to occupy herself in whatever ladylike manner she pleases for the rest of her life: "If I draw less, I shall read more; if I give up music, I shall take to carpet-work." Furthermore, Emma does not fear that she will lack "objects for the affections" just because she will not have children of her own: "I shall be very well off, with all the children of a sister I love so much, to care about. There will be enough of them, in all probability, to supply every sort of sensation that declining life can need" (Austen 2003, 69).

While wealthy young ladies have no need for either marriage or husbands (unless, as Emma indicates, they are unfortunate enough to fall in love) and wild, unladylike women like Lydgate's first love Laure may murder their husbands because they do not wish to be bored, most middle class daughters regard marriage as the only way to advance in life. Just like "it is a truth universally acknowledged, that a single man in possession of a good fortune, must be in want of a wife" (Austen 2004, 1), Austen's female characters operate on the universally acknowledged truth of their need to marry if they want to move up on the economic ladder, or perhaps even merely escape the parental domestic sphere (even if it is to exchange it for an equally paternalistic situation in the new home). Charlotte Lucas, Elizabeth Bennet's friend in *Pride and Prejudice* and one of Austen's most unsentimental characters, is fully aware of this second truth when she marries the preposterous Mr. Collins:

> Mr. Collins, to be sure, was neither sensible nor agreeable; his society was irksome, and his attachment to her must be imaginary. But still he would be her husband. Without thinking highly either of men or matrimony, marriage had always been her object; it was the only

> provision for well-educated young women of small fortune, and however uncertain of giving happiness, must be their pleasantest preservative from want. This preservative she had now obtained; and at the age of twenty-seven, without having ever been handsome, she felt all the good luck of it. (Austen 2004, 9)

Before she meets Lydgate, Rosamond's ideas about her ideal future husband form what the narrator calls a "social romance which had always turned on a lover and bridegroom who was not a Middlemarcher, and who had no connections at all like her own: of late, indeed, the construction seemed to demand that he should somehow be related to a baronet" (Eliot 109). She dreams of her ideal husband's family and the ways in which he might offer her an escape from her father's home and town connections. She does not spare much thought for his person though she is excited by Mary Garth's description of Lydgate's manner as "haughty," which she takes as indicative of his superior social status. Rosamond is used to be fallen in love with and has already rejected all the local eligible bachelors when she meets Lydgate and decides "that this was the great epoch of her life. She judged of her own symptoms as those of awakening love, and she held it still more natural that Mr. Lydgate should have fallen in love at first sight of her" (Eliot 109).

> Here was Mr. Lydgate suddenly corresponding to her ideal, being altogether foreign to Middlemarch, carrying a certain air of distinction congruous with good family, and possessing connections which offered vistas of that middle-class heaven, rank; a man of talent, also, whom it would be especially delightful to enslave: in fact, a man who had touched her nature quite newly, and brought a vivid interest into her life which was better than any fancied "might-be" such as she was in the habit of opposing to the actual. (Eliot 110)

On her way home after her first meeting with Lydgate, Rosamond's mind is occupied with "the costume and introductions of her wedded life," the house she and Lydgate are to live in, and "the visits she would pay to her husband's high-bred relatives at a distance, whose finished manners she could appropriate as thoroughly as she had done her school accomplishments, preparing herself thus for vaguer elevations which might ultimately come" (Eliot 110). Rosamond, star pupil of Mrs. Lemon's school, is ready for the advanced lessons in conduct which she imagines will bring her the greater luxuries befitting these "vaguer elevations." Though her interests are thus clearly economic in nature, "there was nothing financial, still less sordid, in her previsions: she cared about what were considered refinements, and not about the money that was to pay for them" (Eliot 110).

Similar to Rosamond Vincy, Becky Sharp is preoccupied with the economic elevation and rank a husband might bring even before she has met the man who she believes may fill this role. But though Becky, like Rosamond, is aware of all the rules of conduct for fine young ladies, she never lived a life of indulgence. She grew up in poverty and was constantly made aware of her inferior station at Chiswick Hall and this background perhaps explains why she is more to the point than Rosamond in targeting her future spouse. As the narrator in *Vanity Fair* observes: "It is a fact that while she was dressing for dinner, and after she had asked Amelia whether her brother was very rich, she had built for herself a most magnificent castle in the air, of which she was mistress, with a husband somewhere in the background (she had not seen him as yet, and his figure would not therefore be very distinct)" (VF 26).

We all claim to admire true virtue and good character, Smith writes in TMS, but those moral goods are much less visible than status, rank and wealth. Though we may esteem the wise and virtuous in principle, in practice the recipients of our "benevolent attention" tend to be "those who are distinguished by their extraordinary situation," i.e. "the greatly fortunate … the rich and the powerful" (TMS 237). Even though it is problematic from an ethical perspective that "the rich and the great are too often preferred to the wise and the virtuous," Smith believes that "Nature has wisely judged that the distinction of ranks, the peace and order of society, would rest more securely upon the plain and palpable difference of birth and fortune, than upon the invisible and often uncertain difference of wisdom and virtue" (TMS 238).

Smith considers our admiration for the rich and powerful to be a fact of our human psychology. This admiration inspires emulation and in the cases of Becky and Rosamond, their ambition is fixed on obtaining and "enslaving" husbands. If the only way open to middle class women to pursue status and riches is to "marry up," marriage becomes career move. Explicitly or implicitly, marriage is understood to be a contract between the sexes: economic goods (and with them, rank and status) in exchange for a modest, selfless angel. The next section focuses on the "arts" employed by Becky and her literary sisters to make a career for themselves.

The Impassibility of the Artful Minx

Much to his surprise, Lydgate finds that "affection did not make [Rosamond] compliant." Over time, realizing that in matters big and small Rosamond acts in direct defiance of his judgments and opinions, Lydgate becomes "much worried, and conscious of new elements in his life as noxious to him as an inlet of mud to a creature that has been used to breathe and bathe and dart after its illuminated prey in the clearest of waters" (Eliot 550). When he gets angry one night because Rosamond has secretly acted against his wishes, she does not respond in kind but continues to delicately handle the tea-service, looking "at the objects immediately before her with no curve in her face disturbed, and yet with an ineffable protest in her air against all people with unpleasant manners." "For the moment he lost the sense of his wound in a sudden speculation about this new form of feminine impassibility revealing itself in the sylph-like frame which he had once interpreted as the sign of a ready intelligent sensitiveness. His mind glancing back to Laure while he looked at Rosamond, he said inwardly, "Would she kill me because I wearied her?" (Eliot 556).

In the Epilogue to *Middlemarch,* we learn that Lydgate and Rosamond never became the couple either of them had imagined during their courtship. We get a hint that the specter of husband murder continued to haunt Lydgate throughout his married life: "He once called her his basil plant; and when she asked for an explanation, said that basil was a plant which had flourished wonderfully on a murdered man's brains" (Eliot 782). Lydgate has come a long way from the certainty he felt before his domestic troubles began, "that if ever he married, his wife would have that feminine radiance, that distinctive womanhood which must be classed with flowers and music, that sort of beauty which by its very nature was virtuous, being moulded only for pure and delicate joys" (Eliot 153). Rosamond, taught by Mrs. Lemon to project "feminine radiance" and appear like a creature made of music and light, proves immovable and indomitable and is master of the situation despite all Lydgate's supposed masculine virtues.

While Rosamond considers her own behavior at all times as the most proper and irreproachable, always blaming others for their "moodiness" and offensiveness, Becky readily tells her friend Amelia as they leave boarding school together: ""I'm no angel." And," the narrator adds "to say the truth, she certainly was not" (VF 14). Miss Pinkerton, headmistress of Chiswick Hall, considers Becky a "rebel," a "monster," a "serpent," and a "firebrand," to be removed from her school as soon as she can find her a position as a governess elsewhere (VF 20). The headmistress was deceived by Becky's manner when her father was still alive and the girl acted as became her lowly station as the drawing master's daughter. Becky's parentage - an artist father and a mother who was a Parisian "opera girl" – gives the reader a few early clues to Becky's own considerable "art." Throughout *Vanity Fair,* Becky gains power, influence, and status through mimicry and play-acting.[14] She delights in deception and double-talk and is fully aware of her masks and roles, unlike Rosamond who appears to have become (or to always have been) one with her act: "Every nerve and muscle in Rosamond was adjusted to the consciousness that she was being looked at. She was by nature an actress of parts that entered into her physique: she even acted her own character, and so well, that she did not know it to be precisely her own" (Eliot 109).

To better understand Becky's art and artfulness, we must look at the way she is first introduced. We first meet Becky as she and Amelia Sedley are about to leave Miss Pinkerton's academy for young ladies at Chiswick Mall. Amelia is loved by all, but Becky, orphaned and of questionable lineage, leaves no friends behind at Chiswick – even Miss Pinkerton herself is afraid of her. Miss Pinkerton gives Amelia the traditional gift for departing students, Johnson's dictionary. When Becky is asked to come into the headmistress's rooms to say goodbye, she receives no gift and refuses the hand Miss Pinkerton offers her in farewell. Miss Jemima, Miss Pinkerton's timid younger sister, feels sorry for Becky and secretly gives her a copy

[14] Lisa Jadwin notes that "ambitious women … have little choice but to refashion "virtuous" discourse by reinflecting and exaggerating its rhetoric and concealing their unacceptable ideas beneath an acceptable surface. … These women mimic the discourse of the "paragon of virtue," deliberately enlisting the true believer's acquiescent, self-minimizing discourse to camouflage their disbelieving defiance and to achieve power denied them by the masculine declarative discourses they are forbidden to use" (Jadwin 1992, 664). Stephanie Womick argues that Thackeray's "broadest critique" in VF "is of middle-class femininity." "By consciously performing and subverting markers of ideal domesticity, Becky uses them to her own benefit, employing female accomplishments and postures in her arsenal of strategies to seduce, entrap, and manipulate." This makes Becky "both dangerous and fascinating" (Womick 2011, 67).

of the dictionary when Becky and Amelia are about to drive off in their carriage. To Miss Jemima's and Amelia's horror, Becky throws the dictionary out of the carriages back into the yard in front of Chiswick Mall as the carriage pulls away. Miss Pinkerton is vain and pompous and perhaps deserving of Becky's ridicule but Becky's cruelty to Miss Jemima feels unwarranted: "When Miss Sharp had performed the heroical act mentioned in the last chapter, and had seen the Dixonary, flying over the pavement of the little garden, fall at length at the feet of the astonished Miss Jemima, the young lady's countenance, which had before worn an almost livid look of hatred, assumed a smile that perhaps was scarcely more agreeable" (VF 13). Becky does not want or need a dictionary because she intends to come up with her own definitions.[15] She has learned what she could at Chiswick not because she desires to become a proper lady, but to act like one when convenient.

This and other early scenes in *Vanity Fair* show Becky to be neither easily intimidated nor eager to please like her friend Amelia. Becky takes pleasure in making others uncomfortable, especially the people who have wronged her or are (in her opinion) deserving of ridicule because of their subservience, like Miss Jemima to Miss Pinkerton. Becky's main emotion while at Chiswick is rage: forced to live at Chiswick as an "articled pupil" she is surrounded by other girls whose family and fortune give them an (in Becky's eyes) unfair advantage (VF 6, 16). She believes herself to be both more intelligent and more beautiful than her peers. While her father was alive she was free to do as she pleased but now she is confined to the school, bound to live by Miss Pinkerton's rules. Her rage and envy make her lonely and she starts to make plans for her future: to escape her current prison and find a better position for herself. She learns to dissemble and to exercise self-command: to appear "artless" when in fact she is artfully engaging the vanity of others to better her condition. Becky's "artful artlessness" is a recurring theme and it serves to consider a few of the most telling instances.

Vanity Fair's narrator calls Becky a "little artful minx" (VF 58) when she intercepts George Osborne's gaze as he is admiring himself in a mirror. Once Becky has gained a position as governess for Sir Pitt's children Mrs. Bute Crawley (Sir Pitt's sister-in-law), worried about Becky's plans and the family name and fortune, calls her an "artful hussy" (VF 115). She is "an artful and dangerous person" (VF 436), Miss Crawley writes to a French friend of Becky's; "an artful little minx" according an unnamed person at one of the parties at the Rawdons (VF 638). Most of the people suspicious of Becky's "arts" are women, while most men (Captain Dobbin being a notable exception) consider her "artless" exactly when she is most artfully ensnaring them. The narrator frequently and ironically comments on Becky's "artlessness" in her dealings with the opposite sex. The contrast with Amelia is clear: Amelia is the genuine article, "the kind, fresh, smiling, artless, tender little domestic goddess, whom men are inclined to worship" (VF 132). Becky, on the other hand, merely plays the part - and very successfully so. Before Miss Crawley learns of the marriage between Becky and her nephew Rawdon, she expresses the opinion that

---

[15] As Jadwin puts it: Becky throws the dictionary back into the yard "where it belongs:" she will "define her own wor(l)d" (Jadwin 1992, 678).

"Rawdon must … not play with a poor artless girl's feelings" (VF 165). She blesses and admires Becky "as a dear, artless, tender-hearted, affectionate, incomprehensible creature" (VF 185). The new Sir Pitt feels that "it was impossible sometimes to resist this artless little creature's hospitalities, so kindly were they pressed, so frankly and amiably offered" (VF 558). Lord Steyne, the richest among Becky's benefactors, enjoys her arts, fully aware that she is playing a part yet expecting her to play it nonetheless: "Becky came down to him presently; whenever the dear girl expected his lordship, her toilette was prepared, her hair in perfect order, her mouchoirs, aprons, scarfs, little morocco slippers, and other female gimcracks arranged, and she seated in some artless and agreeable posture ready to receive him" (VF 606).

Becky's artlessness is a performance and she is as keenly aware of her spectators as is Rosamond. Smith starts his account of sympathy from the perspective of the spectator: seeing other people's sorrow and joy makes us experience "analogous feelings" even if they are weaker than the originals. Sometimes our sympathy is awakened by a clearly visible "emotion in another person," like grief or joy: "A smiling face is, to every body that sees it, a cheerful object; as a sorrowful countenance, on the other hand, is a melancholy one" (TMS 61). Other behaviors require explanation before we can sympathize with the subject's emotions, like when we are exasperated with someone because we do not know the cause of his anger. Once we know the provocation we may be able to "bring his case home to ourselves" (TMS 62). All of this implies that the spectator has a set of preconceived notions regarding proper behavior and is predisposed to sympathize with some feelings and actions more than others. Our preconceptions may even enable us to have a better sense of what somebody should be feeling than the person concerned, like when "we blush for the impudence and rudeness of another, though he himself appears to have no sense of the impropriety of his own behavior" (TMS 62). While the kind of immediate, bodily sympathy we experience when we see someone about to receive a stroke appears to be independent of society's mores, the sympathy required to feel ashamed in someone else's stead depends on learned standards of propriety.

Applying this insight to the previous sections, it is clear that only proper women will receive the sympathy they crave – the desire for sympathy being universal. More accurately, women have to take care to properly display their emotions, and to appear to feel only those emotions that women are supposed to experience. Only if they conduct themselves in accordance with the common sense rules of the time can their spectators "enter into" their situation and "bring their case home" to themselves. Furthermore, women are not just actors but spectators, too. They have to be careful spectators in order to learn what kind of (female) behavior meets with (dis)approval. They also notice when they themselves are inclined to sympathize with others and when they are not, extrapolating from these observations how they should act themselves. Becky Sharp is an exceptionally keen spectator with experience far more wide-ranging than Rosamond's. She uses her powers of perception to ever further develop her own artless performance and gain the sympathy of those around her. But she is not interested in sympathy for its own sake, nor is she fooled into thinking that the attention she receives is much more than the result of other people's flattered vanity. What then drives Becky to perfect her art and play on the vanity of others?

Becky the Siren will Not Go Unheeded

Becky's first attempts at seduction fail, but only by a hair. The vicar, Mr. Crisp, proposed "something very much like marriage" to her in his intercepted note and Jos Sedley was determined to make her a proposal until he drank a fateful quantity of "rack punch" at Vauxhall and left town in embarrassment the next morning. Had it not been for this unfortunate circumstance, she would certainly have got "the better of him, and at her first entrance into life," as the narrator remarks. We would be wise to regard her as "a young person of no ordinary cleverness" (VF 28).

Becky's cleverness is indisputable but contrary to what the narrator tells us, her foray into the world of the Sedleys is hardly "her first entrance into life" (VF 28). When she entered Chiswick Hall at age sixteen, she "looked like a child" but "she had the dismal precocity of poverty" (VF 17). Used to her father's companions' wild stories, experienced in turning away creditors and greatly admired for her wit all through the "Artists' quarter," "she never had been a girl, she said; she had been a woman since she was eight years old"[16] (VF 17). Before her father's death forces her to move in with the girls at Chiswick, she acted like "the meekest creature" when she joined him for his visits to the Mall. Miss Pinkerton even gave her a doll that, back in the artists' quarter, became Miss Pinkerton's puppet-double (VF 17). Becky is a merciless puppeteer and finds a second doll to mock Miss Jemima, Miss Pinkerton's younger sister who a few years later will give Becky the dictionary: "For though that honest creature had made and given her jelly and cake enough for three children, and a seven-shilling piece at parting, the girl's sense of ridicule was far stronger than her gratitude, and she sacrificed Miss Jemmy quite as pitilessly as her sister" (VF 18).

Becky's father, though a violent and irresponsible drunk who eventually succumbs to delirium tremens, is proud of Becky's wit, which has established her as a favorite in the neighborhood. From a young age she has learned to use her cleverness, wit and powers of mimicry not just to survive but also to be seen and admired. At sixteen she already has a circle of admirers who happily give up other engagements to spend time with her and her puppet show. After a few years at Chiswick Mall she makes her entrance into life as a lady, even though she has already "been a woman," which is to say an artful actress, for a decade. From a very young age, she

[16] Maria Dibattista draws attention to Thackeray's awareness of a "culture whose model of angelic womanhood" creates "freaks" like Becky. "Becky's "disreputable" character represents the potential for a demonic and malevolent female sexuality in contrast to the respectable but no less selfish "love" of her true opposite and double, Amelia, the martyr to the Victorian feminine ideal who dedicates her life to the "corpse" of her love." Dibattista is here referring to Amelia's devotion to the unworthy George years after he dies on the battlefield (Dibattista 1980, 833).

has delighted in play-acting, cleverness, and witty cruelty – not, at least initially, out of envy or resentment, but for the fun of it.

Envy and resentment enter into her life at Chiswick Hall, where she made to feel inferior to girls she considers beneath herself in looks and intelligence. With the "precocity of poverty," Becky is keenly aware of the distinctions of rank and wealth and the propensity, in Smith's words, of "the fortunate and the proud," to "wonder at the insolence of human wretchedness, that it should dare to present itself before them, and with the loathsome aspect of its misery presume to disturb the serenity of their happiness" (TMS 100). Becky also has experienced what it is like to be admired. At Chiswick she finds herself without a proper audience, surrounded by silly young girls of good families, the kind of families who may one day employ her as a governess. Smith claims that "to be seen" "renders greatness the object of envy" (TMS 100). For Becky this insight is a particularly difficult pill to swallow because by her own estimations she is the one who, because of her cleverness, wit, and looks, should be the object of envy of the naïve girls around her. She is outraged by the unfairness of a system that deprecates the very qualities for which she used to be admired when her father was alive. By the standards of Chiswick Mall, Amelia is an angel, Becky a serpent. Though Becky does not care about Miss Pinkerton's opinion in particular, it enrages her to think she might be confined to a humble and hence contemptible station in life. In Smith's words, "compared with the contempt of mankind, all other external evils are easily supported" (TMS 106).

According to Smith, the poor man is not taken notice of and goes "unheeded." This, more than anything, makes poverty "mortifying." Nobody notices the poor man who "in the midst of a crowd is in the same obscurity as if shut up in his own hovel" (TMS 99). Smith recognizes that people wish not to be poor because with poverty commonly come hunger and hardship, but he also emphasizes the shamefulness of poverty and its propensity to make people invisible. The poor man knows himself to be unheeded and this mortifies him. The thought of having his poverty exposed to the world makes his position worse: he desires to be seen, but he knows that increased visibility will only expose him to more contempt. This supposition leads Smith to say the following about our desire to better our condition:

> From whence, then, arises that emulation which runs through all the different ranks of men, and what are the advantages which we propose by that great purpose of human life which we call bettering our condition? To be observed, to be attended to, to be taken notice of with sympathy, complacency, and approbation, are all the advantages which we can propose to derive from it (TMS 99).

If the "great purpose of human life" is to better our condition, and we want to better our condition because it will cause us to be "taken notice of with sympathy," it follows that "bettering our condition" is not the end goal but a means to what we are really after: sympathy, recognition and respect from our fellow human beings. But this makes us susceptible to vanity:

> It is the vanity, not the ease, or the pleasure, which interests us. But vanity is always founded upon the belief of our being the object of attention and approbation. The rich man glories in his riches, because he feels that they naturally draw upon him the attention of the world, and

> that mankind are disposed to go along with him in all those agreeable emotions with which the advantages of his situation so readily inspire him (TMS 99).

The feelings Smith here ascribes to the rich must strike us as a little naïve: why would the rich man suppose that others will share his "agreeable emotions" inspired in him by his wealth, especially if those others have no wealth themselves? Perhaps the rich man wants to believe that since his wealth is agreeable to himself, it must also be agreeable to others, taking himself as the standard for approbation. This certainly would be a comfortable view for the rich man, as he could believe himself to be admired (and not, say, resented). But what evidence might the rich man have to believe himself "the object of attention and approbation"? That he is the object of attention appears to be born out by experience: the rich man "glories in his riches" because of the attention his wealth draws upon him. Centuries after Smith wrote this passage, wealth is still more likely to gain you attention than is poverty. More precisely, we are inclined on the one hand to ignore poverty or at least to deny its accompanying hardships and on the other to assign importance to the actions, opinions, and privileges of the wealthy. If we grant this, then perhaps Smith's suggestion that the wealthy can count on sympathy becomes more plausible. If we do not want to see poor people but focus our attention on the wealthy *and aspire to be like them*, is it a surprise that the rich man believes we approve of him? We may envy him his wealth, but this just shows that we want to *be* him, or at least be in his position.

Rebecca Sharp knows what it is like to be taken notice of, to be seen even without the aid of wealth. An experienced puppeteer and actress at the age of eighteen, she leaves Chiswick Hall to embark on a "campaign" to better her condition. She wants to be wealthy, but to gain riches is not her only and perhaps not even her primary goal. She wants to be taken notice of and, as a means to this end, she wants to exercise and hone her powers of mimicry and deception. Becky's vivacity and spirit appear to find their most natural expression in wit and cruelty, often temporarily hidden underneath a convincing veneer of modesty and artlessness. Though the parts she plays inspire sympathy, her person does not (at least not in the inhabitants of VF; the reader may feel differently): those who fall for Becky's deceptions are invariably shocked to find out that her love and affection for them (so agreeable to their *amour-propre*) was not real. After he has related much of her career, the narrator offers the reader the image of a Siren both to describe Becky and to justify his own narration thus far:

> I defy any one to say that our Becky, who has certainly some vices, has not been presented to the public in a perfectly genteel and inoffensive manner. In describing this Siren, singing and smiling, coaxing and cajoling, the author, with modest pride, asks his readers all round, has he once forgotten the laws of politeness, and showed the monster's hideous tail above water? No! Those who like may peep down under waves that are pretty transparent and see it writhing and twirling, diabolically hideous and slimy, flapping amongst bones, or curling round corpses; but above the waterline, I ask, has not everything been proper, agreeable, and decorous, and has any the most squeamish immoralist in Vanity Fair a right to cry fie? (VF 812)

Half angel and half monster, the mermaid is a suitable double for Becky. But a Siren is of course an angel in appearance only; her true nature is monstrous and her actions above the waterline are mere make-belief. She is not "half angel:" she only plays the angel when it suits her evil ends. The narrator explains:

> When, however, the Siren disappears and dives below, down among the dead men, the water of course grows turbid over her, and it is labour lost to look into it ever so curiously. They look pretty enough when they sit upon a rock, twanging their harps and combing their hair, and sing, and beckon to you to come and hold the looking-glass; but when they sink into their native element, depend on it, those mermaids are about no good, and we had best not examine the fiendish marine cannibals, revelling and feasting on their wretched pickled victims. And so, when Becky is out of the way, be sure that she is not particularly well employed, and that the less that is said about her doings is in fact the better (VF 812-813).

The narrator modestly professes his desire to only talk about what is proper and pleasant, and merely hints at the vicious activities in which Becky is engaged when she is "out of the way" and the story centers on the other inhabitants of VF. This part of the story remains hidden in the "unnarrated depths" (Brink-Roby 2013, 133). Yet in the very same passage that includes these genteel and polite narrative intentions, he describes the underwater world of the mermaid, where she feasts on "dead men," her "wretched pickled victims." Becky is dangerous, monstrous, because she has perfected a role that will help her subvert the system that relies on this kind of performance.[17]

Wives of the Second Best Kind

In a passage from TMS dealing with hypocrisy, Smith uses the seemingly off-hand example of "a wife" who "may sometimes not feel that tender regard for her husband which is suitable to the relation that subsists between them." Fortunately, her lack of regard does not necessarily spell doom for their domestic felicity: "If she has been virtuously educated, however, she will endeavour to *act as if* she felt it, to be careful, officious, faithful, and sincere, and to be deficient in none of those attentions which the sentiment of conjugal affection could have prompted her to perform."[18] Though "such a wife," he adds, is not "the very first" of her kind, she is "perhaps the second" (TMS 185, emphasis added). This virtuously educated wife acts the way she does without "hypocrisy or blamable dissimulation" and from a "sacred regard to general rules." The use of the word "sincere" in this passage is surprising: how is it possible for her simultaneously to be sincere and to pretend?

---

[17] Micael M. Clarke discusses Thackeray's awareness of the cultural construction of (female) identity, arguing that "Thackeray anticipates modernism: he was acutely aware of the way personality, including gender-associated characteristics, may be socially constructed" (1995, 49). It is therefore no coincidence that Thackeray compares Becky and his other female characters to mythological creatures and works of art. "Thackeray's novels were indeed a protest … against an entire system of false social values, including false ideas of male honor and female virtue, and of the role of the novel in shaping a culture" (1995, 47).

[18] For a discussion of the sexual contract described in the conduct literature of the late 18th and early nineteenth century, see Armstrong 1990.

Perhaps she is sincere in her "sacred regard" for the rules dictating proper wifely behavior, and this praiseworthy attitude bestows moral value on her actions (TMS 186). But what, in this context, may be the "general rules" at stake? Clearly they are the same conduct rules governing the genteel feminine behavior and propriety of the Victorian heroines discussed above.

That Smith relegates women to the private sphere of non-economic activities can in part be deduced from the mere fact of their absence from Smith's text. Or, more precisely, from the absence of their labor, which is nowhere in his published work acknowledged as a part of the economy. When women do make an appearance in TMS, their part as Smith describes it bears close resemblance to the role Lydgate thought Rosamond would play in his life. Commenting on proper conduct, Smith writes: "To talk to a woman as we would to a man is improper: it is expected that their company should inspire us with more gaiety, more pleasantry, and more attention; and an entire insensibility to the fair sex, renders a man contemptible in some measure even to the men" (TMS 78). More dramatically, Smith uses a telling example when he laments moral disorder, citing "the eloquent and philosophical bishop of Clermont" who asks: "'does it suit the greatness of God, to leave the world which he has created in so universal a disorder? To see the wicked prevail almost always over the just… the husband expiring under the stroke of a barbarous and faithless wife?'" (TMS 191). Faithless wives, like the wicked, subvert the proper order of things and act against the will of God. This offers a clue to our understanding of Smith's estimation of the play-acting wife as being of the "second best" kind. She may not feel the "tender regard" that is rightly expected of her, but she respects the proper order of things as laid down in the rules for which she has a "sacred regard." Without knowing what, exactly, these rules might be, Smith's comments of proper female conduct combined with his general neglect of women's roles in public life and the economy suggest that they are not dissimilar from the rules laid out by authors like Erasmus cited above. Husband murder is so clear an example of disorder that it needs no further comment: it is an offense against both propriety and morality. And yet: the woman acting as if she feels a tender regard for her husband cannot be called sincere about her feelings, even if she is sincerely following the rules prescribing proper wifely conduct. Elsewhere in TMS, Smith talks about men seeking vain praise, i.e. praise they do not deserve because it does not pertain to who they are in reality:

> The man who applauds us either for actions which we did not perform, or for motives which had no sort of influence upon our conduct, applauds not us, but another person. We can derive no sort of satisfaction from his praises. To us they should be more mortifying than any censure, and should perpetually call to our minds, the most humbling of all reflections, the reflection of what we ought to be, but what we are not (TMS 152).

Though of course Smith wrote at a time when it was common to use words like "man" and "mankind" to include men and women alike, the passage above reveals a tension between Smith's judgment on men and his judgment on women concerning praise for what they ought to be but are not. Smith praises the unloving but dutiful wife for acting *as if* she feels tender regard for her husband, yet by the standards set for men we know she should be mortified for being praised by those who (like her husband?) mistake her play-acting for reality. She is caught in a double bind: on the one hand she is expected to *be* rather than to merely *seem* "good," on the other this "goodness" is defined by a set of rules that together amount to an ideal attainable only through play-acting. Rosamond seems, but turns out not to be, the perfect angel who emerged from Mrs. Lemon's school. Even Amelia, as we shall see, ultimately shows herself to be a vain person, ignoring the man who loves her out of misplaced fidelity to a dead husband. To further complicate things, the unloving but *seemingly* attentive wife from TMS is only the second best kind of wife, while the best kind – who not only feels true tender regard for her husband but also comports herself according to the very rules that demand that she play a part – appears to be both a fiction and a contradiction unto herself. Smith supplies a helpful example in support of this point in TMS where he writes about undeserved praise and the attendant feelings of mortification. Referring to a woman who uses what today we would call make-up, he writes:

> A woman who paints, could derive, one should imagine, but little vanity from the compliments that are paid to her complexion. These, we should expect, ought rather to put her in mind of the sentiments which her real complexion would excite, and mortify her the more by the contrast. To be pleased with such groundless applause is a proof of the most superficial levity and weakness (TMS 152).

Yet this same woman, when she is pretending to love her husband, deserves our praise (even if not our highest praise). Several themes come together here. We all, claims Smith, desire to better our condition because we believe that this will make others acknowledge and "heed" us. But Smith also holds that this acknowledgment from others should be based on our real merits, not on play-acting or make-believe: if we accept their praise and attention knowing that we are unworthy of either, it is a sign of "the most superficial levity and weakness."[19] For most people, Smith holds, it is "mortifying" to accept praise for something they did not do or feel. And yet Smith himself praises the second best kind of wife for deceiving her husband into thinking that she loves him while she does not. This cluster of observations is further complicated by Smith's account of sympathy, which starts from the presupposition that it is our deepest desire "to be seen," to be known for who we truly are. The female characters we have encountered so far cannot "be seen" in this way because they all more or less consciously play a part: some earnestly, others manipulatively but all of them because they have to.[20]

---

[19] Vanity is a vice for women and for the effeminate, which is why Jos Sedley and George Osborne are mocked in *Vanity Fair.* But these men are ridiculous not only because they behave like women but also because they assume a vice reserved for the aristocracy. As Sarah Rose Cole argues, "Thackeray implies that effeminacy and male vanity are appropriate for idle aristocrats, while middle-class men who are vain must be condemned as snobs" (Cole 2005, 152). The middle class man who looks in the mirror thus violates both gender and class norms. Vanity is natural only for aristocrats like Rawdon, but not for city men like George (Cole 2005).

[20] Gilbert and Gubar argue that female authors in the nineteenth century had to apply a similar, even more complicated strategy. They told "their own stories" but "allayed their distinctively female anxieties of authorship by following Emily Dickinson's famous (and characteristically female)

Becky Sharp stands apart because she, more than the other (pre-) Victorian heroines discussed here, takes a delight in deceit, double talk, and manipulation. In some ways she resembles the dashing but untrustworthy male characters from Jane Austen's novels, the ones who are easy to fall in love with but invariably turn out to be no good: Mr. Willoughby in *Sense & Sensibility,* Mr. Wickham in *Pride and Prejudice,* Frank Churchill in *Emma,* and Mr. Elliot in *Persuasion.* Like Becky, these charming gentlemen are duplicitous and talk of love and affection without complete sincerity. But unlike Becky, they are not expected to be angelic, passive, and selfless and they do not have to pay a (large) price for their deceit once it becomes known.

To Be Quiet and Very Much Interested

Smith writes about the heroes of tragedy and romance and our sympathy for them. As spectators, we see the injustice done to them and feel grief and resentment on their behalf just as we experience joy when they are delivered from their trials. We feel pain at their pain, happiness at their happiness, because our feelings are analogous to the feelings of the characters. In his account of sympathy, Smith repeatedly uses the phrases "to bring [a situation] home to oneself" and "to enter into [a situation]" to describe the sympathetic process. When we can bring someone's situation home to ourselves we can enter into it and sympathize with the person's sentiments. The more fully we can sympathize with another person, the more we are apt to agree with them and consider their feelings reasonable and proper. When we cannot relate to or identify with the person's situation we cannot sympathize with him or her and will judge their sentiments as inappropriate or unreasonable. We know no greater joy than to be in harmony with others and feel like they sympathize with us, and no greater mortification than to notice others cannot enter into our sentiments and judge us accordingly. We are therefore often tempted to act a part we think our spectators will approve of, hiding our true feelings for fear that others may look down on us. The result is that we may earn praise and admiration for our performance rather than for the sentiments we actually experience. People may sympathize with what is in effect a façade, a convincing piece of make-believe. This is not the ideal sympathy Smith has in mind when he writes about our just admiration for the wise and virtuous, but rather the misdirected sympathy we tend to feel for the great and powerful. A person's wealth tells us nothing about a person's character and yet most of us admire the wealthy and not only ascribe to them virtues for the existence of which

advice to "Tell all the Truth but tell it slant-" (1980, 51). "In short, like the twentieth century American poet H. D., who declared her aesthetic strategy by entitling one of her novels Palimpsest, women from Jane Austen and Mary Shelley to Emily Bronte and Emily Dickinson produced literary works that are in some sense palimpsestic, works whose surface designs conceal or obscure deeper, less accessible (and less socially acceptable) levels of meaning. Thus these authors managed the difficult task of achieving true female literary authority by simultaneously conforming to and subverting patriarchal literary standards" (1980, 73).

we have no evidence, but forgive them their obvious vices. Status and rank affect our moral evaluation and this goes both ways: we look down on the virtues of the poor and instead of forgiving them their vices we judge them more harshly because they belong to someone in the "inferior ranks."

Substituting the heroines discussed in this chapter for Smith's "heroes of tragedy and romance," we can add a few insights to Smith's doctrine of sympathy. Leaving aside for the moment the reader's ability to enter into their situations and bring their cases home to herself, we see that Rosamond, Becky, and Amelia all receive admiration from a variety of spectators. They all of them are praised for their appearance and feminine conduct, even if the three women are not equally purposeful in their performance. Whatever the difference in their awareness of the instrumentality of their conduct to gain praise, it is clear that in most instances the "sympathy" they receive does not pertain to their (moral) sentiments but to the pictures or images these three women project. Just like a person's wealth or status tells us nothing about a person's character, a person's conduct and appearance tells us nothing about her motivations and feelings – especially when she is a "natural" actress. But Smith evaluates the wealthy person and the "woman who paints" very differently. We can only guess the wealthy person's moral character, and Smith would rather we reserve our praise for the wise and virtuous. Yet in the end "it is well" that we admire our "superiors" because it preserves the order of society. "Nature" has decreed that human psychology works this way. Smith nowhere claims that the wealthy should be ashamed to receive so much undeserved praise. A woman who uses make-up, on the other hand, ought to be mortified at the praise she receives for her complexion. This puts her into a bind not imposed on the wealthy: while one presumably could get to know a rich person and determine the extent of their virtue and wisdom, the woman who paints cannot allow anyone to get close enough to see through the image she has so carefully constructed – neither literally nor figuratively.

The next chapter discusses the importance of blushing and the accompanying expectation that women preserve their youthful innocence not only in character but also in appearance. In the current context it suffices to observe that the woman who paints cannot simply "drop the act" and go about *au naturel,* without make-up. She faces a Catch 22: she must perform the part of the proper lady, expressing a "sacred regard" for the rules made explicit in the conduct literature, but she must also (on Smith's account of undeserved praise) be ashamed at the praise she receives when her performance is successful. How can this woman ever feel the joy Smith describes as resulting from the "harmony of sentiments?" (TMS 70, 75) For someone to feel like the sentiments "of their own breast" are recognized by another person who sympathizes and hence approves of these sentiments, there needs to be some kind of open exchange. The next chapter describes the impossibility of this exchange between the sexes, at least between those members of the sexes who obey the masculine and feminine roles implicit in Smith's theory of the division of labor and education.

These insights also bear on our understanding of Smith's account of vanity. One of the defining characteristics of the vain person is that he or she takes pleasure in undeserved praise. This chapter showed that the "second best kind of wife" must pretend to feelings she does not possess, thus cutting herself off from the harmony of sentiments that is, on Smith's account, essential to happiness. If she takes pleasure in the compliments she receives for being a loving wife, this would make her vain. She has to live with the knowledge that any praise she receives is false praise, and that she will be forever denied the chance of true sympathy.

This is a glum state of affairs, which is why we must remember Becky. As a spectator nothing escapes her attention and as an actor she applies what she has learned with great effect. Specifically, she observes the many different ways in which the people around her are vain and pretends to sympathize with them the way she knows will most delight them. She can give others the sense that she shares their feelings and approves of them in ways other people cannot. At the same time, she knows how to give people the feeling that they can "bring her case home" to them and "enter into" Becky's situation. She applies all the rules of proper female conduct to achieve this effect and to give the people (and especially men) surrounding her the feeling that they have a unique understanding of her, an underappreciated, innocent and angelic woman. Becky does not care that the praise she receives pertains to her performance, not her virtue. In fact, the distinction seems moot to her. Becky's art is her pride and joy and she appears genuinely unconcerned about the discrepancy between her conduct and her ambitions. Furthermore, she does not care about the virtue and wisdom of others either; she is interested in their vanity and rarely has reason to look any further.

Becky's playfulness is in contrast with Smith's grave and pessimistic account of human vice and folly. If she is rarely completely honest with anyone, she is sincere in the lighthearted and energetic pleasure she takes in her puppeteering. She creates her own rules not because she wants to push back on the oppressive morality of her time but because she has never identified with this morality – the mores of Becky's time are constraints she has to take into account, not rules she has internalized. The importance of internalized rules will be a topic of Chap. 7 which discusses Smith's notion of the impartial spectator and suggests that Becky, too, has developed a spectator but one whose rules are primarily aesthetic and who bears little resemblance to Smith's moral ideal.

References

Armstrong, Nancy. 1990. *Desire and domestic fiction: A political history of the novel*. Cary: Oxford University Press.

Austen, Jane. 2003. *Emma*. Oxford: Oxford University Press.

———. 2004. *Pride and prejudice*. Oxford: Oxford University Press.

Bninski, Julia. 2011. *Vanity Fair's* ethic of readerly emotion. *Victorians Journal*: 118–128.

Brink-Roby, Heather. 2013. Psyche: Mirror and mind in *Vanity Fair*. *ELH* 80 (1): 215–147.

Clarke, Micael M. 1995. *Thackeray and women*. Dekalb: Northern Illinois UP.

Cole, Sarah Rose. 2005. The aristocrat in the mirror: Male vanity and bourgeois desire in William Makepeace Thackeray's *Vanity Fair*. *Nineteenth-Century Literature* 61 (2): 137–170.

Darwin, Erasmus. 1798. *A plan for the conduct of female education in boarding schools*. Gale and the British library facsimile edition of the original.

Dibattista, Maria. 1980. The triumph of Clytemnestra: The charades in vanity fair. *PMLA* 95 (5): 827–837.

Dimand, Robert W., Evelyn L. Forget, and Chris Nyland. 2004. Retrospectives: Gender in classical economics. *The Journal of Economic Perspectives* 18 (1): 229–240.

Eliot, George. 1996. *Middlemarch*. Oxford: Oxford University Press.

Gilbert, Sandra M., and Susan Gubar. 1980. *The madwoman in the attic: The woman writer and the nineteenth-century literary imagination*. New Haven: Yale University Press.

Jadwin, Lisa. 1992. The seductiveness of female duplicity in vanity fair. *Studies in English Literature, 1500–1900* 32 (4): 663–687.

Jones, Ann. 1981. *Women who kill*. New York: Fawcett.

King, Nikole. 2011. The male body and heroic manhood in Thackeray's Vanity Fair: A novel without a Hero. *Victorians Journal*: 105–116.

Neocleous, Mark. 2014. "O effeminacy! Effeminacy!:" martial power, masculine power, liberal peace. In *War Power, Police Power*. Edinburgh: Edinburgh UP.

Pujol, Michèle. 1998. *Feminism and Anti-feminism in early economic thought*. Northampton: Edward Elgar.

Rendall, Jane. 1987. Virtue and commerce: Women in the making of Adam Smith's political economy. In *Women in Western Political Philosophy, Kant to Nietzsche*. Brighton: Wheatsheaf Books.

Smith, Adam. 1981. An inquiry into the nature and causes of the wealth of nations. In *Vol. 2 of the Glasgow Edition of the Works and Correspondence of Adam Smith*, ed. R.H. Campbell and A.S. Skinner. Indianapolis: Liberty Fund.

———. 1982a. The theory of moral sentiments. In *Vol. 1 of the Glasgow Edition of the Works and Correspondence of Adam Smith*, ed. D.D. Raphael and A.L. Macfie. Indianapolis: Liberty Fund.

———. 1982b. Lectures on Jurisprudence. In *Vol. 5 of the Glasgow Edition of the Works and Correspondence of Adam Smith*, ed. R.L. Meek, D.D. Raphael, and P.G. Stein. Indianapolis: Liberty Fund.

Thackeray, William Makepeace. 1983. In *Vanity Fair: A novel without a hero*, ed. John Sutherland. New York: Oxford UP.

Womick, Stephanie. 2011. The green silk purse and little Rawdon's shirt: Sartorial literacy and domestic performance in Vanity. *Victorians Journal*: 67–79.

Chapter 4
Educating the Martial Spirit

Abstract Adam Smith condemns the public education of his day as a "useless and pedantick heap of sophistry and nonsense" (WN ii 168). Most of what men learn in public institutions in no way prepares them for their future lives or professions. Women's education, on the other hand, focuses on what it is necessary and useful for women to learn. Becky Sharp in Thackeray's *Vanity Fair* understands that "a virtuous woman is a crown to her husband" and convincingly plays the part of the girlish, guileless loving wife – for as long as it suits her (VF 699). The conduct literature of the late eighteenth and early nineteenth century prescribes that a woman should soften a man's heart and polish his manners, and Becky appears a perfect domestic angel while she is striving to better her condition and gain power through her performance. While Adam Smith laments the decline of what he calls the "martial spirit," Becky shows that women, largely absent from Smith's account, are forced to develop the "masculine firmness" and "Spartan discipline" Smith finds lacking in the male members of commercial society. Women resemble the "savages" Smith describes with some awe: forced to dissimulate, they become unpredictable and dangerous.

The Importance of Blushing

This chapter continues the discussion of proper female conduct but shifts the emphasis from sympathy and vanity to what Smith calls the "martial spirit." Though Smith describes the warlike attitude accompanying this spirit in emphatically masculine terms, the heroines introduced in the previous chapter appear to possess a spirit more martial than the men around them. Smith's account of the martial spirit helps frame the "hypocrisy" that VF's manager detects in women: they are expected to be passive, quietly cheerful, weak, innocent, soft and simple but in order to keep up these appearances they must be active, smart, strong and savvy. Furthermore, their performance requires them to exercise great self-command, perhaps the most manly of all the virtues, to bear the tortures of domestic life without complaint, and never betray the complexity of their inner lives. Against this backdrop, the current chapter will consider Smith's thoughts on education and the division of labor, in

R. Slegers, *Adam Smith's Moral Sentiments in Vanity Fair*, Issues in Business Ethics 49, https://doi.org/10.1007/978-3-319-98731-6_4

particular his notion that education should be suited to the needs of the people educated and the idea that an individual's understanding is formed by his or her employment. Self-command, essential to the martial spirit so admired by Smith, emerges as an unintended and (depending on one's perspective) dangerous side effect of women's education. To understand the hypocrisy essential to a woman's performance, we will first turn to Becky's friend Amelia Sedley who falls on hard times after her husband George Osborne's death.

Amelia's father has been ruined on the stock exchange and has fallen ill after the death of Amelias mother, Mrs. Sedley. Amelia has to part with her young son George because she has no money to raise him. The Manager of the Performance exclaims: "O you poor women! O you poor secret martyrs and victims, whose life is a torture, who are stretched on racks in your bedrooms, and who lay your heads down on the block daily at the drawing-room table; every man who watches your pains, or peers into those dark places where the torture is administered to you, must pity you— and— and thank God that he has a beard" (VF 724).

Many women's lives are spent performing "cheerless duties," watching by "thankless sick-beds" where, like Amelia with her sickly father, they "suffer the harassment and tyranny of querulous disappointed old age." The narrator recognizes that most of the "thousands of people … who are doomed to endure this long slavery" are women: "hospital nurses without wages— sisters of Charity, if you like." These women do not even have "the romance and the sentiment of sacrifice" but "strive, fast, watch, and suffer, unpitied" just to "fade away ignobly and unknown" (VF 725). But while Amelia is resigned to her situation, Becky clearly is not. Instead of being enslaved, she is the one doing the enslaving. She watches by Miss Crawley's sickbed but only because she expects to materially benefit from it, not because she feels it her female or friendly duty. This is contrast to Amelia's sense of daughterly and motherly obligation. Observing Amelia's suffering, the narrator again laments the fate of women:

> What do men know about women's martyrdoms? We should go mad had we to endure the hundredth part of those daily pains which are meekly borne by many women. Ceaseless slavery meeting with no reward; constant gentleness and kindness met by cruelty as constant; love, labour, patience, watchfulness, without even so much as the acknowledgement of a good word; all this, how many of them have to bear in quiet, and appear abroad with cheerful faces as if they felt nothing. Tender slaves that they are, they must needs be hypocrites and weak (VF 720).

Tender slaves, these women are yet strong enough to bear pains a hundred times greater than a man could endure. They have to appear cheerful while they are subjected to cruelty and yet in their cheerfulness they have to appear weak. And they have to manage this complicated mix of feelings and performances without acknowledgment – even though to be acknowledged is, on Smith's account, our deepest desire. Women, the narrator of VF indicates, have to be hypocrites because they have to deceive the world and themselves into thinking that they are something they are not. Because how could someone truly weak bear the kind of torture to which women are subjected?

Chapter 3 briefly touched on a few of the problematic aspects of proper female conduct here alluded to by VF's narrator. On Smith's account in TMS of the "virtuously educated" wife, women who do not love their husbands should nonetheless "endeavor to *act as if*" they felt "the sentiment of conjugal affection" (TMS 185). Contrary to the narrator's views expressed in VF, Smith holds that these women are no hypocrites, nor can we blame them for dissimulating. Yet elsewhere in TMS, Smith refers to "a woman who paints," i.e. uses rouge to enhance her complexion, to make a scathing point about vanity: if this woman receives any compliments about her complexion, Smith states, we should expect her to be mortified because she knows that her real complexion would not receive any such praise. "To be pleased with such groundless applause," Smith concludes, "is a proof of the most superficial levity and weakness" (TMS 152). It is therefore very important for a woman to know when pretense and dissimulation are expected and praiseworthy, and when they are proof of superficial levity and weakness.

Amelia, during her younger years and before her father's ruination, has no need of rouge: "Her face," as we already know, "blushed with rosy health, and her lips with the freshest of smiles" (VF 7). The subject of a woman's complexion is not as trivial as it may at first appear. Very few women make their way into TMS (or WN) and when they do make an appearance we have reason to wonder why Smith chose a female example to make any particular point. Furthermore, Smith is not alone in his condemnation of fake blushes and (we may infer) his appreciation of the genuine article. In a popular conduct book of the late eighteenth century (and a favorite of Jane Austen), Dr. Gregory starts his account of proper female "conduct and behavior" praising "one of the chief beauties in a female character:" "that modest reserve, that retiring delicacy, which avoids the public eye, and is disconcerted even at the gaze of admiration" (Gregory 25). And he continues:

> WHEN a girl ceases to blush, she has lost the most powerful charm of beauty. That extreme sensibility which it indicates, may be a weakness and incumbrance in our sex, as I have too often felt; but in yours it is peculiarly engaging. Pedants who think themselves philosophers, ask why a woman should blush when she is conscious of no crime? It is a sufficient answer that Nature has made you to blush when you are guilty of no fault, and has forced us to love you because you do so. Blushing is so far from being necessarily an attendant on guilt, that it is the usual companion of innocence. (Gregory 26)

Dr. Gregory wrote *A Father's Legacy* after his wife died, leaving him to raise his daughters without a mother. He claims that he and his late wife agreed on everything and that he is merely conveying the girls' mother's thoughts on proper education. In the introduction to the *Legacy,* he states that he holds the female sex in high regard and that he considers his daughters (and women in general) "not as domestic drudges, or the slaves of our pleasures, but as our companions and equals" (Gregory 12). In what apparently did not seem to Dr. Gregory like a statement at odds with the previous, he then goes on to explain that he thinks of his daughters and any other female beneficiaries of his treatise "as designed to soften our [i.e. men's] hearts and polish our manners; and as Thompson [sic] finely says, "To raise the virtues, animate the bliss/And sweeten all the toils of human life" (Gregory 12).[1] Unlike Becky, who has to do her husband hunting without a mother or father to help her, Dr. Gregory's daughters have at their disposal a "system of conduct" which their father believes will not only help them become honorable and happy but also to guide them to "those virtues and accomplishments which render you most respectable and most amiable in the eyes of [their father's] own sex" (Gregory 13).[2] Becky's father, too, was concerned with his daughter's fate and, before he died in a fit of delirium tremens, entrusted her to the care of Ms. Pinkerton at Chiswick Hall. Ms. Pinkerton's education was structured on the same principles as those laid out in conduct books of the period and helped Becky extend and perfect her acting skills. Becky knows when to blush, and how to appear innocent, but for her the conduct rules are never more than guidelines for how to *act*, never prescriptive of how to *be*.

The reader of *A Father's Legacy* gets the feeling that the "virtues and accomplishments" Dr. Gregory points out for his daughters' benefit are meant not so much to help them become happy women but to keep them in a state of childlike passivity for life. That is, he wants them to grow up to run their husbands' households, which presumably will require a good amount of decisiveness and insight. But the good sense and maturity they will need in this quarter should not lessen their soft, modest, and innocent behavior in the presence of men. In her *Vindication of the Rights of Woman,* Mary Wollstonecraft takes issue with the conduct books of her time and addresses her female readers directly:

> My own sex, I hope, will excuse me, if I treat them like rational creatures, instead of flattering their fascinating graces, and viewing them as if they were in a state of perpetual childhood … Dismissing then those pretty feminine phrases, which the men condescendingly use to soften our slavish dependence, and despising that weak elegancy of mind, exquisite sensibility, and sweet docility of manners, supposed to be the sexual characteristics of the weaker vessel, … I wish to shew that elegance is inferior to virtue, that the first object of laudable ambition is to obtain a character as a human being, regardless of the distinction of sex; and that secondary views should be brought to this simple touchstone. (Wollstonecraft 73)

Amelia could serve to illustrate Dr. Gregory's *Legacy* and yet in VF she is described as capable of bearing pains and tortures the likes of which most men could not endure. There need not be a contradiction here, however: Dr. Gregory's prescriptions for his daughters do not preclude the possibility that they will experience the "torture" to which Amelia is subjected in VF. In fact, the requirements laid out in the *Legacy* perhaps help create the "dark places where the torture is administered" to women who have to appear cheerful when they are miserable, and be content with

[1]The lines are from James Thomson, *The Seasons*: "Autumn." See James Thomson, *The Works of James Thomson*, Palala Press, 2016. II.606–9.

[2]The tone and content of Dr. Gregory's *Legacy* make the perfect daughter and the perfect wife sound very much alike. Similarly, it appears that a good husband is very much like a good father. Dr. Gregory tells his daughters how to behave in relation to the opposite sex and explicitly identifies himself with the opposite sex. The inequality Dr. Gregory ascribes to both relationships (the woman childlike and naïve, the man fatherly and wise in the ways of the world) serves to stress the identity between the ideal daughter and the ideal bride.

the praise they receive for their innocent blushes. Smith does not talk about a woman's capacity to bear pain and torture, but he is clear about this virtue in men. The ability to support pain is praiseworthy, the lack of it contemptible:

> No character is more contemptible than that of a coward; no character is more admired than that of the man who faces death with intrepidity, and maintains his tranquillity and presence of mind amidst the most dreadful dangers. We esteem the man who supports pain and even torture with manhood and firmness; and we can have little regard for him who sinks under them, and abandons himself to useless outcries and womanish lamentations. A fretful temper, which feels, with too much sensibility, every little cross accident, renders a man miserable in himself and offensive to other people (TMS 252).

Dr. Gregory praises the "extreme sensibility" that causes women to blush but holds that the same propensity in men is "an encumbrance" (Gregory 25). Similarly, Smith holds that "too much sensibility" in a man makes him not only unhappy but "offensive" to others. And of course he notably (though predictably) condemns as "womanish lamentations" the "outcries" of a man lacking in "manhood and firmness." Thackeray's narrator, by contrast, repeatedly comments on women's ability to bear pain and suffering far beyond what most men are subjected to even on the battlefield. Amelia, who cries at the death of a mouse, of a silly novel, endures great suffering when she is forced to part from her child and to live with her emotionally abusive mother and bankrupt father – all of it without giving vent to "womanish lamentations" but bearing her grief in silence.

Bettering one's Condition through Marriage

Smith holds that it is the "great purpose of human life" to better our condition. This "emulation" "runs through all the different ranks of men" and comes from our desire "to be observed, to be attended to, to be taken notice of with sympathy, complacency, and approbation" (TMS 99). This desire, in turn, can make us vain. Smith does not make explicit what it means for a woman to have an interest in bettering her condition, but he does regard vanity as an "effeminate" vice, a folly occurring in both women and men but one that takes away from a man's manliness. Since vanity "is always founded upon the belief of our being the object of attention and approbation," and since Smith is explicit about the existence of vain women, it follows that on his account women, too, care about being the object of attention (TMS 99). But to be susceptible to vanity, one has to be susceptible to the emulation Smith calls "the great purpose of human life." In short, even though Smith barely mentions women in TMS or WN, his account of the desire to better our condition combined with his comments on (female) vanity make clear that women, too, wish to better their condition.

This is important because reading TMS and WN, one gets the impression that to Smith's mind (if indeed they are on his mind at all), women are content to stay within the domestic sphere. More precisely, we simply do not encounter women in Smith's public sphere – no decent women, that is, or women belonging to the middle and upper classes. This is in line with the conduct books of the time. As Thomas Broadhurst puts it in his *Advice to Young Ladies on the Improvement of the Mind and Conduct of Life*, only a woman "destitute of all amusements with herself, and incapable of perceiving her chief happiness to center at home, in the bosom of her family" will feel the need to "[sally] forth in quest of adventures." But a woman interested in appearing in public does not make a good wife. 'Such women are "regularly seen in the ballroom or at the card-table, at the opera or in the theatre, among the numberless devotees of dissipation and fashion."'[3] Women should not desire to be seen – at least not outside their homes.

Dr. Gregory acknowledges that his female audience, confined to the private sphere, may worry about ever meeting any suitable gentlemen at all. After all, he recommends that his daughters be always reserved in their behavior, and seldom appear in public places. But he does not intend to "cut off all opportunities of your being acquainted with gentlemen," adding: "I am very far from intending this. I advise you to no reserve, but what will render you more respected and beloved by our sex" (Gregory 79). And yet in what follows, Dr. Gregory only presents more reasons to believe that his daughters would be right to be concerned about finding a suitable husband: "without an unusual share of natural sensibility, and very peculiar good fortune, a woman in this country has very little probability of marrying for love" (Gregory 59). Since "love is not to begin" on the woman's part, but she must wait for a man to love her first, it is very unlikely that the man who happens to fall in love with her will also be someone she esteems. Men are "exceedingly capricious" in whom they choose to love and "it is extremely improbable" that the man who becomes "particularly attached" to a woman of "sense and taste" "should be the man in the world her heart most approved of" (Gregory 59). Fortunately, Nature has granted women "a greater flexibility of taste" than she has granted men. A woman feels gratitude when she perceives an agreeable man's attachment to her and "this gratitude rises into a preference, and this preference perhaps at last advances to some degree of attachment" (Gregory 60). This attachment may make it possible that a woman can marry for love, but only if the attachment first "meets with crosses and difficulties." Without obstacles and "a state of suspense" to help love grow, "there is not one of a million of you that could ever marry with any degree of love" (Gregory 60). A man may marry a woman because he loves her, but "a woman of equal taste and delicacy marries him because she esteems him, and because he gives her that preference" (Gregory 61).[4]

---

[3]Thomas Broadhurst, Advice to Young Ladies on the Improvement of the Mind and Conduct of Life (1810), cited in Armstrong (1990). Armstrong comments on this passage: "That, in a word, is their crime: these women either want to be on display or simply allow themselves to be "seen." It is not that the conduct books disapprove of dancing, enjoying music, playing cards, or even attending theatrical performances when they are enjoyed in the sanctuary of one's parlor. … It is a woman's participation in public spectacle that injures her, for as an object of display, she always loses value as a subject" (Armstrong 1990).

[4]This certainly appears to be the case for Amelia and Dobbin in *Vanity Fair,* though it takes Amelia a very long time to finally feel the gratitude which (Dr. Gregory might argue) is Dobbin's due.

Dr. Gregory recommends social passivity throughout his *Legacy,* cautioning his daughters against going out in public, being witty, or even speaking much at all (fortunately "people of sense and discernment will never mistake such silence for dullness" (Gregory 26)). But if (recalling Smith) women, like men, desire to better their condition, and if marriage is the only real means at their disposal to achieve what Smith calls this "great purpose of human life," where does this leave them? Chap. 3 suggested that women have no choice but to resort to play-acting: to carefully follow the rules while secretly using them to their advantage. The childlike, blushing woman described in the conduct literature thus takes on an ambiguous and perhaps even a frightening aspect: vicious, plotting women may deceive men into bestowing their "exceedingly capricious" love on them. The emphasis Dr. Gregory and other authors of conduct books place on modesty, reserve, and general passivity sounds less fatherly and when regarded in light of a statute passed by Parliament in 1770:

> All women of whatever age, rank, profession, or degree, whether virgin maid or widow, that shall from and after such Act impose upon, seduce, and betray into matrimony any of His Majesty's subjects by means of scent, paints, cosmetics, washes, artificial teeth, false hair, Spanish wool, ironstays, hoops, high-heeled shoes, or bolstered hips, shall incur the penalty of the law now in force against witchcraft and like misdemeanors, and that the marriage upon conviction shall stand null and void.[5]

The text of the statute mirrors the opinion expressed by the narrator in *Vanity Fair*: "A woman with fair opportunities and without an absolute hump, may marry WHOM SHE LIKES. Only let us be thankful that the darlings are like the beasts of the field, and don't know their own power. They would overcome us entirely if they did" (VF 34). But the statute also shows what Dr. Gregory feared his daughters might become without the benefit of his *Legacy*: women employing witchlike artifices to trick unwitting men into marrying them. Perhaps it is this fear that motivates him to write: "I know nothing that renders a woman more despicable than her thinking it essential to happiness to be married" (Gregory 74). Later in the same paragraph, however, he shares that he is "of opinion, that you may attain a superior degree of happiness in a married state, to what you can possibly find in any other" (Gregory 74). Dr. Gregory appears to share Harriet's concern on her friend's behalf in *Emma* cited in the previous chapter. Emma, however, believes that celibacy is "contemptible to a generous public" only when it is accompanied by poverty. "A single woman of good fortune," on the contrary, "is always respectable" (Austen, Emma 69). In *Pride and Prejudice,* the same sentiment drives Charlotte Lucas to marry the preposterous Mr. Collins because matrimony is "the only provision for well-educated young women of small fortune, and however uncertain of giving happiness, must be their pleasantest preservative from want" (PP 94). Dr. Gregory does not want his daughters to become "old maids" even though he indicates that they

[5]Cited in Barbara M Swords (1988). Swords adds: "A widely held opinion about women's legal rights was expressed by Dr. Samuel Johnson, renowned man of letters and much admired by Jane Austen as well; he said: "Nature has given women so much power that the law has wisely given them little.""

will be provided for financially upon his death. He fears that they will be subject to peevish tempers, unable to make "a transition with dignity and cheerfulness, from the period of youth, beauty, admiration and respect, into the calm, silent, unnoticed retreat of declining years" (Gregory 75). Unmarried women, even the ones with "vigorous minds, and great vivacity of spirits" are apt to degrade themselves through dissipation or by becoming insufferable busybodies and gossips.[6] Had their "exuberant activity of spirit" but found "employment at home," it "would have rendered them respectable and useful members of society." Other, less vivacious old maids, "blessed with sense, taste, delicacy and every milder feminine virtue of the heart, but of weak spirits" are apt to sink "into obscurity and insignificance, ... gradually losing every elegant accomplishment" (Gregory 76). Why do these women sink?

> For this evident reason, that they are not united to a partner who has sense, and worth, and taste to know their value; one who is not able to draw forth their concealed qualities, and shew them to advantage; who can give that support to their feeble spirits which they stand so much in need of; and who, by his affection and tenderness, might make such a woman happy in exerting every talent and accomplishing herself in every elegant art that could contribute to his amusement. (Gregory 76)

The last part of this sentence is particularly noteworthy, as it makes clear that this woman's happiness consists at least in part in exerting herself to contribute to her husband's amusement. Her happiness is essentially derivative: she cannot attain happiness as an "old maid," by herself, but only as a married woman exerting herself to amuse her husband. If a woman desires to better her condition (as on Smith's account all people do), the best way for her to go about achieving this goal is to marry (as it is the only "career" open to middle class women at the time). But (on Dr. Gregory's account) she should not actively seek a husband, nor even believe marriage to be essential to her happiness. Even though happiness is not the same as bettering one's condition, the pursuit of the desire to better one's condition is the most common way in which people strive for happiness. So though marriage is the best way to better one's condition and achieve (some kind of) happiness, a woman should not actively seek to achieve either of these goals. Additionally, she should not even desire to be "seen" – both in the sense of being "on display" in public and in the deeper sense of being sympathized with as explained in Smith's account of sympathy. And even when she is married, a woman should never relinquish "that reserve and delicacy which always left the lover something farther to wish, and often made him doubtful of your sensibility or attachment" (Gregory 89). Even a married woman should always guard her true feelings in order to keep her husband's love. And even if she truly loves her husband, perhaps even "violently" so, a wife should not let this feeling show because it would result in "satiety and disgust" on her husband's part (Gregory 16). Dr. Gregory feels it necessary to add this cautionary note even though women are naturally reserved: "Nature in this case, has laid the reserve on you" (Gregory 64).[7]

---

[6] Emma in Jane Austen's *Emma* appears to be in danger of becoming this kind of woman but is saved when she marries Mr. Knightley (Austen 2003).

[7] Even Jane Eyre (who will feature prominently in Chap. 7), fiery and rebellious in comparison to the readership Dr. Gregory appears to have in mind for his book, appears to heed a version of this

The complexity of this cluster of prescriptions, warnings, rules and principles is at odds with the supposed "simplicity" of the female nature and of a woman's life. On Smith's and Dr. Gregory's accounts, men's lives are complex because they are part of the bustle of public life, while a woman's existence is neatly bounded by the domestic sphere. The same distinction defines men's and women's education: women's education is always private, never public. The next section outlines Smith's views on public education and its usefulness in WN to highlight the importance he attaches to order – both the order of society and the order of the sexes.

Public Education and the Martial Spirit

Women's education – be it in boarding schools or through conduct literature - was a private matter in Smith's time. Smith's paragraph about the education of women cited in the previous chapter should be considered in full and in context to better understand its relevance. The paragraph is part of Book V of WN, Chap. 1, Part III, entitled "Of the Expense of publick Works and publick Institutions." Parts I and II of Chap. 1 are devoted to "the publick institutions and publick works necessary for the defence of the society, and for the administration of justice" respectively (WN ii 131). Part III considers the public institutions that facilitate "the commerce of the society" and those that promote "the instruction of the people." The latter is the topic of the second Article of Part III: "Of the Expense of the Institution for the Education of Youth." Smith explains that public schools and universities were originally "intended only for the education of a particular profession, that of churchmen" (WN ii 163). Though the quality of the education offered at these institutions left something to be desired even from the perspective of someone interested in becoming a churchman, "they gradually drew to themselves the education of almost all other people, particularly of almost all gentlemen and men of fortune." Smith explains that education of this kind became the obvious way for young men to spend the years making up "the long interval between infancy and that period of life at which men begin to apply in good earnest to the real business of the world." Not because the education they received at university was suited to the "real business of the world" in which they were supposed to engage later in life, nor because it was

piece of advice. In response to Rochester's insistence on his love for her, Jane says: "For a little while you will perhaps be as you are now – a very little while; and then you will turn cool; and then you will be capricious; and then you will be stern, and I shall have much ado to please you: but when you get well used to me, you will perhaps like me again – like me, I say, not love me. I suppose your love will effervesce in six months, or less. I have observed in books written by men, that period assigned as the furthest to which a husband's ardour extends. Yet, after all, as a friend and companion, I hope never to become quite distasteful to my dear master." Rochester replies that he will not merely like her but love her with "truth, fervour, constancy." Jane sensibly suggests that if Rochester has never before loved anyone like Jane, he has no grounds for his predictions (Brontë 2016, 5675).

in any other way particularly beneficial to their character, but because "no better method, it seems, could be fallen upon" (WN ii 163).

In part because of the poor quality of education, it had become the fashion in Smith's time for young men to travel abroad for several years instead of attending university. This practice did not improve a young man's character, according to Smith: any improvement in these young men was due merely to the passing of time and the natural maturation process. The years away from home were much more likely to make young men conceited and forget the good habits of their childhood. As a contrast, Smith holds up educational practices in ancient Greece where young men were hardened "by gymnastic exercises" which also helped "sharpen" young men's courage. Importantly for Smith's argument, "as the Greek militia was, by all accounts, one of the best that ever was in the world, this part of their publick education *must have answered completely the purpose for which it was intended*." (WN ii 164, emphasis added). The educational system Smith criticizes lacks this sense of purpose and does nothing to prepare young men for their future "business." It is in this context that Smith briefly turns to the education of women touched on in Chap. 3. The full paragraph concerning women's education reads as follows:

> There are no publick institutions for the education of women, and there is accordingly nothing useless, absurd, or fantastical, in the common course of their education. They are taught what their parents or guardians judge it necessary or useful for them to learn, and they are taught nothing else. Every part of their education tends evidently to some useful purpose; either to improve the natural attractions of their person, or to form their mind to reserve, to modesty, to chastity, and to economy; to render them both likely to became the mistresses of a family, and to behave properly when they have become such. In every part of her life, a woman feels some conveniency or advantage from every part of her education. It seldom happens that a man, in any part of his life, derives any conveniency or advantage from some of the most laborious and troublesome parts of his education (WN ii 168).

Read in isolation, this passage first and foremost strikes one as conveying Smith's low esteem of women's minds and disregard of any aspect unrelated to being a good (future) wife. The only things that are necessary or useful for a woman to learn are related to her appearance or the cultivation of her womanly virtues of reserve, modesty, chastity and economy (the latter understood to mean the ability to run a household – which was not part of the greater economy according to Smith). But Smith's text leading up to this passage highlights the importance of the last two sentences: a woman's education is much better suited to her future life than is the education of most men to theirs. There are no public institutions to educate women, but the public institutions to educate men are largely useless and a remnant from the past. If there were no public schools at all, Smith argues, then only those sciences and systems would be taught "for which there was … some demand" – because of their necessity, convenience or even just because it was "fashionable" to learn them. "A private teacher could never find his account in teaching either an exploded and antiquated system of a science acknowledged to be useful, or a science universally believed to be a mere useless and pedantick heap of sophistry and nonsense" (WN ii 168).

The rich have the time and means to educate themselves if they want, but the "common people" do not. Children have to start working at a young age and if they attend school at all, it is to learn "a little smattering in Latin... which can scarce ever be of any use to them." It would be better if "they were instructed in the elementary parts of geometry and mechanics" which would serve them in later life (WN ii 171). Smith suggests that "the most essential parts of education" could be made mandatory by "the publick" which could oblige "every man to undergo an examination or probation in them, before he can obtain the freedom in any corporation, or be allowed to set up any trade, either in a village or town corporate". Smith again points to the "Greek and Roman republics" as examples: they "maintained the martial spirit of their respective citizens" by making "military and gymnastic exercises" mandatory (WN ii 171).

Though it first appears that Smith is making the comparison to ancient Greece and Rome to make a point about "the publick" setting certain requirements for the education of all (male) citizens (whatever those requirements may be), Smith is interested in the "martial spirit" in particular, as well as in the way he believes it to be connected to masculinity and the intellectual faculties. The lack of martial spirit makes a man into a coward: "a man incapable either of defending or of revenging himself," lacking "one of the most essential parts of the character of a man." A coward "is as much mutilated and deformed in his mind as another is in his body, who is either deprived of some of its most essential members, or has lost the use of them" (WN ii 172). But to be deformed in one's mind is worse than any physical deformation because bodily injuries do not necessarily impact one's happiness, while a deformed mind cannot be happy.

Even more contemptible than a coward is a "man without the proper use of the intellectual faculties." Implicit in this ranking of the stupid and ignorant below even the cowards is the reasoning that the mental deformity of the former surpasses that of the latter. In Smith's words, the man without the proper use of his mental faculties "seems to be mutilated and deformed in a still more essential part of the character of human nature" than the coward. The "inferior ranks of people" should receive at least some education to ward off this evil, not just because to instruct them would be the proper thing to do in and of itself, but also because "the state ... derives no inconsiderable advantage from their instruction:"

> The more they are instructed, the less liable they are to the delusions of enthusiasm and superstition, which, among ignorant nations frequently occasion the most dreadful disorders. An instructed and intelligent people, besides, are always more decent and orderly than an ignorant and stupid one (WN ii 172).

Just like a state comprised of citizens schooled in the "martial spirit" is better equipped for war, a state with educated men is more stable and orderly. Educated people are less likely to rise up against their government and less prone to faction. "Instructed and intelligent people" feel more respectable and also feel like their "lawful superiors" are more likely to respect them. As a result, educated, self-respecting citizens are "more disposed to respect those superiors" (WN ii 172). Smith's preoccupation with order, and an ordered society in particular, is the topic of the next chapter. The next section of the current chapter shows that Becky, instructed and intelligent though she may be, does not respect her lawful superiors but seeks to usurp their place.

Striving for What Is Not Worth the Having

An instructed populace is "more disposed to examine, and more capable of seeing through, the interested complaints of faction and sedition; and they are, upon that account, less apt to be misled into any wanton or unnecessary opposition to the measures of government." Educated people are less likely to "judge rashly or capriciously concerning" its government (WN ii 173). When Smith argues for the need for basic public education of the "inferior ranks of people," he is talking about men. Judging from the paragraph cited from WN, Smith believes that women's education is sufficient as is and that there is no need for the public to interfere the way he believes it necessary to reorganize men's education. Girls already learn what they need to know privately and benefit from their education in later life, unlike boys of inferior rank who learn a useless "smattering of Latin" if they learn anything at all (WN ii 171). Smith's concern with the order of society plays a role here, too: if everyone feels themselves respectable and respected, there will be less cause for sedition or rebellion of any kind. This means that everyone should know his or her place and, it appears, be content with it.

Becky is not content with her place and very much interested in bettering her condition. As Becky is moving up the social ladder in London after she and Rawdon have returned from the continent, her protector Lord Steyne warns her: "you are bent on becoming a fine lady. You pester my poor old life out to get you into the world. You won't be able to hold your own there, you silly little fool. You've got no money" (VF 607). Thanks to Becky's business skills, she and Rawdon are living very well "on nothing a year," being invited along with the "best people" in town and throwing exclusive parties at their own home on Curzon Street (VF 636). But Lord Steyne, responsible for Becky's introduction into the highest circles and even at Court, predicts that in the end Becky's lack of fortune will stop her upward mobility. Conspicuous consumption and the trappings of wealth and luxury go a long way but do not provide the kind of security of status Lord Steyne enjoys because of his wealth and family name. He tells Becky:

> You've got no money, and you want to compete with those who have. You poor little earthenware pipkin, you want to swim down the stream along with the great copper kettles. All women are alike. Everybody is striving for what is not worth the having! Gad! I dined with the King yesterday, and we had neck of mutton and turnips (VF 607).

There is a tension between Smith's sketch of an educated, self-respecting, calm populace respectful of its superiors, and the desire to "better one's condition" described in WN. Though an "augmentation of fortune" is the "most vulgar" means by which people can obtain this apparently universal end, it is also "the most obvious." It is perhaps because they are uneducated that "the greater part of men" desire to better their condition in this vulgar way but Smith does not make this explicit, nor does he propose how instruction in "the elementary parts of geometry and mechanics" would enable or encourage people to reach their end by different, more virtuous, means (WN ii 171). If people commonly want to better their condition, this means that they are not satisfied with their station but want to rise above it as does Becky. It is difficult to see how being educated (to whatever extent) would make one more satisfied with one's position in society – in fact, one could argue that the more one learns about the world, the more one is likely to desire a change in one's situation. Becky sets her sights ever higher the more knowledge she acquires, though her real world education is clearly not the same as the schooling Smith proposes for the "inferior ranks" of people, let alone the women among them.

Lord Steyne discerns in Becky the (in his opinion) common tendency to strive "for what is not worth the having." As someone who has everything that people of lower status commonly desire, he dismisses it as vanity. Yet Lord Steyne admires Becky for her unstoppable ambition. With him as her benefactor and protector, Becky reaches the greatest heights of her career at a party at Lord Steyne's house, where she plays the role of Clytemnestra in one of the charades performed before the high society audience invited to the gathering.[8] In the crucial scene, her husband Rawdon plays Agamemnon. When Aegisthus hesitates to murder the sleeping hero, Becky as Clytemnestra "scornfully … snatches the dagger out of Aegisthus's hand and advances to the bed. You see it shining over her head in the glimmer of the lamp, and— and the lamp goes out, with a groan, and all is dark" (VF 646). Thunderous applause ensues. Becky's peak career performance coincides with her acting the part of Clytemnestra, not only killing her onstage husband but showing herself to be more decisive than her cowardly lover who hesitates to act on the couples' plan to murder Agememnon. Lord Steyne recognizes the significance of the scene: ""Brava! brava!" old Steyne's strident voice was heard roaring over all the rest. "By—, she'd do it too," he said between his teeth (VF 646)."[9] Becky is willing and able to upset the order of society in several ways: by climbing high above the social rank to which her lack of money and name would normally condemn her, by enslaving and mock-murdering her husband, and by using her education not to become more virtuous but to manipulate ever more powerful people.

According to Smith, women's education in his time is unproblematic because it is suited to the role women play in his world, while men's education can be improved upon to better serve both the individual and society at large. Women appear to have it better than men in this respect that they do not toil at Latin or any other useless

[8] For an insightful analysis of the charades in *Vanity Fair,* see Dibattista (1980).

[9] Kit Dobson explains that Becky is one of the "characters who attempt to perform what they perceive as an acceptable identity." But while these characters are usually "undercut by others who recognize and denounce their performances as such, and thereby negate their supposed naturalness," Lord Steyne primarily admires Becky for her performance – he sees through it but enjoys it and does not want to expose Becky because her performance entertains and flatters him (Dobson 2006).

subjects that will never be of any use to them in life. Their private education is suited to their station. Smith does not appear to give any thought to the fact that women, too, may want to better their condition. Their activities take place within the home (first as daughters, then as wives) and they are not part of the economy properly speaking; their "toil" does not register as significant. Women's "natural" inferiority to men is made explicit in Smith's *Lectures on Jurisprudence* where he writes: "As in almost all contracts of marriage the husband has a considerable superiority to the wife, the injury done to his honor and love will be more grievous, as all injuries done to a superior by an inferior are more sensibly felt than those which are done to an inferior by one whom they look upon as above them" (Smith Lectures 149). Yet as we know from the 1770 statute cited above, these inferior women were feared as well: they could use their powers of deception to upset the natural order of things and trick superior men into marrying them. Order is so important to Smith that he agrees with the spirit of the 1770 statute: it is worse for an inferior to hurt her superior than for a superior to hurt his inferior. The former action violates the order of things in addition to hurting the victim, while the second confirms the existing order, making the injury to the victim less offensive to common moral sensibility.[10]

Though Rawdon is slow to catch on to the full extent of his wife's involvement with Lord Steyne and the benefits she has received from him, Rawdon's brother Pitt acutely feels the sting of Becky's preferring Steyne to himself. At Lord Steyne's party, "Becky hardly so much as spoke to him" and Pitt "declared her behaviour was monstrously indecorous, reprobated in strong terms the habit of play-acting and fancy dressing as highly unbecoming a British female" (VF 667).[11] But the real reason he leaves the party early, together with his wife, is Becky's neglect now that she has found a more highly ranked man to help her secure a better condition in life. Becky appears "monstrously indecorous" to him only once she stops flattering his vanity and directs her attentions elsewhere. She uses her playacting skills on and off stage to better her condition, drawing on her education to great effect but outside its proper domestic sphere. In public, the skills she has acquired become dangerous to the societal and moral order.

When Rawdon finally becomes suspicious of his wife and starts accompanying her everywhere to make sure she is faithful to him, Becky is "charmed with Rawdon's gallantry" and even tells him "Let us always go on so, dear Rawdon." Wherever they go and whomever they meet, whatever his mood, "she had always a kind smile for him and was attentive to his pleasure and comfort. It was the early days of their marriage over again: the same good humour, prevenances, merriment, and artless confidence and regard." We know Becky well enough by now to recognize that her artlessness must be very artful indeed, as the narrator confirms when he lifts Becky's mask for just a moment: "[Rawdon] fell asleep after dinner in his chair; he did not see the face opposite to him, haggard, weary, and terrible; it lighted

[10] Rendall convincingly argues that Smith nowhere in his works suggested that "natural justice required any principle of equality" (Rendall 1987, 64).

[11] The irony here is that playacting is condemned only when it occurs on a stage – the playacting required in everyday life, on the other hand, is expected of decent females.

up with fresh candid smiles when he woke. It kissed him gaily" (VF 667). In Dr. Gregory's words, Becky knows that "an inviolable fidelity, good humour, and complacency of temper … outlive all the charms of a fine face, and make the decays of it invisible" (Gregory 108). Not just the "decays" are hidden but so is Becky's martial spirit, stronger or at least more active in her than it is in her husband the dragoon.

Becky uses her specifically female education to subvert the order that education is meant to support. She seeks to better her condition using the skills she was meant to use only to acquire a husband and then run a virtuous household. The recipients of Becky's "benevolent attention" tend to be "those who are distinguished by their extraordinary situation… the greatly fortunate … the rich and the powerful" (TMS 237). Extraordinary, that is, relative to her own situation. Once Becky has acquired a more powerful benefactor in Lord Steyne, she no longer needs Rawdon's brother and ignores him (until she falls from grace and is forced to set her sights lower). Chapter 8 will go into more detail about Becky's relationship to Lord Steyne and Chap. 3 already showed how Becky conquered her brother in law. Expressing interest in his tedious pamphlets, Becky remarks: "Poor little penniless, I have got a little interest—and who knows, perhaps the mouse may be able to aid the lion" (VF 570). Here and elsewhere, Becky does not miss the opportunity to remark on her poverty while at the same time making clear her awareness of her inferior position to her intended victim. Calling herself a mouse is as laughable as calling Pitt Crawley a lion and yet "Pitt Crawley was amazed and enraptured with her speech. "How that woman comprehends me!" he said. "I never could get Jane to read three pages of the malt pamphlet. She has no idea that I have commanding talents or secret ambition"" (VF 570).

Becky flatters Pitt by referring to her inferior station and her resultant admiration of his intellect. Had a man spoken those words ("Poor little penniless…. aid the lion"), the result would hardly have been the same. It is not just or even primarily Becky's inferior social rank that makes her speech effective, it is her being a woman – and one who better than anyone appears to know her place as an admirer of superior men like himself. Becky's case casts in a new light Smith's ideas about the division of labor. The following takes as its point of departure Smith's famous example of the pin factory to help frame a discussion of the sexual division of labor underlying Smith's proposed economic system.

Invisible Women and the Division of Labor

In WN, Smith famously illustrates the principle of the division of labor with an account of the manufacturing of pins. "The important business of making a pin is, in this manner, divided into about eighteen distinct operations," he explains, and ten or more people each performing one, two, or three of these operations become so dexterous at their craft that together they can produce many times more pins a day than they ever could have made completing all eighteen steps alone (WN i 67).

Smith hypothesizes that each of the ten men employed in his example could individually manufacture perhaps one pin, but certainly not more than twenty a day. Working together, the division of labor enables these ten men to make forty-eight thousand pins a day. Smith recognizes that in other arts and kinds of manufacture, "the labour can neither be so much subdivided, nor reduced to so great a simplicity of operation." Furthermore, agriculture "does not admit of so many subdivisions of labour, nor of so complete a separation of one business from another, as manufactures." The same person generally takes care of the plowing, the harrowing, the sowing and the reaping, while "the spinner is almost always a distinct person from the weaver" (WN i 67).

In this passage we get a first hint of the invisibility of women in WN – spinners and weavers were often women, though here they are listed among typically male laborers. Though these female spinners and weavers worked for wages, Smith here and elsewhere talks about all wage earners as if they are exclusively male. Surprisingly, women's wage work simply goes unmentioned even though laboring women were a common phenomenon of which Smith must have been aware.[12] Smith in fact shows his awareness of women laborers elsewhere in WN:

> The lowest species of common labourers must everywhere earn at least double their own maintenance, in order that one with another they may be enabled to bring up two children; the labour of the wife, on account of her necessary attendance on the children, being supposed no more than sufficient to provide for herself. (WN i 110)

Smith here recognizes that common laborers would simply die out after one generation if they did not earn enough to keep their children alive, but notably he also includes the off-hand remark about "the wife" who is supposed to make enough to "provide for herself." She, presumably, has a job outside the home and also is the one providing care within the home, an occupation so time consuming that it makes it impossible for her to earn additional wages through her labor outside the domestic sphere. Smith's comment takes on additional significance in light of another passage from the first chapter of WN in which he asks us to "consider what a variety of labour is employed" in the production of tools and household items (WN i 71). Even the "very meanest person in a civilized country" uses all manner of things the production of which involve "the assistance and cooperation" of many. Take, for example:

> the coarse linen shirt which he wears next his skin, the shoes which cover his feet, the bed which he lies on, and all the different parts which compose it, the kitchen-grate at which *he* prepares his victuals, the coals which *he* makes use of for that purpose, dug from the bowels of the earth, and brought to him, perhaps, by a long sea and a long land-carriage, all the

[12] Michèle Pujol writes: "Women are as invisible in Smith's work as in the work of succeeding economists, with the exception of J. S. Mill. Their economic contribution through participation in wage work is ignored, and their fundamental role in reproducing the nation's 'human capital' is taken for granted" (Pujol 1992, 21). Sumitra Shah confirms Pujol's fidings: "Combing through Smith's writings to find references to women's wage work does not yield many results. Pujol (1992) has listed the few places where it is barely mentioned. I was able only to find corroboration of her thesis that based on Smith's comments, women of poor class who worked for wages was a commonplace phenomenon and he was fully aware of it" (Shah 2006, 238).

> other utensils of his kitchen, all the furniture of his table, the knives and forks, the earthen or pewter plates upon which *he* serves up and divides his victuals, the different hands employed in preparing his bread and his beer, the glass window which lets in the heat and the light (WN i 71, emphasis added).

The "different hands" preparing this man's meal most likely were woman's hands, the same employed at the kitchen-grate and serving up and dividing his victuals. This almost certainly female work becomes invisible on Smith's account.[13] Feminist critics have pointed out that Smith overlooks a division of labor without which the economy as he describes it could not exist: the sexual division of labor, separating men's work outside the home from women's work within the home.[14] Smith takes for granted and does not discuss the fact that men can only go out to "labour" outside the home because someone inside the home manages the household. Given his comments on the suitability and sufficiency of the existing educational opportunities for women and his general lack of concern with the way households are run, we can assume that Smith did not think this part of the system in need of overhaul or revision.

This part of the common order of society, and the sexual division of labor it entails, is so obvious that it is invisible. But the sexual division of labor bears little resemblance to the division of labor Smith finds in the pin factory. There, the making of a pin is divided up in the smallest possible steps to increase output and productivity. A man working in the pin manufacturing business spends his day performing the same action or couple of actions over and over again. His wife's day, presumably, could not be more different as she is engaged in all the aspects of the household. Even if she is not a laborer's wife but a middle class woman with household staff, she is supposed to manage domestic affairs in all their variety. At least at first glance, the sexual division of labor differs from the division of labor found in the pin factory because it concerns two (artificially) separated spheres – the public and the private – rather than one segment of the manufacturing business.

This difference between the sexual division of labor and the division of labor discussed in the *Wealth of Nations* has implications for the concerns Smith expresses about the effect the division of labor can have on uneducated people. Despite his attachment to social order and hierarchy, Smith does not believe that there is any

---

[13] About this passage Shah comments: "For a political economist who has gained the reputation of being an acute observer of the panorama of people's daily lives, this shows a degree of blindness to the facts, which must be a conscious choice on his part. Although one can make concessions for the use of masculine pronoun in all discourse as was the custom of the times in which Smith lived, this depiction of reality seems to go beyond the unconscious level, given his particular methodological preference" (Shah 2006, 230). And she adds: "The actuality that the author's famed realism stops at the door of the household. All the tasks of domestic production and reproduction are made invisible in his analysis; and if they are mentioned as examples of consumption, by their very non-mention, women who perform those tasks are made doubly invisible" (Shah 2006, 231).

[14] See for example Paula England: "The sexism here is in failing to see how much traditionally female activities or dispositions contribute to the economy, society or polity. Examples include failing to see how much child rearing, household work, and volunteer work contribute to the 'wealth of nations'" (1993, 39). See also Bodkin (1999) and Justman (1993).

essential difference between the natural capacities of men. This reveals an (apparent) tension in Smith's work as he seems to be concerned about the regrettable social effects of the division of labor, his foundation for the system set forth in the *Wealth of Nations*. We next turn to this tension and Smith's proposed solution before revisiting the issue of women's education and the sexual division of labor as it relates to Becky Sharp.

Stupid and Ignorant as Possible

Taken in isolation, Smith's comments on the importance of order in society make him sound like Dives, a character occasionally trotted out by VF's narrator when he wants to take aim at a self-satisfied reader of "the present work." Addressing this hypothetical reader directly, the narrator asks:

> You who see your betters bearing up under this shame every day, meekly suffering under the slights of fortune, gentle and unpitied, poor, and rather despised for their poverty, do you ever step down from your prosperity and wash the feet of these poor wearied beggars? The very thought of them is odious and low. "There must be classes— there must be rich and poor," Dives says, smacking his claret (it is well if he even sends the broken meat out to Lazarus sitting under the window). Very true; but think how mysterious and often unaccountable it is— that lottery of life which gives to this man the purple and fine linen and sends to the other rags for garments and dogs for comforters. (VF 724)

But even in the first pages of WN, Smith recognizes that social differences are not based on merit but on luck. Nature has endowed all men with approximately the same talents: "the difference of natural talents in different men is, in reality, much less than we are aware of." If mature men appear to have very different talents, it is not because they started out differently. Rather, the distinction between men in this respect "is not upon many occasions so much the cause, as the effect of the division of labour" (WN i 73). One person is not born a philosopher and another a "common street porter" - they become one or the other "from habit, custom, and education." It is merely the philosopher's vanity that refuses to "acknowledge … any resemblance." If it were not for the division of labor, "everyone had the same duties to perform, and the same work to do," and most men would have the same talents (WN i 73). This is the case among the savages, but then savages have no economy to speak of.

Immediately following the passage on women's education, Smith asks: "Ought the public, therefore, to give no attention, it may be asked, to the education of the people?" (WN ii 168) The "therefore" refers to the point Smith has just made about women learning only useful things and therefore enjoying a more suitable education than most men. To make men's education suited to men's lives, Smith suggests that the public may have to interfere. In some societies this is not necessary because individuals are formed by circumstances and the government need not interfere. In other societies, like in Smith's own, "some attention of government is necessary, in order to prevent the almost entire corruption and degeneracy of the great body of the people" (WN ii 168). Again it should be kept in mind that "the great body of the people" is comprised of "common men" – women, we already know, are not in need of government interference as they already have all the education they need.

To emphasize the importance of properly educating laborers, Smith highlights the mind-deadening effects of the division of labor. "Confined to a few very simple operations," the laboring masses become "as stupid and ignorant as it is possible for a human creature to become." Smith's argument is constructed on the same lines as his point about talents in the opening pages of WN: differences in ability are not the cause but the result of the circumstances in which we find ourselves.

> But the understandings of the greater part of men are necessarily formed by their ordinary employments. The man whose whole life is spent in performing a few simple operations, of which the effects, too, are perhaps always the same, or very nearly the same, has no occasion to exert his understanding, or to exercise his invention, in finding out expedients for removing difficulties which never occur. He naturally loses, therefore, the habit of such exertion, and generally becomes as stupid and ignorant as it is possible for a human creature to become. The torpor of his mind renders him not only incapable of relishing or bearing a part in any rational conversation, but of conceiving any generous, noble, or tender sentiment, and consequently of forming any just judgment concerning many even of the ordinary duties of private life. (WN ii 168)

Hence Smith is concerned about the effects of the very principle underpinning the system he lays out in WN. These unfortunate effects threaten the laboring poor in every "improved and civilized society," "unless government takes some pains to prevent it" (WN ii169). A laborer, made "stupid and ignorant" by a life spent performing just a few simple tasks, has lost his power of judgment: "Of the great and extensive interests of his country he is altogether incapable of judging." Also, "he is equally incapable of defending his country in war." Again the lack of mental ability and martial spirit are mentioned in the same breath:

> The uniformity of his stationary life naturally corrupts the courage of his mind, and makes him regard, with abhorrence, the irregular, uncertain, and adventurous life of a soldier. It corrupts even the activity of his body, and renders him incapable of exerting his strength with vigour and perseverance in any other employment, than that to which he has been bred. His dexterity at his own particular trade seems, in this manner, to be acquired at the expense of his intellectual, social, and martial virtues (WN ii 169).[15]

---

[15] Mark Neocleous cites Smith's contemporary Adam Ferguson, who shared Smith's concern about the effect of the division of labor on the martial spirit of the people: "There is a danger, for Ferguson, in making 'a kind of separation between the civil and the military character'. 'The subdivision of arts and professions, in certain examples, tends to improve the practice of them, and to promote their ends. By having separated the arts of the clothier and the tanner, we are the better supplied with shoes and with cloth. But to separate the arts which form the citizen and the statesman, the arts of policy and war, is an attempt to dismember the human character ... By this separation, we in effect deprive a free people of what is necessary to their safety.'" (Neocleous 2014, 96; Ferguson 1767, 229–30) Neocleous adds: "The division of labour that is so crucial to commercial order and a liberal civil society is thus, in another fundamental way, also a *threat* to that order" Neocleous sums up Smith's and Ferguson's shared opinion that "the good citizen – the liberal, commercially driven citizen – needs to remain a warrior" (Neocleous 2014, 97–98).

Dr. Gregory claimed to regard women "not as domestic drudges, or the slaves of our pleasures, but as our companions and equals; as designed to soften our hearts and polish our manners" (Gregory 12). The bulk of his *Legacy* bears out only part of this claim: if he does not wish his daughters to become drudges, he does mean for them to be thoroughly domestic; if not slaves of their future husbands' pleasures, he does intend them to mold themselves according to his own explicitly male standards. Without artifice they should yet "design" themselves to soften men's hearts and polish their manners. If Smith is correct that our "understandings" are formed by our "ordinary employments," then the sexual division of labor implicit in his work and made explicit in conduct books like the *Legacy* would form the female understanding in accordance with their daily tasks. But while the pin-maker's life is "spent in performing a few simple operations," a middle class woman's activities are much less straightforward or easy to describe. If she is married she needs to run her husband's household, delegating tasks to a number of staff depending on her husband's wealth. As a manager, she has to perform and/or divide a variety of tasks, none of them as simple or repetitive as the pin maker's. At the same time, she needs to pay attention to her conduct, specifically her conduct as a (future) wife. This means, for example, that a woman should accustom herself "to an habitual neatness, so that in the most careless undress, in [her] most unguarded hours, [she] may have no reason to be ashamed of [her] appearance" (Gregory 44). Even when there are no men around, a woman should at all times conduct herself as if a man might see her, and judge her by the standards laid out by Dr. Gregory.

The drudgery involved in pin making prevents the laborer employed in this kind of manufacture from "exercising his invention, in finding out expedients for removing difficulties which never occur." The middle class woman, on the contrary, perpetually acting as if her artlessness and simplicity come naturally, does not have opportunity to lose "the habit of such exertion." Not, at least, when she is someone like Becky who wishes to actively better her condition. Her activities, efforts, and inventions keep her mind exercised and shape her into someone who could not be more different from Smith's laborer who "generally becomes as stupid and ignorant as it is possible for a human creature to become." Her mind is sharp and astute, not in a "torpor" rendering her incapable of rational conversation. But her habit of invention and quickness of mind also do not spur in her the conception of "any generous, noble, or tender sentiment." Becky's intellectual and social skills are well developed, but not at all along the virtuous lines that either Smith or Dr. Gregory would deem proper in a woman. Not to speak of her "martial virtues" and her self-command, the latter to be discussed in Chap. 6.

Sympathizing with Savages, Women

In the last chapter of Part V of TMS, "Of the influence of Custom and Fashion upon Moral Sentiments," Smith states: "when custom and fashion coincide with the natural principles of right and wrong, they heighten the delicacy of our sentiments, and increase the abhorrence for every thing which approaches to evil" (TMS 216). Those of us who were brought up in "really good company" are therefore more outraged by immoral acts than are those "who had the misfortune to be brought up amidst violence, licentiousness, falsehood, and injustice." People in the latter group have likely not lost their sense of right and wrong entirely, but they are apt to be less shocked at improper conduct. They may dismiss immoral behavior as "the way of the world," regarding those who refrain from this kind of conduct entirely as "dupes of [their] own integrity" (TMS 216).

Becky clearly belongs to this class of people even though she would probably choose to describe her upbringing in different terms, placing the emphasis on the skills and traits that she acquired early on and that enabled her to avoid becoming a dupe of her own integrity. Becky did not exactly lose her sense of right and wrong but never really had it in the first place. She is aware of the way the people around her regard right and wrong, but this awareness shows her rather that right and wrong are contingent on situation and rank. Smith makes the same observation when he comments on our propensity to forgive "the great" their vices while we despise the virtues of the poor. Vice and virtue, Becky learns even before she officially "enters the world," are in the eyes of the spectator. If the spectator is our social equal they will detect in us different virtues and vices than do the people who are either above or below us in the hierarchy. And even people in our own class are measured by the standards appropriate to whatever subset they belong to. Again Smith uses the language of "bringing home" someone's case to ourselves, reiterating the ideas behind his opening remarks on sympathy: "The propriety of a person's behaviour, depends not upon its suitableness to any one circumstance of his situation, but to all the circumstances, which, when we bring his case home to ourselves, we feel, should naturally call upon his attention" (TMS 217). To illustrate this point, Smith talks about the behavior we expect from a clergyman and a military man: when the former does not comport himself with a certain gravity of manner we feel uncomfortable, just like we do when the latter does not act with the levity we expect from someone in the military.[16] When our expectations regarding someone's behavior are not met, we "cannot entirely go along with" their conduct and hence do not fully sympathize with them. Similarly we can sympathize with a parent who grieves over the loss of "an only son," but we do not feel that the same grief is appropriate in a commander who lost one of his men in battle. We enter into a person's situation, bringing their case home to ourselves to see if we can enter into it with sympathy and approbation (TMS 218). When this effort of the imagination fails and we cannot sympathize

[16]George Wickham in Jane Austen's *Pride and Prejudice* is a good example. Having "accepted a commission" in the corps, the narrator remarks: "This was exactly as it should be; for the young man wanted only regimentals to make him completely charming. His appearance was greatly in his favour; he had all the best part of beauty, a fine countenance, a good figure, and very pleasing address. The introduction was followed up on his side by a happy readiness of conversation—a readiness at the same time perfectly correct and unassuming" (Austen 2004, 54). But Mr. Darcy is familiar with the blameworthy side of Mr. Wickham's levity: "Mr. Wickham is blessed with such happy manners as may ensure his making friends—whether he may be equally capable of retaining them, is less certain" (Austen 2004, 70).

with someone, "We are embarrassed, and put to a stand, and know not how to address ourselves to a character, which plainly affects to be of a different species from those with which we should have been disposed to class it" (TMS 219).

Considering these comments against the backdrop of the current and previous chapters, we can more accurately define the difficult situation a woman finds herself in: if she does not behave the way we expect of her given her rank and class, "we do not know how to address ourselves" to her. And things presumably get worse still when a woman is not behaving like a woman at all. Becky is aware of our general tendency to categorize people and to be put off when they do not behave the way we expect them to. The consummate actress, Becky effortlessly changes her behavior to suit the expectations of her spectators, never duped by her sense of integrity because she has none – at least not on Smith's account of integrity as dictated by the impartial spectator (discussed in Chap. 7). He holds that our moral sentiments may be affected by "custom and fashion," but never to a very great extent. When we come across a custom that clearly constitutes a violation of our moral sentiments, like the infanticide common in the otherwise civilized Greek and Roman societies, it is an exception to the rule: "No society could subsist a moment, in which the usual strain of men's conduct and behaviour was of a piece with the horrible practice I have just now mentioned" (TMS 224). Even though we know of historical examples of "horrible practices" persisting in civilized societies, we should not therefore believe that the moral sentiments of society as a whole could be perverted.

Two of Smith's claims in this passage are of importance here: on the one hand, there is no "particular practice so gross" that custom cannot authorize it for a time. On the other, "the general style and character of conduct and behavior" in a society will never sink to the level of a grossly immoral practice like infanticide. Smith holds that a society can only continue to exist because its overall character is, if not morally excellent, at least not "horrible." What is at stake here is the virtue Smith calls "humanity." This virtue will return in Chap. 6 where it will be discussed in contrast with its counterpart, generosity. In this passage of TMS, Smith suggests that the humanity of societies increases as they become more civilized but that the "hardiness" demanded of "savages" diminishes it. "The masculine firmness" of character diminishes in civilized nations because there is less need for self-denial and "the command of the passions." In civilized nations there is room for kindness, friendliness and other virtues "founded upon humanity" while in "rude and barbarous nations" the savage has to rely on "Spartan discipline" to survive (TMS 223). In what appears to be an effort to convince his reader of the almost inhuman toughness of the members of these uncivilized societies, Smith relates that the savage regards the "weakness of love" as "unpardonable effeminacy" and maintains his composure even when he is "hung by the shoulders over a slow fire," refusing to show pain but instead calmly mocking his tormentors. "Every savage is said to prepare himself from his earliest youth for this dreadful end" (TMS 221).[17]

[17] Smith has in mind especially the native North American tribes. "Fortune never exerted more cruelly her empire over mankind, than when she subjected those nations of heroes to the refuse of the jails of Europe" (TMS 221).

Yet for all the presumably extremely masculine behaviors Smith assigns to these savages, they bear closer resemblance to Becky and her literary sisters than to the men that surround them. About the savage, Smith writes: "His circumstances not only habituate him to every sort of distress, but teach him to give way to none of the passions which that distress is apt to excite. He can expect from his countrymen no sympathy or indulgence for such weakness" (TMS 220). Amelia may frequently burst into tears, she rarely expects sympathy from her parents or even her husband, and certainly not from her husband's family who force her to give up her son to them. She keeps her tortures to herself and receives neither acknowledgment nor praise for the way she bears her hardships. "This heroic and unconquerable firmness, which the custom and education of his country demand of every savage, is not required of those who are brought up to live in civilized societies" (TMS 221). In the "civilized society" of VF, women are to expect no sympathy but bear their suffering in silence. There is of course no perfect parallel between the behavior of savages in barbarous societies on the one hand and women in civilized societies on the other. But we can use VF to highlight a difficulty in Smith's thinking about so-called civilization. Smith argues that civilized societies are more humane and encouraging of the display of sympathy. People in these societies are more open about their feelings and so can form friendships more easily, expecting to both give sympathy to and receive sympathy from the people close to them. But these people must be men, because as we know women are forced to be hypocrites: not only should they not give vent to their feelings but they should dissemble, feigning sympathy (or even love) when they feel none. Furthermore, they should respect no acknowledgment in return. If they play their part convincingly, others will never be aware of their real troubles and the self-command required to hide them. Like Rawdon, they will only see the "fresh candid smiles," never the "haggard, weary, and terrible" face that Becky wears when nobody is watching (VF 667).

Continuing our reading of Smith's passage on the behavior of savages, we find that barbarians talk to each other "with the reserve of strangers" because they cannot afford the luxury of indulging in or expressing emotions. Since they are "obliged to smother and conceal the appearance of every passion," they "necessarily acquire the habits of falsehood and dissimulation." Chapter 8 and the Conclusion will build on Smith's observations about the mutual mistrust among savages and pursue the subject of horizontal aggression among women. Of primary interest here are the "habits of falsehood and dissimulation," essential elements of the hypocrite's arsenal (TMS 222). These habits make the women who have perfected them dangerous. Becky is like the savage who "seldom shows any symptoms of anger, yet his vengeance, when he comes to give way to it, is always sanguinary and dreadful" (TMS 222).

The Desire to Bewitch and Enslave

This chapter discussed several contrasts. On the one hand there is the tender, passive, cheerfully weak and innocent woman who is (as a wry observer comments in VF) "a crown to her husband," softening his heart and polishing his manners (VF 699). On the other, we find the slave who through hypocrisy gains power over her husband and master, using her education (suited to her station as daughter and wife) to better her condition within the constraints of a system that presupposes her lack of ambition and martial spirit. Because the drive to strive for higher station and status is regarded as obviously masculine, the clever playacting woman can work her way up the social ladder – suspected of her true motivations only by other women, her peers. The slave becomes master, a dynamic that in Charlotte Brontë's *Jane Eyre* Rochester seems to have understood, at least in part, when he tells his former employee and soon to be wife Jane:

> I never met your likeness. Jane, you please me, and you master me – you seem to submit, and I like the sense of pliancy you impart; and while I am twining the soft, silken skein round my finger, it sends a thrill up my arm to my heart. I am influenced – conquered; and the influence is sweeter than I can express; and the conquest I undergo has a witchery beyond any triumph I can win (Brontë 5685).

Jane Eyre, who features prominently in Chap. 7, insists on calling Rochester her master even after she has stopped working for him as a governess, but Rochester knows that he has been mastered in turn. The silken skein binds the conqueror as well as the conquered. The "sense of pliancy" reminds us of Rosamond in *Middlemarch* and Lydgate's chilling realization that the "soft white substance" he has married does not at all confirm to the ideally submissive wife he had imagined (Eliot 324). He had assumed that "his superior knowledge and mental force" would be for Rosamond "a shrine to consult on all occasions" (Eliot 549). Yet where he had expected pliancy he finds a tenacity so strong he wonders whether Rosamond might one day be the death of him. In the passage cited above, Rochester speaks of Jane's "witchery" as sweet but we know that Becky can achieve the same effect with her signature intrigues. Like Becky, Jane is a conqueror, showing great courage and self-command in the pursuit of her goals. A man may believe, with old Casaubon in *Middlemarch,* that he will take "a wife … to adorn the remaining quadrant of his course, and be a little moon that would cause hardly a calculable perturbation" (Eliot 88). But how many women would, if they were to lay aside their hypocrisy, agree with Laure and say "I do not like husbands. I will never have another"? (Eliot 142).

Becky regards husbands as instrumental to her ambition. She would have married old, boorish Sir Pitt if she had had the chance. Never in her life is she sidetracked by love or romance. The next chapter provides a study of Becky's ambition in the context of the machinery and order of "civilized" society.

References

Armstrong, Nancy. 1990. *Desire and domestic fiction: A political history of the novel*. Cary: Oxford University Press.

Austen, Jane. 2003. *Emma*. Oxford: Oxford University Press.

———. 2004. *Pride and prejudice*. Oxford: Oxford University Press.

Bodkin, R.G. 1999. Women's Agency in Classical Economic thought: Adam Smith, Harriet Taylor Mill and J.S. Mill. *Feminist Economics* 5 (1): 45–60.

Brontë, Charlotte. 2016. *Jane Eyre*. Kindle Edition. New York: W.W. Norton.

Dibattista, Maria. 1980. The triumph of Clytemnestra: The charades in vanity fair. *PMLA* 95 (5): 827–837.

Dobson, Kit. 2006. 'An insuperable repugnance to hearing vice called by its proper name': Englishness, gender, and the performed identities of Rebecca and Amelia in Thackeray's *Vanity Fair*. *Victorian Review* 32 (3): 1–25.

Eliot, George. 1996. *Middlemarch*. Oxford: Oxford University Press.

England, Paula. 1993. The separate self: Andocentric Bias in neoclassical assumptions. In *Beyond economic man*, ed. Marianne A. Ferber and Julie A. Nelson, 37–53. Chicago: U of Chicago Press.

Ferguson, Adam. 1966 [1767]. *An essay on the history of civil society*. Edinburgh: Edinburgh University Press.

Gregory, John. 2008 [1796]. *A father's legacy to his daughters. By Dr. Gregory*. Facsimile edition. Ann Arbor: University of Michigan Text Creation Partnership.

Justman, S. 1993. *The autonomous male in Adam smith*. London: University of Oklahoma Press.

Neocleous, Mark. 2014. "O effeminacy! Effeminacy!:" martial power, masculine power, liberal peace. In *War power, police power*. Edinburgh: Edinburgh UP.

Pujol, Michèle. 1992. *Feminism and anti-feminism in early economic thought*. Northampton: Edward Elgar.

Rendall, J. 1987. Virtue and commerce: Women in the making of Adam Smith's political economy. In *Women in western political philosophy: Kant to Nietzsche*, ed. E. Kennedy and S. Mendus, 44–77. New York: St. Martin's Press.

Shah, Sumitra. 2006. Sexual division of labor in Adam Smith's work. *Journal of the History of Economic Thought* 28 (2): 221.

Smith, Adam. 1981. In *An inquiry into the nature and causes of the wealth of nations*, eds. R. H. Campbell and A. S. Skinner, vol. 2 of the *Glasgow Edition of the Works and Correspondence of Adam Smith*. Indianapolis: Liberty Fund.

———. 1982a. In *The theory of moral sentiments*, eds. D.D. Raphael and A.L. Macfie, vol. 1 of the *Glasgow Edition of the Works and Correspondence of Adam Smith*. Indianapolis: Liberty Fund.

———. 1982b. In *Lectures on Jurisprudence*, eds. R. L. Meek, D. D. Raphael and P. G. Stein, vol. 5 of the *Glasgow Edition of the Works and Correspondence of Adam Smith*. Indianapolis: Liberty Fund.

Swords, Barbara M. 1988. "Woman's place" in Jane Austen's England 1770–1820. *Persuasions* 10: 76–82.

Thackeray, William Makepeace. 1983. In *Vanity fair: A novel without a hero*, ed. John Sutherland. New York: Oxford UP.

Wollstonecraft, Mary. 2009. *A vindication of the rights of woman and a vindication of the rights of men*. Oxford: Oxford University Press.

Chapter 5
Ambition, the Poor man's Son, and the Poor man's Daughter

Abstract In *Vanity Fair,* Becky Sharp enjoys what Adam Smith calls the "toil and bustle" of commercial society. She wants to better her condition and seeks to increase her fortune, but most of all she desires power over others. Becky has a keen sense of hierarchy and believes her rightful place is at the top of the power pyramid. What sets her apart from other ambitious people is the pleasure she takes in working the machinery of society on her way to the top. Becky knows how to manipulate the vain people around her and happily uses them as means to her end. She enjoys the fitness of her skills to the goals she wants to achieve. Becky is the vivacious, ironic counterpart of Smith's famous "poor man's son" who strives to obtain the luxuries flaunted by the rich. The poor man's son's ambition drives him to work hard his entire life just to find that he was deluded about the happiness these luxuries seemed to promise. Becky, on the other hand, finds pleasure in the toil and bustle itself; she is ambitious and a social climber but ultimately it is her desire to dominate others that motivates her. Like Smith, Becky recognizes that vanity drives industry, but unlike the poor man's son in TMS and the many vain characters in VF who lack self awareness, she is not a cog in the machine but a master of it.

The Tendency to Hide our Sorrow

In his opening remarks about sympathy cited in Chap. 3, Smith refers to the heroes of tragedy and romance to explain that our fellow feeling concerns not only sorrow but joy as well. He revisits this claim a little later in TMS, noting that "our sympathy with sorrow, though not more real, has been more taken notice of than our sympathy with joy" (TMS 94). When we see someone suffer, we can rarely entirely "go along with" the feelings of the sufferer because their sorrow is too great for us to enter into. We cannot achieve a "perfect harmony" of sentiments with the sufferer, especially when we are confronted with extravagant expressions of grief, but we can go along with their feelings at least part of the way. When, on the other hand, we witness somebody who "skips and dances about with that intemperate and senseless joy," we feel only "contempt and indignation" (TMS 94). We have no respect for the extravagantly joyous. And yet despite our contempt of overly enthusiastic public

R. Slegers, *Adam Smith's Moral Sentiments in Vanity Fair*, Issues in Business Ethics 49, https://doi.org/10.1007/978-3-319-98731-6_5

displays of cheerfulness, we would rather sympathize with pleasure than with sorrow because the former is a pleasant emotion. Sympathizing with sorrow makes us sorrowful and since we do not enjoy (vicarious) pain we often wish to be rid of this kind of sympathy. Sympathizing with joy makes us joyful, and for this reason we often wish we had more of this kind of sympathy. So how is it that sympathy with joy is more pleasant than sympathy with sorrow yet more difficult achieve? Smith claims: "the observation … which it naturally falls in our way to make, is, that our propensity to sympathize with sorrow must be very strong, and our inclination to sympathize with joy very weak" (TMS 95). Though joy is a more pleasant emotion than sorrow, we find ourselves more affected by the latter than by the former.

But this is not all: our propensity to go along with the happiness of others is often further weakened by envy. "When there is no envy in the case, our propensity to sympathize with joy is much stronger than our propensity to sympathize with sorrow" (TMS 95). Hence the reasons we frequently feel more strongly for people in their sorrow than in their joy are therefore twofold. First, because the original emotion is strong in the sufferer, even a weak and incomplete fellow feeling will make us experience a degree of sorrow ourselves. Second, our fellow feeling with another person's sorrow is unobstructed by envy the way our fellow feeling with another person's joy often is. If it were not for envy, our joy on other people's behalf would be both more common and more in harmony with the feelings of the people concerned. "It is agreeable to sympathize with joy; and wherever envy does not oppose it, our heart abandons itself with satisfaction to the highest transports of that delightful sentiment" (TMS 96). The theme of envy will be taken up again in Chap. 8. In the current chapter we are interested primarily in the way sympathy relates to ambition and the workings of commercial society.

We know how difficult it is to suppress expressions of grief and we are patient with people who at times fail to tone down their emotions so that the spectator may more easily enter into them. We have no such patience with people who fail to master their joy, which we know is much easier to achieve. Intemperate joy annoys us since it appears to us more out of proportion than intemperate grief: "adversity … necessarily depresses the mind of the sufferer much more below its natural state, than prosperity can elevate him above it" (TMS 95). This explains why the spectator has more difficulty going along with sorrow than with joy: he or she has to make a much bigger departure from his or her "ordinary temper of mind in the one case than in the other" (TMS 96). Drawing an analogy with the theater, Smith reminds us that even as spectators of a tragedy we enter into the heroes' grief "with reluctance." If, after struggling "against that sympathetic sorrow" which the action on stage inspires in us, "we give way to it at last," we try to hide our feelings from the other spectators. "If we shed any tears, we carefully conceal them, and are afraid, lest the spectators, not entering into this excessive tenderness, should regard it as effeminacy and weakness." Just like we are afraid that our fellow spectators may not enter into our feelings of sympathetic sorrow, any "wretch whose misfortunes call upon our compassion feels with what reluctance we are likely to enter into his sorrow, and therefore proposes his grief to us with fear and hesitation" (TMS 96). Everyone knows that pain, even the pain experienced indirectly through sympathy, is unpleasant, and so we are reluctant to impose our pain on others. Since we further know that the mere sight of sorrow can evoke sympathetic pain, we try to "smother" the expression of it.

Because we know how our spectators are likely to feel about our sorrow and our joy, and because we live in a world in which poverty is linked with sorrow and joy is linked with prosperity, "we make parade of our riches, and conceal our poverty: "Nothing is so mortifying as to be obliged to expose our distress to the view of the publick, and to feel, that though our situation is open to the eyes of all mankind, no mortal conceives for us the half of what we suffer. Nay, it is chiefly from this regard to the sentiments of mankind, that we pursue riches and avoid poverty" (TMS 99). So it is that sympathy drives the pursuit of wealth, be it indirectly. The following sections offer an analysis of this dynamic with a focus on ambition, which according to Smith is a corruption of sympathy related to vanity.

Wealth, Power, and "Preheminence"

Becky understands that most of the people around her are motivated by vanity and she plays them accordingly. It stands to reason that if we were not vain, people like Becky would not have a hold on us. But what would remain of society if vanity were eradicated? The narrator of VF tells us: "All the delights of life, I say, would go to the deuce, if people did but act upon their silly principles and avoid those whom they dislike and abuse" (TMS 642). If we acted in accordance with our principles, "what a howling wilderness and intolerable dwelling Vanity Fair would be!"[1] The narrator continues:

> The benefits of civilization would be done away with. We should be quarrelling, abusing, avoiding one another. Our houses would become caverns, and we should go in rags because we cared for nobody. Rents would go down. Parties wouldn't be given any more. All the tradesmen of the town would be bankrupt. Wine, wax-lights, comestibles, rouge, crinoline-petticoats, diamonds, wigs, Louis-Quatorze gimcracks, and old china, park hacks, and splendid high-stepping carriage horses—all the delights of life, I say, - would go to the deuce. (VF 642)

We may privately abuse someone we disagree with on principle and call him "the greatest rascal unhanged," but when we meet him in the street we shake his hand and "if his cook is good we forgive him." "Thus trade flourishes—civilization advances; peace is kept; new dresses are wanted for new assemblies every week;

[1]The narrator's signature irony is obvious in this passage and there are few earnest defenders of vanity as a (public) virtue. Julius Henri Browne is an example of an author defending vanity as a trait that builds character and "enables us to live in a harsh, barren world." If we repress the "bad kind" of vanity and nurture the good kind, human progress, civilization and the "perpetuity of the race" are ensured. Reflecting the narrator's comments about the "howling wilderness" that would result if vanity were to be done away with, Browne states: "Imagine a man without vanity and you have the likeness of a barbarian." Vanity conjures dreams and "dreams are often the best part of existence" (Browne 1891).

and the last year's vintage of Lafitte will remunerate the honest proprietor who reared it" (VF 643).

Chapter 3 touched on the propensity of the rich and famous to believe themselves the object of "attention and approbation" (TMS 100). Deluded by our imagination, we see "the abstract idea of a perfect and happy state" in the "condition of the great" (TMS 100). We desire to be like them and identify with them, regarding them as the kind of person we might one day be ourselves. Because we see our own future in them, we want the rich and powerful to be immortal and we are indignant when something bad happens to them.[2] But it is not only our tendency to identify with them that makes us sympathize with their lot. According to Smith, we are "eager" to help these fortunate people complete "a system of happiness:"

> Upon this disposition of mankind, to go along with all the passions of the rich and the powerful, is founded the distinction of ranks, and the order of society. Our obsequiousness to our superiors more frequently arises from our admiration for the advantages of their situation, than from any private expectations of benefit from their good-will. Their benefits can extend but to a few, but their fortunes interest almost every body. We are eager to assist them in completing a system of happiness that approaches so near to perfection; and we desire to serve them for their own sake, without any other recompense but the vanity or the honour of obliging them. (TMS 101)

Smith suggests that we take pleasure in contributing to the near-perfect happiness of these superior individuals. Furthermore, the "system of happiness" which we are helping to complete is part of the larger "order of society," founded on the "distinction of ranks." Our aesthetic delight is thus linked to two systems: the system of happiness of the individual (group of) rich people to which we are contributing directly, and a larger system encompassing the first, the order of society. Our own admiration for the rich and powerful, together with our vanity, has the happy (if perhaps unintended) effect of founding and maintaining the hierarchy of rank that keeps the society machine running.

In *Vanity Fair*, the narrator has a more cynical perspective on our admiration for the rich and powerful: "It is money you love, and not the man; and were Croesus and his footman to change places you know, you poor rogue, who would have the benefit of your allegiance" (VF 167). If we serve the rich, it is not "for their own sake," nor solely for "the vanity or the honour of obliging them." About Miss Crawley, the rich dowager who receives everyone's eager assistance and obsequiousness, the narrator observes: "The great good quality of this old lady has been mentioned. She possessed seventy thousand pounds" (VF 111). While Smith holds that "nature would teach us to submit to [the rich] for their own sake, to tremble and bow down before their exalted station," Miss Crawley's relatives do not "regard [her] smile as a reward sufficient to compensate any services" (TMS 101). They "dread [her] displeasure," but not because, as Smith suggests, it would prompt them to feel "the severest of all mortifications;" rather, they fear they will lose their inheritance (TMS 101). Miss Crawley herself takes the services she receives for granted: "Gratitude among

[2] This is why, Smith explains, the murder of a king is much worse than the murder of a common person.

certain rich folks is scarcely natural or to be thought of. They take needy people's services as their due" (VF 167). This attitude appears to be a natural fit for Smith's "distinction of ranks, and the order of society". For the narrator, however, this lack of gratitude does not flow from the natural order of things but from simple mercenary motives: "Nor have you, O poor parasite and humble hanger-on, much reason to complain! Your friendship for Dives is about as sincere as the return which it usually gets" (VF 167). If there is a "natural order" in Vanity Fair, it appears at first glance to be an order in which wealth is the highest good and the main motive for action.

This appearance is deceiving, however, because it mistakes the means for the ends. As Smith points out, the purpose of "all the toil and bustle in this world," is "to be observed, to be attended to, to be taken notice of with sympathy, complacency, and approbation" (TMS 99). Miss Crawley's relatives want her money and flatter and indulge her in order to increase their chances of a portion of her seventy thousand pounds. But according to Smith, they want the money because they expect it to increase their social status. The "toil and bustle in this world," Smith explains, is driven not only by "avarice" but also by "ambition;" we pursue not just wealth but also "power and preheminence" (TMS 99). Avarice and ambition may appear like very different traits, but they are aimed at the same kind of objects, which "differ only in their greatness. A miser is as furious about a halfpenny, as a man of ambition about the conquest of a kingdom" (TMS 195). Whether through the pursuit of wealth, the pursuit of power and "preheminence," or a combination of all three, our "toil and bustle" is aimed at gaining approbation. This, then, is the advantage which we hope to gain in achieving that "great purpose of human life which we call bettering our condition" (TMS 99).[3]

The desire to better our condition, Smith writes in the *Wealth of Nations,* "comes with us from the womb, and never leaves us till we go into the grave." Between birth and death, "there is scarce… a single instance" in which we are perfectly satisfied with our situation and "an augmentation of fortune is the means by which the greater part of men propose and wish to better their condition." Smith claims that "frugality" is a dominant principle in "the greater part of men" and that this tendency to augment one's fortune through savings "is the means the most vulgar and the most obvious" to bettering one's condition (WNi 294). Whether we call it "avarice" or "frugality," the desire to accumulate wealth flows from the desire to better our condition, that is, our desire for approbation. But as we know from TMS, we can better our condition and gain the respect of others through other means as well, namely through power and preeminence.[4]

Our capacity for sympathy, and our wish to be sympathized with, is at the root of our desire for approbation: we want to be acknowledged, heeded, and respected. But

[3]This is the only place in the *Theory* where Smith mentions our desire to better our condition. Daniel Luban observes that this "allows us to connect the account of approbation in the *Theory* to the account of self-interest in the Wealth of Nations" (2012).

[4]And hence "The economic self-interest that is so foundational to the Wealth of Nations is simply the most widely prevalent of a larger set of social esteem-seeking behaviors" (Luban 2012, 284).

this natural desire can be corrupted when we seek to gain praise we do not really deserve, when, in other words, we are less concerned with who we really are and more concerned with how we come across to others. We then sacrifice the pursuit of wisdom and virtue to the pursuit of wealth, power, and preeminence. It is status that now concerns us first and foremost. It follows that in all our "toil and bustle," it must be "the vanity, not the ease, or the pleasure, which interests us" (TMS 99).

No Vanity, no Civilization: The Fable of the Bees

According to Smith, we are naturally disposed to "admire, and almost to worship, the rich and the powerful, and to despise, or, at least, to neglect persons of poor and mean condition." This disposition is "necessary both to establish and to maintain the distinction of ranks and the order of society," but it is also "the great and most universal cause of the corruption of our moral sentiments." The esteem we feel for "wealth and greatness" should be reserved for "wisdom and virtue," just like the contempt with which we unjustly regard "poverty and weakness" should only be bestowed on "vice and folly." This "has been the complaint of moralists in all ages," as it is of Smith (TMS 99). Smith's complaint puts him in an interesting position because he regards the "order of society" based on the "distinction of ranks" as necessary and natural. Clearly, it would be better to have an order in which "wisdom and virtue" were the determinants of rank. However, since these traits are much less visible than social status and fortune, they fail to inspire sufficient enthusiasm for emulation. Wisdom and virtue are undoubtedly more deserving of praise and admiration than wealth and status, but most of us would rather have the pomp and circumstance of a large fortune than the quiet gratification of knowing ourselves to be a morally good person. This is especially obvious in Vanity Fair, but Thackeray was far from the first to point out the vicious foundation of societal prosperity.

The passage from *Vanity Fair* describing the "howling wilderness and intolerable dwelling" that would be the result of principled, honest living, calls to mind an older and equally scathing account of vice as the driver of our economy. In his famous and controversial poem *The Fable of the Bees*, Bernard Mandeville describes how a thriving, productive and dynamic beehive is a dominant economic force because many of its members are to some degree vicious. He first published the fable in 1714 and, after the poem had been widely criticized, added an introduction eight years later to explain the meaning of the fable. He writes:

> They that examine into the Nature of Man, abstract from Art and Education, may observe, that what renders him a Sociable Animal, consists not in his desire of Company, Good-nature, Pity, Affability, and other Graces of a fair Outside; but that his vilest and most hateful Qualities are the most necessary Accomplishments to fit him for the largest, and, according to the World, the happiest and most flourishing Societies. (Mandeville 0014-01_324)[5]

[5]And Mandeville adds: "For the main Design of the Fable … is to shew the Impossibility of enjoying all the most elegant Comforts of Life that are to be met with in an industrious, wealthy and powerful Nation, and at the same time be bless'd with all the Virtue and Innocence that can be

The *Fable* starts by describing a flourishing society of bees occupied in many different trades and admired by foreigners who know the hive for its economic success and prowess in battle. But this successful society is not a virtuous one; in fact "every Part was full of Vice /Yet the whole Mass a Paradise." Just like a musical harmony encompasses jarring notes, a flourishing society comprises vices like gluttony and avarice, "whilst Luxury / Employ'd a Million of the Poor/ And odious Pride a Million more/Envy it self, and Vanity/Were Ministers of Industry." And yet these vicious bees "brazenly" pray for honesty, a prayer granted by Jupiter who "with Indignation mov'd /At last in Anger swore, He'd rid/The bawling Hive of Fraud; and did." This has immediate and serious consequences:

> But, Oh ye Gods! What Consternation,
> How vast and sudden was th' Alteration!
> In half an Hour, the Nation round,
> Meat fell a Penny in the Pound. (Mandeville 0014-01_2465)

All of this was written, Mandeville claims, "without the least design of being Witty" – the fable is "a Story told in Dogrel" to illustrate his point that a happy, thriving society is composed of vicious elements (Mandeville, 0014-01_325). Once Jove has made all bees honest, all lawsuits are dropped because the criminals admit their guilt and the victims no longer seek vengeance; jails are closed down and all the people employed by the prison system lose their jobs. No-one lives beyond their means anymore and nobody buys on credit; prices drop, luxuries are no longer desired and trade comes to a halt. Everything is made to be durable and nobody covets products they do not really need – vanity has been eradicated so nobody feels the need to show off. Thus weakened, the hive is soon attacked by a rival nation and after a valiant fight the decimated group of honest bees moves into a hollow tree where they can live out their virtuous lives in peaceful poverty.

Adam Smith opposes Mandeville's claim that the public good is served by private vice but also admits that Mandeville's account would not have appealed to so many people had it not contained a grain of truth (Griswold 1999, 43).[6] Smith talks at length about certain character traits that, though never praiseworthy, admit of degrees and encompass a range of more and less vicious variations. In some cases a trait normally deemed vicious may even tend toward the virtuous or at least hold a promise of virtue, and this is true especially of the vice of vanity. Though vanity

---

wish'd for in a Golden Age; from thence to expose the Unreasonableness and Folly of those, that desirous of being an opulent and flourishing People, and wonderfully greedy after all the Benefits they can receive as such, are yet always murmuring at and exclaiming against those Vices and Inconveniences, that from the Beginning of the World to this present Day, have been inseparable from all Kingdoms and States that ever were fam'd for Strength, Riches, and Politeness, at the same time" (Mandeville 1988).

[6] Samuel Fleischaker states that "if Griswold is right" (as I believe that he is), "Smith urges us throughout TMS to see the pursuit of wealth as morally corrupting and conducive to unhappiness, but also applauds a social system that depends upon, and encourages, that very pursuit" (Fleischaker 2004, 104).

drives industry and has the potential to corrupt our moral sentiments, it can also be redirected to proper objects and even in some cases result in greatness. Thus like Becky Sharp, Smith recognizes that vanity can and even should be manipulated. But while Becky uses other people's vanity for her own ends, Smith suggests that this "social passion" contains moral promise. He observes: "Vanity is very frequently no more than an attempt prematurely to usurp glory before it is due." Your twenty-five year old son may be a "coxcomb," Smith writes, but it is not uncommon for young coxcombs to turn into "wise and worthy" forty year olds (TMS 263). Smith therefore cautions us not to discourage our young coxcombs too much – they may be estimating themselves too highly but we should see some promise in their pretensions: contained within their vanity may be an earnest desire to be great. The trouble is that most of the time, this earnest desire to *be* great is not as strong as the desire to *appear* great.

Our desire for approbation is generally so strong that people like Becky can gain power over us through flattery and by being "very quiet ... very much interested" (VF 29). Engaging our vanity, Becky makes us feel esteemed while she is using us as a rung on the social ladder she intends to climb. Becky, more than anyone else in VF, is aware that money is not the end but merely one of the means to attain higher status and to help her take the place in society she believes she deserves. She knows that for her to rise, others will have to "fall undermost," and for Becky this is hardly a regrettable side effect. Rather, Becky has a "desire of real superiority, of leading and directing" and takes pleasure in establishing her own "system of happiness" in which she is in control (TMS 326). Even when she appears to be aiming for a stable situation, like a marriage in which she could repose in luxury, she delights in the dynamic "scramble for preeminence" and "bustle of industry" (TMS 326). Becky's desire to "better her condition" finds expression, in part, in a "vulgar" desire to augment her fortune, but she is not governed by avarice. Ambition is a better fit for Becky, who strives at all times to gain power and preeminence.

Of the "two different characters" Smith describes, "the one of proud ambition and ostentatious avidity" and "the other of humble modesty and equitable justice," Becky clearly emulates the former (TMS 107). But her ambition delights not only – and perhaps not even primarily – in obtaining the goals she sets for herself. Rather, she takes pleasure in manipulating people and the system they serve with their vanity. Most of us are like cogs in a machine, unaware that our vanity keeps society's mechanisms running. Becky's understands that "civilization" is based on vanity and she takes pleasure in her mastery of the system and its component parts. The following section offers a study of some of the machines and systems at work in VF and TMS to better understand the nature of Becky's ambition.

For the Love of Machines

After Becky Sharp leaves Amelia and the Sedleys, she enters the household of Sir Pitt Crawley, Baronet, as a governess. In a letter to her friend, Becky describes Sir Pitt's second wife, "daughter of Mr. John Thomas Dawson, ironmonger, of Mudbury:" "She looks as if she had been handsome once, and her eyes are always weeping for the loss of her beauty" (VF 91). The narrator is no kinder to the second Lady Crawley:

> As the only endowments with which Nature had gifted Lady Crawley were those of pink cheeks and a white skin, and as she had no sort of character, nor talents, nor opinions, nor occupations, nor amusements, nor that vigour of soul and ferocity of temper which often falls to the lot of entirely foolish women, her hold upon Sir Pitt's affections was not very great. Her roses faded out of her cheeks, and the pretty freshness left her figure after the birth of a couple of children, and she became a mere machine in her husband's house of no more use than the late Lady Crawley's grand piano. (VF 98)

To marry Sir Pitt, Rose Dawson gave up Peter Butt, a man who loved her and with whom she could have been a "cheery lass," "in a snug farm, with a hearty family; and an honest portion of pleasures, cares, hopes and struggles." But, the narrator goes on, "a title and a coach and four are toys more precious than happiness in Vanity Fair: and if Harry the Eighth or Bluebeard were alive now, and wanted a tenth wife, do you suppose he could not get the prettiest girl that shall be presented this season?" (VF 98).

Two details of particular importance to the argument presented in this chapter are the narrator's offhand comment that in Vanity Fair, "toys" like "a title and a coach and four" are more "precious" than happiness and his calling the second Lady Crawley a machine. Together, these details help clarify Smith's account of a society fueled by vanity. Rose Dawson gave up Peter Butt and "true" happiness in order to gain the title and coach belonging to Sir Pitt, presumably because these flashy possessions appealed more to her vanity than the humble (but happy) life Peter Butt could have offered her. Sir Pitt may not be quite as bad as Bluebeard, but it is clear that he never had much to recommend him besides his title and his fortune – or, in Smith's words, his "wealth, power, and preheminence." Worse yet, in marrying him, Rose Dawson gave up not just her happiness, but also her personhood: she has become a machine. And making matters worse still, by the time Becky meets her, she is a *useless* machine, like the grand piano left behind by the first Lady Crawley after she died. The suggestion that the second Lady Crawley is just going through the motions the way a lifeless machine would is strengthened by the chilling description of her death: "Her heart was dead long before her body. She had sold it to become Sir Pitt Crawley's wife. Mothers and daughters are making the same bargain every day in Vanity Fair" (VF 176). When she finally expires, forgotten in her sick chamber on the second floor of the house, unattended by either her husband or her children, her death is not person's passing but a machine's ceasing to function.

This language of systems, order and machinery common to *Vanity Fair* and TMS reveals that in a society founded on vanity, rank and fortune human values like happiness, virtue, and wisdom are less important than the mechanism supporting the system. The second Lady Crawley embodies this principle and has herself become a machine. Though this mechanism crushes people like Rose Dawson, it apparently allows others to flourish. The contrast between the second Lady Crawley and Becky Sharp could scarcely be greater, as no-one in Vanity Fair appears more alive than the young governess. Instead of being sapped by the system that eradicated Rose Dawson's personhood, Becky's vivacity appears only to increase as she learns how to operate its machinery. She takes pleasure in her mastery, feeling herself to be a good fit for the superior position she is working to obtain. To be sure, her delight has significant mercenary aspects, but it also has an aesthetic quality related to the satisfaction Becky so clearly gains from her "art." TMS offers a few clues that help us understand Becky's love of society's system and machinery.

Smith opens the chapter "Of the Beauty which the Appearance of Utility bestows upon all the Productions of Art, and of the extensive Influence of this Species of Beauty" with the claim that "every body" agrees that "utility is one of the principal sources of beauty" (TMS 199). He continues: "That the fitness of any system or machine to produce the end for which it was intended, bestows a certain propriety and beauty upon the whole, and renders the very thought and contemplation of it agreeable, is so very obvious that nobody has overlooked it" (TMS 199). Bolstering these opening remarks, Smith observes that it hurts our sense of propriety to see a house with windows of different sizes, and an off-center door. The possessor of a proper, well-regulated and useful object takes pleasure in its "fitness" to promote "conveniency." As outsiders, we sympathize with the happy possessor and view "the object under the same agreeable aspect" (TMS 199). In an earlier passage Smith used similar language to describe the pleasure we take in observing things we "regard as having no peculiar relation to either of us," for example "the beauty of a plain, the greatness of a mountain, the ornaments of a building, the expression of a picture, the composition of a discourse, the conduct of a third person, the proportions of different quantities and numbers" (TMS 70). Because we have no vested interest in these natural, artistic, personal, and mathematical examples, we feel ourselves free to enjoy their aesthetic merits. Especially natural beauty, on display in "the various appearances which the great machine of the universe is perpetually exhibiting" have "no peculiar relation" to us and so we can regard them with disinterested satisfaction (TMS 70). Similarly, it gives us pleasure to see the palaces belonging to the very rich, who presumably are so far removed from our own sphere that we can regard their dwellings almost as natural phenomena (TMS 199). These supposedly common sense observations out of the way, Smith makes what he takes to be an original point:

> That this fitness, this happy contrivance of any production of art, should often be more valued, than the very end for which it was intended; and that the exact adjustment of the means for attaining any conveniency or pleasure, should frequently be more regarded, than that very conveniency or pleasure, in the attainment of which their whole merit would seem to consist, has not, so far as I know, been yet taken notice of by any body. (TMS 200).

We are not, Smith holds, interested primarily in the end but in the means and the "fitness" of "any production of art: a thousand instances" show this to be the case. When, for example, you enter a room and you find that your servant has left all the chairs in the middle of the floor, you will (perhaps angrily) get to work and arrange the chairs against the wall. Rather than waiting for your servant to do the job for you, you clear the floor – not because the convenience of a clear floor is immediately practical but because you take pleasure in the proper arrangement of things. You could of course have placed yourself on any of the chairs if all you wanted was to sit down. But this was not your objective. What you wanted, Smith writes, "was not so much this conveniency, as that arrangement of things which promotes it." It was "conveniency" that inspired the arrangement of the chairs along the walls instead of in the middle of the room, but it is the arrangement itself (and not the goal it serves) that "bestows upon it the whole of its propriety and beauty" (TMS 200).

Smith's second example showing the importance and aesthetic value of the "fitness" of means to ends concerns watches. The purpose of a watch, and hence its "conveniency," is to tell you the time and so help you keep appointments. Nevertheless, the most avid lovers of watches, those most concerned with their accuracy, are not necessarily the most punctual people or even the ones most anxious about being on time. What interests the watch lover "is not so much the attainment of this piece of knowledge, as the perfection of the machine which serves to attain it" (TMS 200). We love machines like we love mountain ranges, disinterested in their utility but taking pleasure in their "fitness" and perfection.

These two examples, involving the proper distribution of chairs in a room and the accuracy of timepieces, make our interest in fitness appear relatively harmless. But Smith detects a serious danger in our love of fitness: "How many people ruin themselves by laying out money on trinkets of frivolous utility?" For practical purposes, a watch which falls behind "two minutes in a day" is about as useful as one that "will not lose above a minute in a fortnight," yet "one curious in watches" will sell the former for "a couple of guineas" and purchase another "at fifty." "What pleases these lovers of toys is not so much the utility, as the aptness of the machines which are fitted to promote it" (TMS 200). These people, Smith adds with a degree of contempt, "contrive new pockets" in their clothes for these "trinkets," even though their utility in no way compensates for the trouble of carrying them around.

VF's narrator and Smith agree on the importance of "toys" in commercial society and the threat posed to our happiness by our seemingly innocent interest in the "fitness" of "machines" meant to increase our "conveniency." Rose Dawson is a sobering example of what happens to a person who chooses toys (e.g. "a coach and four") over a humble but happy life: in becoming Lady Crawley, she becomes a machine – but not even a "fit" machine, pleasant to owner and spectator alike because of its perfection as a means. Useless as an unplayed piano, she has been chewed up and spat out by the society of which she had hoped to become a part. Becky, resolved to "make friends" with everyone in Sir Pitt's household who could "at all interfere with her comfort," soon realizes that "Lady Crawley was not one of these personages, and a woman, moreover, so indolent and void of character as not to be of the least consequence in her own house" (VF 105). Perhaps the most important feature distinguishing Becky from the second Lady Crawley is that though she also loves "toys," she takes an even greater delight in bringing about order – an order in which she, of course, reigns supreme.

Sir Pitt, Becky, and the Natural Order of Things

Smith observes that "it is scarce agreeable to good morals, or even to good language, perhaps, to say, that mere wealth and greatness, abstracted from merit and virtue, deserve our respect." However, since our experience shows that wealth and greatness "almost constantly" obtain it, Smith points out that they must "in some respects [be] the natural objects" of it (TMS 108). This gives us a clue about Smith's use of the word "natural" in this context: because wealth and greatness do in fact obtain our respect, it follows that it is normal for us to feel this way and to act in accordance with this feeling. The natural order of things may not correspond to the moral order of things but it is an order nevertheless. Smith acknowledges that the "exalted stations" which are the natural objects of our respect "may, no doubt, be completely degraded by vice and folly." But as Sir Pitt Crawley shows, "the vice and folly must be very great, before they can operate this complete degradation" of exalted stations (TMS 108):

> Vanity Fair—Vanity Fair! Here was a man, who could not spell, and did not care to read—who had the habits and the cunning of a boor: whose aim in life was pettifogging: who never had a taste, or emotion, or enjoyment, but what was sordid and foul; and yet he had rank, and honours, and power, somehow: and was a dignitary of the land, and a pillar of the state. He was high sheriff, and rode in a golden coach. Great ministers and statesmen courted him; and in Vanity Fair he had a higher place than the most brilliant genius or spotless virtue. (VF 103)

Firmly ensconced in his "exalted station," Sir Pitt maintains the outward signs of his rank: "Boor as he was, Sir Pitt was a stickler for his dignity while at home, and seldom drove out but with four horses, and though he dined off boiled mutton, had always three footmen to serve it" (VF 101). Engaging Pitt's vanity, Becky quickly finds "many different ways of being useful" to her new master, far exceeding the duties of a governess. Sir Pitt is always engaged in lawsuits and she reads all the relevant papers and copies his letters, altering "the spelling of them so as to suit the usages of the present day" (VF 110). She becomes "so delightful a companion" that "the Baronet would seldom take his after-breakfast walk without her (and the children of course), when she would give her advice as to the trees which were to be lopped in the shrubberies, the garden-beds to be dug, the crops which were to be cut, the horses which were to go to cart or plough." As this sentence shows, the children – supposedly the focus of her attentions – are a mere afterthought. She is a governess in name only but even though she is "almost mistress of the house," she takes care, "in her new and exalted situation," "not to offend the authorities of the kitchen and stable, among whom her behaviour was always exceedingly modest and affable"

(VF 110). Becky learned her lesson at the Sedleys', where the servants suspected her ulterior motives almost from the start:

> She was quite a different person from the haughty, shy, dissatisfied little girl whom we have known previously, and this change of temper proved great prudence, a sincere desire of amendment, or at any rate great moral courage on her part. Whether it was the heart which dictated this new system of complaisance and humility adopted by our Rebecca, is to be proved by her after-history. A system of hypocrisy, which lasts through whole years, is one seldom satisfactorily practised by a person of one-and-twenty; however, our readers will recollect, that, though young in years, our heroine was old in life and experience, and we have written to no purpose if they have not discovered that she was a very clever woman. (VF 111)

Becky convincingly plays the part of the helpful domestic angel. When nature "formed man for society," Smith observes, she "endowed him with an original desire to please, and an original aversion to offend his brethren" (TMS 153). That Sir Pitt and Becky are no "natural" creatures in this regard is clear: they both enjoy giving offense more than they like being pleasant. In fact, giving offense seems to be its own reward for both the Baronet and his governess. Nature may, as Smith suggests, have rendered approval from others "most flattering and most agreeable" to some of us, but Sir Pitt and Becky do not seem to be very susceptible to "this desire of the approbation, and this aversion to the disapprobation of [their] brethren." But these feelings do not go to the heart of Smith's concern: even people in whom the desire for approval and the aversion to disapproval is strong are not always "fit for that society for which" they were "made." To make us fit for society, Smith claims, nature has endowed "man" with a further, more important desire, namely that "of being what ought to be approved of; or of being what he himself approves of in other men" (TMS 153). Here Smith makes an important distinction between appearance and reality. Man "naturally" is subject to two desires: "The first desire could only have made him wish to *appear* to be fit for society. The second was necessary in order to render him anxious to *be* really fit. The first could only have prompted him to the affectation of virtue, and to the concealment of vice. The second was necessary in order to inspire him with the real love of virtue, and with the real abhorrence of vice" (TMS 153, emphasis added).

Rose Dawson wished to appear fit for society and by marrying Sir Pitt became a lifeless machine. If she ever felt a "real love of virtue," it was overshadowed by her desire to "fit in" with the great and powerful. Becky, on the contrary, manages to work the system instead of falling prey to it herself the way Rose Dawson did. The system has no grip on her because she lacks the vanity that makes people susceptible to the workings of the machinery. Whether she feels no vanity at all is as of yet an open question. On the one hand she clearly does not seek the approbation of those around her for its own sake: the Pitt-Crawley family may be superior in rank but Becky does not admire any of its members. She primarily wants to correct a disorder in the system and rise to the rank that suits her. On the other hand, Becky is interested in status and the main advantage of having status is that other people look up to you. Who, if anyone, does Becky seek to impress by taking her proper place in the order of society? Or is this the wrong question, and is it Becky's primary goal not to gain admirers but to perform and practice her art? Smith tells the story of the "poor man's son," "whom heaven in its anger has visited with ambition" and who, at least in some respects, appears to be Becky's unfortunate double (TMS 200).

The Poor man's Daughter and the Poor man's Son

Smith sees our desire for riches and status as an expression of a deeper desire for the acknowledgment and esteem of others. If Smith is correct in his analysis, his claim that this desire for recognition can be redirected makes sense: if wealth and status are merely *possible* (but not the *only*) objects of vanity, then vanity could find expression in other pursuits as well. Smith suggests as much but is pessimistic: the value of wealth, power, and status may be contingent on the society one lives in, but in his society this value is so well-established that few will be able to resist its temptation. In the passage following the examples of the (dis)ordered chairs and (in) accurate watches, Smith asks us to consider the "poor man's son" to illustrate the grave implications of our desire for the "conveniencies" afforded by wealth and greatness.

The poor man's son "admires the condition of the rich" and imagines that he would be more comfortable in a palace than in his father's cottage, less inconvenienced if instead of walking or riding on horseback he could be "carried about in machines." His indolence makes him consider that "a numerous retinue of servants would save him from a great deal of trouble" and he believes that "if he had attained all these, he would sit still contentedly, and be quiet, enjoying himself in the thought of the happiness and tranquillity of his situation." Becky is far from indolent but shares the poor man's son desire for certain "machines" of convenience: a well-appointed house, a carriage (and four) and a retinue of servants. In missing her chance to marry Sir Pitt she regrets losing the prospect of these happy possessions. Smith's description of the poor man's son continues:

> He is enchanted with the distant idea of this felicity. It appears in his fancy like the life of some superior rank of beings, and, in order to arrive at it, he devotes himself for ever to the pursuit of wealth and greatness. To obtain the conveniencies which these afford, he submits in the first year, nay in the first month of his application, to more fatigue of body and more uneasiness of mind than he could have suffered through the whole of his life from the want of them. He studies to distinguish himself in some laborious profession. With the most unrelenting industry he labours night and day to acquire talents superior to all his competitors. (TMS 102)

Becky, too, wants to obtain these "conveniencies," and has distinguished herself in a "laborious profession," i.e. that of modest, unassuming domestic angel. She labors with "unrelenting industry" and beats out the competition, becoming mistress of the house and the favorite of everyone in the Crawley household. She too builds "castles in the sky," and inhabits them in her imagination. But unlike the poor man's son, she seems to enjoy her labors and industry. Becky does not "suffer" like the poor man's son, who deprives himself of pleasures that he could have enjoyed had he not been enthralled by the "superior rank of beings." His "fatigue of body" and "uneasiness of mind" are, in Smith's account, not only unnecessary but not worth the trouble: a life lacking the "conveniencies" the poor man's son is aiming to obtain would have been more comfortable. But unlike the poor man's son, Becky enjoys the "bustle" of her industry and though she keeps her eye on the prize, the game itself energizes her. She likes her "laborious profession" of artful mimicry and play-acting. Continuing his account of the poor man's son, Smith's writes:

> He endeavours next to bring those talents into public view, and with equal assiduity solicits every opportunity of employment. For this purpose he makes his court to all mankind; he serves those whom he hates, and is obsequious to those whom he despises. Through the whole of his life he pursues the idea of a certain artificial and elegant repose which he may never arrive at, for which he sacrifices a real tranquillity that is at all times in his power, and which, if in the extremity of old age he should at last attain to it, he will find to be in no respect preferable to that humble security and contentment which he had abandoned for it (TMS 201).[7]

Wherever she goes – as a guest at the Sedleys', a governess in Sir Pitt's household, and later as protégée of Lord Steyne – Becky finds opportunities to bring her talents "into public view" and "makes [her] court to all mankind." Like the poor man's son, she is at times obsequious to those she despises if she feels she can benefit from them. Yet on a deeper level Becky and the poor man's son differ: Becky does not appear to sacrifice "a real tranquility," nor does she ever reach the conclusion that "humble security" would have been preferable to her busy and laborious life. Knowing Becky's drive and vivacity, the "artificial and elegant repose" which she might have obtained in becoming Jos Sedley's or Sir Pitt's wife would not have satisfied her. It is more likely that she would have used these husbands like she uses Rawdon, i.e. to continue operating the system of society to further elevate herself.

Smith indicates that the poor man's son is a victim not only of ambition but also of delusion, and that at the end of his life he reaches the insight that all his toil was misguided.[8] He started his labors "enchanted with the distant idea" of happiness belonging to the "superior rank of human beings" and he pursues "wealth and greatness" to become like them. The object of the poor man's son's ambition at first therefore appears to lie in wealth and greatness but turns out to be concerned with the instruments that appear to bring about the happy state of the rich. The poor man's son's desires resemble those of people "curious about watches:" both the poor man's son and the watch lover admire "the ingenious and artful adjustment of those means to the end for which they were intended." So it is that the poor man's

[7] This leads Daniel Diatkine to observe: "The poor man's son is not seeking happiness. He likes machines. But he does not know that, and that is why he *thinks* that he is seeking future happiness" (2010, 400).

[8] As Luban argues, the "love of system is generally unconscious. The philosopher can think of himself as publishing for the benefit of humanity, and the poor man's son can think of himself as working for his future happiness, but both are victims of a deception that confuses happiness with models and machines" (2012, 401).

son is more interested in being "carried about in machines" like the rich and less in their presumed happiness:

> If we examine, however, why the spectator distinguishes with such admiration the condition of the rich and the great, we shall find that it is not so much upon account of the superior ease or pleasure which they are supposed to enjoy, as of the numberless artificial and elegant contrivances for promoting this ease or pleasure. He does not even imagine that they are really happier than other people: but he imagines that they possess more means of happiness. And it is the ingenious and artful adjustment of those means to the end for which they were intended, that is the principal source of his admiration. (TMS 202)

Becky appears to understand that the acquisition and maintenance of power, status, and riches demand constant attention and care. She is never mistaken about her goal, however: she is interested in power and riches but not primarily because of the "trifling conveniences" they produce. Becky takes pleasure first and foremost in the running of the "enormous and operose machines" and her dynamic energy is perfectly suited to their maintenance. She therefore avoids the fate of the poor man's son who in "the weariness of old age" finally realizes that "power and riches" are merely "enormous and operose machines contrived to produce a few trifling conveniencies to the body, consisting of springs the most nice and delicate, which must be kept in order with the most anxious attention, and which in spite of all our care are ready every moment to burst into pieces, and to crush in their ruins their unfortunate possessor" (TMS 202).[9]

Not long after Becky marries Rawdon Crawley, the couple attends an auction in Russell Square. Mr. Sedley, Amelia's father, invested unwisely and has been ruined: "His name had been proclaimed as a defaulter on the Stock Exchange, and his bankruptcy and commercial extermination had followed" (VF 205). All the family's possessions are now on display and sold to the highest bidder. The family has moved and is hiding in a poor part of town. Mr. Sedley has been "crushed" by the machinery of his wealth and Becky goes to see the "ruins:" "the comfortable old house where she had met with no small kindness, ransacked by brokers and bargainers, and its quiet family treasures given up to public desecration and plunder" (VF 207). Becky and Rawdon bid on one of the smaller items, "Portrait of a gentleman on an elephant." "I wonder it ain't come down with him," says someone to the general delight of the audience, "he's anyhow a precious big one" (VF 202). And so Becky has her private revenge, buying this "work of art" depicting Jos atop an elephant,

---

[9]Diatkine claims that "the "machines" that the poor man's son so loves are clearly business enterprises" which can ruin and "crush" their owners (2010, 399). On this interpretation Amelia's father, Mr. Sedley, bears resemblance to the poor man's son: Mr. Sedley goes bankrupt and spends his old age longing for his former "happiness," i.e. his time operating the machinery of the stock market. But the "noble House of Gaunt" is perhaps a more interesting instance of people being crushed by the "enormous operose machines" of their wealth and power. Lord Steyne, Becky's mentor and admirer, lives a life of debauchery and dissipation, the narrator suggests, to avoid the thought that he might go insane just like his son. Lord Steyne realizes that his riches and status cannot protect him from madness and that he may lose everything at any time, should the disease manifest itself in him. The members of the House of Gaunt all live in fear. Some retreat into solitude, others try to lose themselves in debauchery to forget their unhappiness.

hunting tigers: "the attitude of the gallant animal quite according to natur'; the gentleman in a nankeen jacket, his gun in his hand, is going to the chase" (VF 202).[10] The machinery of the Stock Exchange has crushed Mr. Sedley, the patronizing gentleman who mocked Becky when she first entered his home. As Smith explains in the *Lectures on Jurisprudence*, "in this generall scramble for preeminence, when some get up others must necessarily fall undermost," and though Becky's rise is not the cause of Sedley's bankruptcy, it shows that the "scramble for preeminence" makes for a dynamic system and "keeps in continual motion the industry of mankind" (Lectures 306; TMS 202).

Labors of Love and Hypocrisy

Chapters 3 and 4 established that the pursuit of a husband was the most obvious way for middle class women to move up in the world. If Becky, an "unprotected orphan," is to some degree selfish in her calculations upon entering Sir Pitt's home, "who can say but that her prudence was perfectly justifiable?" It is unfair, the narrator mockingly suggests, to judge Becky's intentions of making a good match for herself, especially since she has no mother to arrange a husband for her.

> "I am alone in the world," said the friendless girl. "I have nothing to look for but what my own labour can bring me; and while that little pink-faced chit Amelia, with not half my sense, has ten thousand pounds and an establishment secure, poor Rebecca (and my figure is far better than hers) has only herself and her own wits to trust to. Well, let us see if my wits cannot provide me with an honourable maintenance, and if some day or the other I cannot show Miss Amelia my real superiority over her. Not that I dislike poor Amelia: who can dislike such a harmless, good-natured creature?—only it will be a fine day when I can take my place above her in the world, as why, indeed, should I not?" (VF 105)

Becky, like Smith, is interested in the proper order of things. Unlike Smith, she is open about (and primarily concerned with) what she regards as her own proper place within that order. Becky considers herself "really fit" for society and desires to occupy a position suited to the kind of person whose role she has learned to play so well at Chiswick and at the Sedleys': a middle class lady suited to make a genteel match. She knows she is superior to Amelia, yet as a governess she finds herself below her friend in station. In the proper and, to Becky, "natural" order of the world,

[10] The passage in VF describing Jos atop his elephant is one of the many instances at which his vanity is the subject of mockery. Here it is of particular interest because it shows how for Jos, the preeminence Smith writes about is to be found in the admiring gaze. As Cole suggests, the Victorian Bourgeoisie in *VF* "was driven not by utilitarian calculation or domestic ideology, but by the desire for aristocratic status." "Rather than striving for professional success, moral earnestness, or marital bliss, T's bourgeois men are generally in pursuit of an admiring gaze – often a male gaze – that will validate their own fantasies of a Brummell-like physical perfection and social ascent" (138). Jos and George, mirror-gazing bourgeois, hope to see an aristocrat reflected in the glass. This implies a gender reversal: Thackeray's male characters are the biggest coquettes (Cole 2005, 147; see also King 2011).

she would rank above Amelia. But as an unconnected orphan, her own "labour" is the only means available to her to align societal appearance with her own reality. The seduction of Jos Sedley, her first attempt at taking her proper position in the world, fails. Becky knows that a husband is the most effective means to the end she has in mind and that her labor is therefore best spent in securing one. We must not be scandalized by "romantic" Becky's "visions of the future for herself," the narrator tells the readers. "Of what else have young ladies to think, but husbands? Of what else do their dear mammas think? "I must be my own mamma," said Rebecca" (VF 105).

But in setting her sights on a new husband, Becky miscalculates. When Sir Pitt unexpectedly proposes to her, she has to refuse him because she has already secretly married Rawdon Crawley, the whiskered dragoon and favorite of his very rich aunt Miss Crawley. Though she never before "in the course of this history" has lost "her presence of mind," she now weeps "some of the most genuine tears that ever fell from her eyes" (VF 178). Alone in her room, Becky experiences "some very sincere and touching regrets" at her misfortune.

> In this natural emotion every properly regulated mind will certainly share. What good mother is there that would not commiserate a penniless spinster, who might have been my lady, and have shared four thousand a year? What well-bred young person is there in all Vanity Fair, who will not feel for a hard-working, ingenious, meritorious girl, who gets such an honourable, advantageous, provoking offer, just at the very moment when it is out of her power to accept it? I am sure our friend Becky's disappointment deserves and will command every sympathy (VF 186).

Becky had not counted on Lady Crawley dying so soon, vacating the position for a third Lady Crawley. "In all the woes of repentance," Becky considers: "I might have been my lady! I might have led that old man whither I would." And speculating about the advantages (including what Smith would call the "conveniencies") she has lost in marrying the son instead of the father, she thinks about the new furniture and carriage she would have bought and the box she would have had at the opera. Fortunately, Becky is not one to dwell on the past:

> Rebecca was a young lady of too much resolution and energy of character to permit herself much useless and unseemly sorrow for the irrevocable past; so, having devoted only the proper portion of regret to it, she wisely turned her whole attention towards the future, which was now vastly more important to her. And she surveyed her position, and its hopes, doubts, and chances (VF 186).

Once it becomes known that Becky refused Sir Pitt Crawley because she has already married his son Rawdon Crawley, Rawdon loses his aunt's favor and with it the prospect of inheriting her large fortune. In marrying the wrong Crawley, Becky loses her chance at a title and "four thousand a year." Rawdon Crawley did not make a prudent choice either as his aunt disowns him for marrying a mere governess.[11]

[11] This despite Miss Crawley's liberal suggestion to Becky when she does not yet suspect the match: "That was the most beautiful part of dear Lord Nelson's character," Miss Crawley said. "He went to the deuce for a woman. There must be good in a man who will do that. I adore all impudent matches.— What I like best, is for a nobleman to marry a miller's daughter, as Lord Flowerdale

But, as the narrator observes: "If people only made prudent marriages, what a stop to population there would be!" (VF 189) This statement echoes the passage from VF cited at the beginning of this chapter: if people followed their principles, VF would be a "howling wilderness" and "all delights would go to the deuce" (VF 642). Prudence is one of the main obstacles to the delights referred to in this passage, and prudent marriages generally do not stimulate the economy the way imprudent marriages do. The union of Becky and Rawdon Crawley is a prime example of this phenomenon and though it hardly results in a significant population increase (they will have only one child), their married life is suited exactly to Mandeville's beehive. Becky and Rawdon live on credit and in great luxury, consuming the kinds of goods that the narrator claims would be absent from "principled" society: "He lived comfortably on credit. He had a large capital of debts, which laid out judiciously, will carry a man along for many years, and on which certain men about town contrive to live a hundred times better than even men with ready money can do" (VF 209).

Meanwhile, Becky thinks to herself: "'If he had but a little more brains … I might make something of him'; but she never let him perceive the opinion she had of him" (VF 208). She listens to all his "stories of the stable and the mess" and laughs "at all his jokes." Here we are reminded of the degree to which Becky has perfected her art, a "laborious profession" as Smith calls it in his description of the poor man's son. But unlike the deluded poor man's son, Becky is fully aware of the true goals of her "unrelenting industry." She, too, "labours night and day to acquire" and exercise "talents superior to all [her] competitors:" When Rawdon "came home she was alert and happy: when he went out she pressed him to go: when he stayed at home, she played and sang for him, made him good drinks, superintended his dinner, warmed his slippers, and steeped his soul in comfort" (VF 208). Becky is the wife *Middlemarch*'s Lydgate thought he was marrying when he engaged himself to Rosamond, the woman he will later in life compare to a basil plant flourishing on a dead man's brain. But it will take Rawdon many years to begin to suspect his wife's intentions. He finally becomes aware of Becky's true feelings (or lack thereof) because of the interference of Lady Jane, Rawdon's kind hearted sister in law and Becky's unlikely nemesis. Becky's trouble with women in general and Lady Jane in particular will be the topic of Chap. 8. At the time of Sedley's ruin, Lady Jane is still a marginal figure in the story of Becky's success when "that veteran rake, Rawdon Crawley, found himself converted into a very happy and submissive married man." The narrator offers us the following insight:

> The best of women (I have heard my grandmother say) are hypocrites. We don't know how much they hide from us: how watchful they are when they seem most artless and confidential: how often those frank smiles which they wear so easily, are traps to cajole or elude or disarm— I don't mean your mere coquettes, but your domestic models, and paragons of female virtue. Who has not seen a woman hide the dulness of a stupid husband, or coax the

---

did—it makes all the women so angry—I wish some great man would run away with you, my dear; I'm sure you're pretty enough" (VF 128).

> fury of a savage one? We accept this amiable slavishness, and praise a woman for it: we call this pretty treachery truth. A good housewife is of necessity a humbug (VF 207-8).

Chapters 3 and 4 discussed "the second best kind of wife" according to Smith, the woman who does not love her husband but acts as if she feels the "tender regard" befitting a dutiful wife. Becky here appears as a perfect example of Smith's second best wife, but the narrator (distancing himself from the claim in ascribing it to his grandmother) goes a step further and calls her "the best of women." Smith holds that we generally should be contented only with the praise we deserve when we are what we seem, but seems to make an exception for those women who play-act their "tender regard" out of a "sacred respect" for the rules governing female behavior. This leaves us with a problem regarding the morality of female behavior in general, as women are relegated to the domestic sphere where they are supposed to always act a part, being "all things to all people" (Armstrong). With no opportunity to ever be themselves, but always acting in compliance with conduct rules, women can never be rightly praised because they are never allowed to show themselves as they really are. In Vanity Fair, this problem does not exist because the narrator explodes Smith's ideal of the best kind of wife, i.e. the one who not only appears to be but really *is* a perfect domestic angel. Smith's ideal is exposed as hypocritical in two senses: first because the best woman is, on the narrator's account, a hypocrite and second because "we call this pretty treachery truth." Husbands (and presumably everyone familiar with the concept, including unmarried philosophers like Smith) are hypocrites for accepting woman's "amiable slavishness" because they know that it is an act. In this picture, everyone is a humbug.[12]

Ambition and the Love of Dominion

Becky, a "hard-working, ingenious, meritorious girl," is ambitious. But in her ambition she is less like the poor man's son and more like the "great statesman" Caesar. Even Rawdon, not normally the keenest observer, is aware of her "masculine" and "martial" qualities: "By Jove, Beck, you're fit to be Commander-in-Chief, or Archbishop of Canterbury, by Jove" (VF 190). Becky's first encounter with George Osborne after she has left the Sedleys (and with them the prospect of marrying Jos) is a powerful example of the strategic prowess that marks her as a commander in chief. It reveals not only her command of the rules governing proper behavior, but also her awareness of the system within which George is her (undeserving) superior. An early scene between Becky and George captures both Becky's keen understanding of her situation and her cleverly aggressive response to it.

Walking up to Becky "with a patronising, easy swagger," George means to "be kind to her and protect her." George even intends to honor her with a handshake and

[12] Smith observes "That the world judges by the event, and not by the design, has been in all ages the complaint, and is the great discouragement of virtue" (TMS 145). Yet to focus all "designs" on the "event" is the only way for a woman to appear "virtuous."

"saying, "Ah, Miss Sharp! how-dy-doo?"' he holds out "his left hand towards her, expecting that she would be quite confounded at the honour. Miss Sharp put out her right forefinger, and gave him a little nod, so cool and killing" that Rawdon, witnessing the power struggle from across the room, has trouble suppressing his laughter (VF 172).[13] Things only get more awkward for George when he opens the conversation by "agreeably" asking Becky "how she liked her new place," referring to her position as governess at Sir Pitt Crawley's. "My place?" said Miss Sharp, coolly, "how kind of you to remind me of it!" (VF 172) Observing that the people in Hampshire are not as wealthy as "you lucky folks in the city," she adds: "But then I am in a gentleman's family— good old English stock" (VF 173). The remark is meant to sting: it signals to George that she knows his father's fortune consists of "new money," what Smith would classify as the most "vulgar" basis for esteem. When George parries with an allusion to Becky's interest in Jos Sedley and his "City folk" money, Becky counters: "What an honour to have had you for a brother-in-law, you are thinking? To be sister-in-law to George Osborne, Esquire, son of John Osborne, Esquire, son of— what was your grandpapa, Mr. Osborne?" (VF 173) Despite his initial, condescending intention to be "kind to her and protect her," George finds himself "patronised him and persiffled." Becky admits that she would have married Jos if she had had the chance, "for could a poor penniless girl do better?" Having shown herself to be "frank and open" about her circumstances and her past intention of marrying Jos Sedley, she adds: "It was very kind of you to allude to the circumstance— very kind and polite" (VF 173).

In a section of TMS on the "selfish passions," Smith discusses the "man of enterprise," who distinguishes himself from "the man of dull regularity" by his "spirit and keenness" to get "an extraordinary job" (TMS 195). The man of enterprise is like a prince anxious to conquer a province, or a private gentleman making an effort to "gain an estate." Conquests of these kinds can change the rank of a person and are the "objects of the passion properly called ambition." Ambition is "a passion, which when it keeps within the bounds of prudence and justice, is always admired in the world" (TMS 195). In her conversation with George, Becky confesses to her own ambition of marrying Jos and makes George feel ashamed about drawing her out. Who could blame a penniless girl for her desire to better her condition in this perfectly just and prudent manner?

The poor man's son lets ambition ruin his life because he is deluded about the objects he has in view and spends his entire life pursuing them. Ambition, Smith writes, "when once it has got entire possession of the breast, will admit neither a rival nor a successor" (TMS 104). This example of ambition breaking the bounds of prudence shows that it is a dangerous passion and one that can destroy the person subject to it, much like it destroyed the second Lady Crawley. But there is another,

[13] Peter J. Capuano writes about the "formal relationship between Becky's manual activity and Thackeray's narrative strategy in Vanity Fair." The narrator may "claim to be the sole "Manager" of Vanity Fair's complicated marionette production" but "while this is true to a certain literal extent," Capuano's "contention is that Becky challenges this authority by taking over the controlling "hand" of the puppet-master at crucial junctures in the narrative" (Capuano 2008, 180).

grander way in which ambition can run amok, and with a greatness that "dazzles the imagination." This kind of ambition "is not only unjust but extravagant" and tends to occur primarily in "heroes and conquerors," and in "statesmen, whose projects have been very daring and extensive, though altogether devoid of justice" (TMS 195). Whether Becky's projects are unjust remains to be seen, but she certainly shows a lot of daring in her adventures. "To those who have been accustomed to the possession, or even to the hope of public admiration," Smith writes, "all other pleasures sicken and decay" (TMS 104). We know from Becky's history that as a young girl she enjoyed great public admiration in the Artist's Quarter for her quick wit and powers of mimicry. A woman since the age of eight, she has played her various roles to great effect and applause, and her conversation with George Osborne shows both awareness of her "place" in society and a hostility against those who have impeded her ambition.

Smith claims that nobody despises "rank, distinction pre-eminence … unless he is either raised very much above, or sunk very much below, the ordinary standard of human nature" (TMS 104). And since rank, distinction and preeminence usually go hand in hand with prosperity, we hope to gain the "respect and admiration of mankind" by becoming rich ourselves (TMS 109). So important are respect and admiration to the ambitious person that they may "endeavour, therefore, not only by fraud and falsehood, the ordinary and vulgar arts of intrigue and cabal; but sometimes by the perpetration of the most enormous crimes, by murder and assassination, by rebellion and civil war, to supplant and destroy those who oppose or stand in the way of their greatness" (TMS 109). While the poor man's son of Smith's story appears to hurt nobody but himself in his pursuit of "conveniencies," the ambitious "hero," "conqueror," and "statesman" are prepared to destroy all (human) obstacles in their way. Because we are often blinded by the success of great people, we admire them for what in someone else we would call rashness and imprudence. Yet when these greatly admired people eventually fail, we suddenly become aware of all their shortcomings and judge them with as much feeling as we had praised them before. Had Caesar lost instead of won after he crossed the Rubicon, "the insolence and injustice of his all-grasping ambition would have darkened and extinguished the glory of all that real merit" (TMS 258). Fortune, Smith argues, influences the moral sentiments of mankind and can make the same character hated or loved depending on the circumstances.

Our admiration as readers for Becky is complicated because we know about her intentions and feelings. We witness not only her actions but also know about her sentiments – or at least about the ones consistent with the narrator's intention of being "perfectly polite" in the telling of his story. Still, if we admire and respect her, it is not because we are deceived about her moral virtue. Becky's shaming of George Osborne is satisfying because she bests him at his own game, making "the British Lion" feel ashamed (in so far as George is capable of that sentiment) about his condescending attitude toward her. Becky could have used George to effect a rekindling of Jos Sedley's tender feelings towards her, but instead she chooses to have her revenge and put him in his place. In WN Smith points out that people are apt to overlook their economic interests when they have a chance to subjugate others. This is why slavery in both the literal and figurative sense will never be eradicated: "The pride of man makes him love to domineer" (WN i 325). This is helpful in understanding Becky, who is often imprudent when propriety might have been safer from an economical perspective. But though Becky is interested in the "conveniencies" afforded by wealth, her desire for rank and power is stronger. And rank only exists in a hierarchy, where those on top dominate over those below: "Slavery therefore has been universall in the beginnings of society, and the love of dominion and authority over others will probably make it perpetuall" (Lectures 180). Smith's pessimism on this topic is clear: History shows that even though it would be in a slave-owner's "real" (i.e. economic) interest to free his slaves and instead have "free servants or tenents" cultivate his land, "yet the love of domination and authority and the pleasure men take in having every thing done by their express orders ... will make it impossible for the slaves in a free country ever to recover their liberty" (Lectures 179).[14] Becky likewise sacrifices "real" economic interests to her desire to subjugate, mock, and enslave.

How Not to Be Driven Insane by the Machine

The next chapter will discuss Smith's notion of self-estimation, central to his account of vanity and pride. "Great success in the world, great authority over the sentiments and the opinions of mankind, have very seldom been acquired without some degree of this excessive self-admiration" (TMS 257). Alexander the Great and Caesar present interesting examples of a vanity feedback loop: admiration feeds vanity, vanity causes people to do things that (sometimes) inspire more admiration, which in turn feeds their vanity, etc. Vanity may encourage us to do exceedingly stupid and rash things, but when fortune is on our side and our vain endeavors happen to be successful, the praise we receive confirms our vanity. Smith reflects that vanity "was, perhaps, necessary, not only to prompt [people like Alexander the Great and Caesar] to undertakings which a more sober mind would never have thought of, but to command the submission and obedience of their followers to support them in such undertakings" (TMS 257).

Just like it keeps industry in motion, vanity spurs people into action and, sometimes, great deeds are the result. But eventually both Caesar and Alexander the Great allowed their presumptions to betray them "into a vanity that approached almost to insanity and folly" (TMS 257). Alexander the Great expected people to worship him as a god; Caesar claimed to be a descendant of Venus. This degree of vanity encourages assassins, Smith observes, and so it is that the same principle that encourages people to great undertakings often spells their downfall. But the downfall

[14] See also the *Wealth of Nations:* "For though management and persuasion are always the easiest and the safest instruments of government, as force and violence are the worst and the most dangerous, yet such, it seems, is the natural insolence of man, that he almost always disdains to use the good instrument, except when he cannot or dare not use the bad one" (WN ii 180–1).

of these great statesmen is nothing like the second Lady Crawley's demise, nor does it resemble the faith of the poor man's son. The poor man's son simply grows old and, perhaps, comes to realize his delusion. He has helped to keep in motion the industry of mankind, but remains an anonymous cog in the machine, behaving predictably and unremarkably. Similarly, nobody takes "any notice at all" of the second Lady Crawley even when she is "exceedingly ill" and she is left "fading away in her lonely chamber, with no more heed paid to her than to a weed in the park" (VF 163). Both Rose Dawson and the poor man's son are deluded, but neither of them has the self-esteem that drives the great undertakings of statesmen. More precisely, if they ever had great self-esteem, it was not sustained or fed by the people around them: the second Lady Crawley is ignored even by her children, while the poor man's son spends all his time and energy obtaining "conveniencies."

If Becky is more like Caesar and Alexander the Great, and less like the poor man's son, then she is prone to a particular kind of ambition and, on Smith's account, a particular kind of vanity. Yet the previous chapter suggested that Becky can take advantage of other people's vanity at least in part because she is not herself vain. The next chapter offers an analysis of self-estimation (and self-love) to resolve this apparent problem.

References

Browne, Julius Henri. 1891. The value of vanity. *The North American Review* 153 (418): 379–381.

Capuano, Peter J. 2008. At the hands of Becky sharp: (In) visible manipulation and *Vanity Fair*. In *Faculty publications–department of English*, vol. 88. Lincoln: DigitalCommons@University of Nebraska-Lincoln. http://digitalcommons.unl.edu/englishfacpubs/88.

Cole, Sarah Rose. 2005. The aristocrat in the mirror: Male vanity and bourgeois desire in William Makepeace Thackeray's *Vanity Fair*. *Nineteenth-Century Literature* 61 (2): 137–170.

Diatkine, Daniel. 2010. Vanity and the love of system in *Theory of Moral Sentiments*. *European Journal of History of Economic Thought* 17 (3): 383–404.

Fleischaker, Samuel. 2004. *On Adam Smith's wealth of nations*. Princeton: Princeton University Press.

Griswold, Charles. 1999. *Adam Smith and the virtues of enlightenment*. Cambridge: Cambridge University Press.

King, Nikole. 2011. The male body and heroic manhood in Thackeray's *Vanity Fair: A novel without a hero*. *Victorians Journal*: 105–116.

Luban, Daniel. 2012. Adam smith on vanity, domination, and history. *Modern Intellectual History* 9 (2): 275–302.

Mandeville, Bernard. 1988. *The fable of the bees or private vices, publick benefits*. Vol. 2. Indianapolis: Liberty Fund. http://oll.libertyfund.org/titles/846#Mandeville.

Smith, Adam. 1981. An inquiry into the nature and causes of the wealth of nations. In *Vol. 2 of the Glasgow Edition of the Works and Correspondence of Adam Smith*, ed. R.H. Campbell and A.S. Skinner. Indianapolis: Liberty Fund.

———. 1982a. The theory of moral sentiments. In *Vol. 1 of the Glasgow Edition of the Works and Correspondence of Adam Smith*, ed. D.D. Raphael and A.L. Macfie. Indianapolis: Liberty Fund.

———. 1982b. Lectures on Jurisprudence. In *Vol. 5 of the Glasgow Edition of the Works and Correspondence of Adam Smith*, ed. R.L. Meek, D.D. Raphael, and P.G. Stein. Indianapolis: Liberty Fund.

Thackeray, William Makepeace. 1983. In *Vanity fair: A novel without a hero*, ed. John Sutherland. New York: Oxford UP.

Chapter 6
The Self-estimation and Self-command of a Mighty Conqueror

Abstract In his *Theory of Moral Sentiments,* Adam Smith suggests that high (perhaps even excessive) self-esteem may be a requirement for great undertakings. We revere even "barbaric" conquerors like Genghis Khan who, with their acts of "fortunate violence," won the submission and obedience of their followers and so brought about order. But excessive self-estimation is not a sufficient condition for greatness, barbaric or otherwise; the vain and the proud also esteem themselves too highly but are not therefore necessarily the objects of our admiration. This chapter discusses Smith's understanding of self-estimation, pride, vanity, and the related feelings of shame and mortification. It also introduces the (for Smith) masculine virtue of generosity and the feminine virtue of humanity. *Vanity Fair's* Becky Sharp challenges Smith's gendered theory built around these virtues, traits and feelings. She is neither generous nor humane, esteems herself most highly, never experiences shame or mortification, and is a mighty conqueror in her own right. Most importantly, she has a level of self-command that for Smith marks the "character of dark and deep dissimulation."

The Presumption of Mighty Conquerors

In TMS, Smith explains that we can compare our own merit either to "the idea of exact propriety and perfection," or to "that degree of approximation to this idea which is commonly attained in the world" (TMS 254). The wise man uses the first standard and is constantly at work to remove moral "blemishes" on his character because he is "enamored" of the "exquisite and divine beauty" of the first standard. The wise man is therefore always aware of his own imperfections and "sees, with grief and affliction, in how many different features the mortal copy falls short of the immortal original"[1] (TMS 255). More commonly, people focus on the second,

[1] The wise man's "grief and affliction" resemble the despair of women trying (but of course always failing) to live up to the "immortal" ideal of the perfect domestic angel described in Chaps. 3 and 4. It is difficult to see how Smith's ideal of "tranquility" could be achieved by either wise men or women since both groups appear to be condemned to a life of striving without ever succeeding.

R. Slegers, *Adam Smith's Moral Sentiments in Vanity Fair*, Issues in Business Ethics 49, https://doi.org/10.1007/978-3-319-98731-6_6

obtainable standard and as a result they think more highly of themselves than wise men do, even though the former are usually the latter's inferiors. Most people aim at "ordinary" instead of "ideal" perfection and in their arrogance and presumption overlook their own flaws. They are "great admirers of themselves, and great contemners of other people." Their self-admiration is such that it "dazzles the multitude, and often imposes even upon those who are much superior to the multitude." Many "quacks" have shown that it is easy to impress "the multitude" with "the most extravagant and groundless pretensions" (TMS 256).

Smith here repeats his conviction that virtue often loses out to vanity and pretension. Moreover, "great success in the world, great authority over the sentiments and the opinions of mankind, have very seldom been acquired without some degree of this excessive self-admiration" (TMS 257.) Though virtue and wisdom are more deserving of praise, excessive self-admiration not only receives praise but also achieves "success in the world." "This presumption was, perhaps, necessary, not only to prompt them to undertakings which a more sober mind would never have thought of, but to command the submission and obedience of their followers to support them in such undertakings." Becky undertakes adventures that would not have occurred to "more sober minds" and she gains submissive and obedient followers wherever she goes. She clearly does not suffer from low self-esteem, but can her self-admiration be called "excessive"? Smith writes: "When crowned with success, accordingly, this presumption has often betrayed them into a vanity that approached almost to insanity and folly" (TMS 257). For Becky to fit into this category, she would have to be presumptive and led to folly by her successes. Thus far, she has not lost control over her situation – only when she reaches Paris is she to be "intoxicated" by her success. But even there she cannot be called insane and she remains in control; she merely slights the acquaintances she now considers beneath her. Still, it is not clear that her self-estimation is excessive. Even her enemies esteem her and consider her dangerous. She does not appear to be a victim of either folly or insanity.

Smith gives examples of the kind of excessive self-estimation that leads to folly and insanity: Alexander the Great, who wanted people to worship him as a god; Socrates, who claimed (or so Smith believes) to be privileged by some divine Being; and Caesar, who claimed to be descended from Venus. The "insolence" and "almost childish vanity" of the latter was such that it "emboldened" his assassins. According to Smith, the principle that leads to great undertakings can drive a person over the edge. Up to what point is excessive self-estimation to one's advantage and when does it become a problem?

Several people in her acquaintance call Becky insolent but she never gives way to "childish vanity" (TMS 257). She enjoys frivolous trinkets but they do not distract her from her grander ambitions. As readers we are not blinded by her success, or at least not like the "multitudes" described by Smith in the case of Caesar and Alexander. We know too much about Becky's intentions and feelings to mistake her actions for generosity or benevolence. Nor do we mistake her for a wise person who wants to adhere to "the idea of exact propriety and perfection." Rather, we admire her but not because "success covers from [our] eyes, not only the great imprudence, but frequently the great injustice of [her] enterprises" (TMS 258).[2] We are aware of Becky's imprudence and injustice (by Smith's standards) but we are impressed nonetheless by her success. And it is well that we are: just like we naturally respect "wealth and greatness," we admire success and so help establish and maintain "the distinction of ranks and the order of society." So even though our admiration for ill-gotten success may betray a "great disorder in our moral sentiments," it is "by no means … without its utility; and we may on this, as well as on many other occasions, admire the wisdom of God even in the weakness and folly of man." The "mob of mankind" looks up to Caesar and Alexander with "a very weak and foolish admiration." This is not very remarkable, but Smith points out that we do not reserve our admiration for "splendid characters" like these. We "regard with reverence, and sometimes even with a sort of respectful affection, that fortunate violence which we are no longer capable of resisting" even when the perpetrator is a "savage barbarian:" "an Attila, a Genghis, or a Tamerlane" (TMS 258).

What then, is the "utility" of our disposition to admire "mighty conquerors" and the fortunate violence they perpetrate even when they are barbaric? It is so we may "submit more easily to those superiors, whom the course of human affairs may assign to us." Since we would not in any case be able to resist their violence, it is as well that we are inclined to submit to them. The violence these mighty conquerors perpetrate is "fortunate" because it brings about order and establishes a hierarchy. Once again we are made aware of the importance of the society machine described in the previous chapter.

Becky has already shown herself to be a "mighty conqueror" to whom many people will readily submit. She has no interest in attaining to the ideal standard that makes wise men perpetually aware of their shortcomings. Nor does she particularly care about the much lower standard to which people commonly aspire. Becky has her own standards, or rather: she sets them herself. She is not in doubt about her moral merit like the anxious wise man, nor is she self-satisfied the way the common man is about his worldly success. The latter is too much wrapped up in the system, unable to operate the machinery of society because his scope and understanding are limited. This chapter considers the Smithian themes of self-esteem and pride and offers a sketch of the standards Becky devises for herself.

---

[2] When the fortunes of the great fail them, however, "things change their colours and their names" (TMS 258). No longer do we turn a blind eye to the injustice of their enterprises but we judge them more harshly than we perhaps would have done had we not first admired them to an unreasonable degree. Becky Sharp experiences this fall from grace when her protector Lord Steyne turns against her. Becky's downfall is described in Chap. 8.

Captain Dobbin's Low Self–esteem

Categorizing people in accordance with their level of self-estimation, Smith first describes "the man who neither ascribes to himself, nor wishes that other people should ascribe to him, any other merit besides that which really belongs to him." This person "fears no humiliation, dreads no detection; but rests contented and secure upon the genuine truth and solidity of his own character" (TMS 259). Lacking the pomp and circumstance of people of wealth, power, and status, he does not have many admirers, but being wise, sober, and just, he is satisfied with the admiration of one or more of his fellow wise men.

Second, there is "the man of excessive self-estimation." About this person, Smith writes: "The wise men who see him the nearest, admire him the least." The man of excessive self-estimation interprets as envy the wise man's failure to admire him. By the standards of the man of excessive self-estimation, the wise man's self-esteem is piteously low and is taken as an indication of his minimal merit. The man of excessive self-estimation seeks the company of "flatterers and traitors, who pretend to idolize his vanity and presumption" (TMS 259). Over time, this man's character becomes odious and contemptible even if it was not all that bad to begin with.

Third, there is the "man who under-rates himself." People are inclined to make this person suffer "all the injustice which he does to himself, and frequently a great deal more" (TMS 265). Smith observes: "men of no more than ordinary discernment never rate any person higher than he appears to rate himself. He seems doubtful himself, they say, whether he is perfectly fit for such a situation or such an office; and immediately give the preference to some impudent blockhead who entertains no doubt about his own qualifications" (TMS 264). Wise men are few and far between and though they are to be admired for their virtue and wisdom, they tend to lead quiet lives out of the public eye. They do not, like the "mighty conquerors," establish order in society because the multitude does not submit to them. So though "wise men" set the standard for correct self-estimation, they do not contribute much to the hierarchy required for an ordered society. Perhaps this is part of the reason why Smith believes that where it comes to self-estimation, it is better to err on the side of excess than defect: "In almost all cases, it is better to be a little too proud, than, in any respect, too humble; and, in the sentiment of self-estimation, some degree of excess seems, both to the person himself and to the impartial spectator, to be less disagreeable than any degree of defect" (TMS 265).

If there are people in Vanity Fair who fit the first category of wise men who judge themselves correctly neither thinking too much or too little of themselves, they are minor characters.[3] Examples of "impudent blockheads," on the other hand, are

[3]The good-natured Major O'Dowd and his Irish wife Peggy fall in this category. Major O'Dowd leads George and Dobbin's regiment and is reliably good humored, level-headed, and neither vain nor proud. Mrs. O'Dowd evolves from an initially silly character to a model army wife, brave in her own right and as capable of leading an army, the narrator observes, as her husband. It would perhaps go too far to call her "wise" in the full Smithian sense, but she comes a lot closer than most of the other characters in VF.

plentiful. The third category, people who under-rate themselves, has at least one notable member: Captain (and later Major) William Dobbin.[4] Dobbin looks up to George Osborne and is in love with Amelia, who barely notices him. He is also the only man in Vanity Fair who is impervious to Becky's artfulness. Though Dobbin underrates himself, he is not one of "those unfortunate persons" Smith describes "whom nature has formed a good deal below the common level" (TMS 264). Dobbin is admired and beloved by his regiment and known for his valor and levelheadedness on the battlefield. If anything, he is above the common level in courage and understanding. But where Amelia is concerned he rates himself so far below her that he regards her rudeness to him as perfectly natural. When Becky is pursuing Jos Sedley and George is courting Amelia at Vauxhall, Dobbin tags along but is entirely forgotten for the duration of the visit. He carries the ladies' coats and shawls and after the meal, of which he did not partake, he dispatches of the inebriated Jos. When Mr. Sedley is ruined and all the Sedleys' possessions are sold at auction, Dobbin buys Amelia's old piano and has it sent to her at her new address. She and her mother believe it to be a gift from George and Dobbin does not correct Mrs. Sedley when she mentions the piano and Amelia's supposed benefactor. Though he is in love with her himself, Dobbin encourages George to marry Amelia before the regiment leaves for Belgium. After the marriage is a fact, Dobbin visits both Mr. Sedley and Mr. Osborne (Amelia's and George's father, respectively) to try to bring about a rapprochement between the gentlemen, who neither of them agreed to the match. Why did he bring about this marriage, which could easily have been postponed until after the regiment's return? "Because he loved her so much that he could not bear to see her unhappy: or because his own sufferings of suspense were so unendurable that he was glad to crush them at once" (VF 278). Amelia travels to Belgium with George and Dobbin's regiment and Dobbin keeps her company or tries to show her attention while George is away, flirting with Becky. Though Amelia suffers as a result of George's inattention, she does not respect Dobbin or see his sympathy for her and her situation:

> Little Amelia, it must be owned, had rather a mean opinion of her husband's friend, Captain Dobbin. He lisped— he was very plain and homely-looking: and exceedingly awkward and ungainly. She liked him for his attachment to her husband (to be sure there was very little merit in that), and she thought George was most generous and kind in extending his friendship to his brother officer. George had mimicked Dobbin's lisp and queer manners many times to her, though to do him justice, he always spoke most highly of his friend's good qualities. ... Not knowing him intimately as yet, she made light of honest William— and he knew her opinions of him quite well, and acquiesced in them very humbly. (VF 293)

In his relationship to Amelia, Dobbin's humility sinks him "into idiotism." "Whoever has taken the trouble to examine idiots with attention," writes Smith, has found that "many idiots" can be "taught to read, write, and account tolerably well," while many

[4]Though his attitude matches Smith's description of the person who underrates himself, Dobbin's fate differs from Smith's prediction: "A youth, too unassuming and too unambitious, is frequently followed by an insignificant, complaining, and discontented old age" (TMS 264). It is only because Dobbin eventually (though only after many years of humility and humiliation) stands up for himself that his old age is not discontented (though neither is does it appear very happy).

people who are not considered idiots have trouble acquiring these skills to a satisfactory degree. The difference between the people considered idiots and those not considered idiots appears to be their "instinct of pride," which encourages them to "set themselves upon a level with their equals in age and situation; and, with courage and firmness, maintain their proper station among their companions" (TMS 264). Though reading, writing, and accounting are not the relevant skills in this situation, Dobbin clearly lacks the pride to set himself "upon a level" with his equals, or even (in some cases) with his inferiors.

When they were children, Dobbin fought the boy bullying George at school and became George's protector, admirer, and friend. George borrows money from Dobbin and often treats him like a servant (as he does at Vauxhall) and Dobbin "humbly acquiesces" in this role much like he does in respect to Amelia. "The want of proper indignation is a most essential defect in the manly character," Smith writes (TMS 251). Dobbin might even be mean-spirited by Smith's standards: "The man …, who, in matters of consequence, tamely suffers other people, who are entitled to no such superiority, to rise above him or get before him, is justly condemned as mean-spirited" (TMS 251–2). At the same time, Captain Dobbin's love for Amelia, combined with his lack of pride and vanity, give him at least one advantage over the other men in VF: he is unsusceptible to Becky's stratagems. Becky senses this instinctively avoids him. The following section teases out the differences between (excessive) self-estimation, pride, and vanity.

The Vain, the Proud, and the Right to Think Highly of Oneself

The previous chapters explained how Becky Sharp exploits the vanity of others, giving people the feeling that they deserve praise, admiration, privilege, luxuries, etc. – at a price, of course. Mandeville and Thackeray (and Smith, though reluctantly) hold that without this kind of vanity there would be no industry to speak of. People providing luxury goods and services rely on vanity for their business, while their own desire to make money and achieve status is an expression of the same driving force. Smith suggests that vanity's objects are contingent on our situation and though our vanity encourages us to take "shortcuts" to fame and fortune, in theory we could be guided to value and pursue worthier objects. Smith therefore regards vanity as a malleable passion, one that can be manipulated for better or for worse. To better understand the malleability of vanity we need an account of pride, a vice which does not lend itself to manipulation according to Smith. In the *Theory*, Smith presents vanity and pride alongside each other as two forms of "excessive self-estimation." While Captain Dobbin shows himself to be defective in his self-estimation, George and Jos are prone to excess, as the following few examples will show.

We commonly admire the vain and call them "spirited" and "high-minded" when in fact they are reckless and impudent. People like Rawdon Crawley, his aunt Miss Crawley and of course Becky see George Osborne for what he really is: a young "city man," new money without bona fides. Amelia, on the other hand, sympathizes with him because she sees in him what Smith describes as "a great and distinguished superiority above the common level of mankind" (TMS 260). But excessive self-estimation without real "distinguished superiority" is disgusting and revolting, according to Smith. When someone esteems himself too highly, he is proud or vain. Vanity always, and pride "for the most part," involves in its meaning a "considerable degree of blame" (TMS 260). When, just after arriving at the Sedleys', Becky whispers to Amelia that she considers Jos "very handsome," Jos hears her and "(thinking in his heart that he was a very fine man) the praise thrilled through every fibre of his big body, and made it tingle with pleasure." But Jos's self-estimation is not as stable as George's: "Then, however, came a recoil. 'Is the girl making fun of me?'" (VF 28) George is never prey to insecurities of this kind.

George has always been his father's pride and joy: "His dearest vanities, ambitious hopes, had all been here. What pride he had in his boy! He was the handsomest child ever seen. Everybody said he was like a nobleman's son. A royal princess had remarked him, and kissed him, and asked his name" (VF 283). The older Osborne always supplies George with ample funds so his son can spend time in good company:

> I don't grudge money when I know you're in good society, because I know that good society can never go wrong. There's no pride in me. I was a humbly born man— but you have had advantages. Make a good use of 'em. Mix with the young nobility. There's many of 'em who can't spend a dollar to your guinea, my boy. (VF 155)

Father and son alike believe that the company of the "young nobility" will elevate their own family's status, like "the vain man" who "sees the respect which is paid to rank and fortune, and wishes to usurp this respect" (TMS 261).[5] George and Mr. Osborne take the most obvious route to usurp this respect by buying their way into a social class. The vain person realizes that respect is also extended to certain "talents and virtues," which is probably why George wants to appear honorable, claiming to be a gentleman and marrying Amelia because he wants to be a man of his word. When Dobbin lends him money to buy a gift for Amelia, George instead buys a diamond pin for himself (which Amelia thinks looks beautiful on him). "His dress, his equipage, his way of living accordingly, all announce both a higher rank and a greater fortune than really belong to him," Smith writes of people like George, and

---

[5] Mr. Osborne and his son George are "not always very delicate" and seek to please their social superiors with "unnecessary ostentation" (TMS 262). Even less delicate and more ostentatious in his attempts to flatter "the great" is Mr. Collins in *Pride and Prejudice*. Like George Osborne, "He is fond of being admitted to the tables of the great, and still more fond of magnifying to other people the familiarity with which he is honored there" (TMS 261). But while George has at least a few social graces that make him pleasant company to most, Mr. Collins's vanity makes him insufferable even to the woman he is trying to court, like when he advises Elizabeth before her first encounter with Lady Catherine deBourgh: "Do not make yourself uneasy, my dear cousin, about your apparel. Lady Catherine is far from requiring that elegance of dress in us, which becomes herself and her daughter. I would advise you merely to put on whatever of your clothes is superior to the rest, there is no occasion for anything more. Lady Catherine will not think the worse of you for being simply dressed. She likes to have the distinction of rank preserved" (Austen 2004, 124).

he adds that vain people often reduce themselves to poverty because they are eager to look good to the world. George dies on the battlefield just six weeks after marrying Amelia, and so does not have the chance to ruin himself financially – though he leaves his wife nothing (TMS 261).[6]

George shows that there is a subset of vain people unencumbered by insecurity. "His vanity is delighted with viewing himself, not in the light in which you would view him if you knew all that he knows; but in that in which, he imagines, he has, by his own address, induced you actually to view him" (TMS 261). George does not appear to have enough of an inner life to reflect on the difference between the admiration he receives and his actual admirability – he simply takes the attention and praise at face value: "This is certain, that Amelia believed her lover to be one of the most gallant and brilliant men in the empire: and it is possible Lieutenant Osborne thought so too" (VF 146). One of the main features that set George apart from the proud person is that he is considered decent or at least entertaining company both by his admirers and by the people who mock him and take advantage of him. As Smith observes: "Not withstanding all its groundless pretensions, however, vanity is almost always a sprightly and gay, and very often a good-natured passion. Pride is always a grave, a sullen, and a severe one" (TMS 262). This distinction corresponds to the contrast between the way people look at George Osborne (who is very popular but also known as a dandy) and the way they regard Jane Austen's Mr. Darcy (who is almost universally disliked but respected nonetheless).

Mr. Darcy's pride is a topic of conversation early on in Jane Austen's *Pride and Prejudice*. The following excerpt is instructive as it touches on several elements of Smith's theory: proud people often have some greatness to boast of, even if their self-estimation is excessive; the proud person demands that others acknowledge his or her superiority; and the proud person differs from the vain person.

> "His pride," said Miss Lucas, "does not offend me so much as pride often does, because there is an excuse for it. One cannot wonder that so very fine a young man, with family, fortune, everything in his favour, should think highly of himself. If I may so express it, he has a right to be proud."
>
> "That is very true," replied Elizabeth, "and I could easily forgive his pride, if he had not mortified mine."
>
> "Pride," observed Mary, who piqued herself upon the solidity of her reflections, "is a very common failing, I believe. By all that I have ever read, I am convinced that it is very common indeed; that human nature is particularly prone to it, and that there are very few of us who do not cherish a feeling of self-complacency on the score of some quality or other, real or imaginary. Vanity and pride are different things, though the words are often used synonymously. A person may be proud without being vain. Pride relates more to our opinion of ourselves, vanity to what we would have others think of us." (Austen 2004, 13)

Miss Lucas's estimation of Mr. Darcy's pride reflects Smith's observation that people with excessive self-estimation often are above the norm. The problem, as will be discussed below, is that their relative greatness does not justify their exaggerated self-estimation. Still, Miss Lucas can forgive Mr. Darcy's pride because his good

[6] Becky, meanwhile, has received many gifts from George which she plans to sell should Rawdon leave her a widow.

looks, his material wealth, and his ancestry justify most or all of it. Elizabeth Bennet suggests that she could forgive him his pride on these grounds, but as Mr. Darcy has just publicly dismissed her as a dance partner at the ball, her own pride is mortified – she may not be as proud as Mr. Darcy himself, but she has enough pride to be offended at Darcy's open refusal to acknowledge and respect her.

Most interesting for our purposes is Mary's statement. Mary is one of the younger Bennet sisters and is described as both vain and pedantic: "Mary had neither genius nor taste; and though vanity had given her application, it had given her likewise a pedantic air and conceited manner, which would have injured a higher degree of excellence than she had reached" (Austen 2004, 17). One way in which Mary's vanity manifests itself is through her tendency to offer up pieces of wisdom gathered from her readings. Though she does not mention her source, it appears that Mary has been reading Smith: her little lesson about vanity and pride is a perfect summary of Smith's initial distinction between the two closely related character traits and hence Mary's comment encourages us to consider *Pride and Prejudice* from the perspective of Smith's theory.[7]

Sincerity and Mortification

In his descriptions of pride and vanity, Smith refers to a host of other character traits that tend to accompany the two "vices of excessive self-estimation." The first trait Smith mentions in his account of pride is, perhaps surprisingly, a virtue: sincerity. He writes:

> The proud man is sincere, and in the bottom of his heart, is convinced of his own superiority; though it may sometimes be difficult to guess upon what that conviction is founded. He wishes you to view him in no other light than that in which, when he places himself in your situation, he really views himself. He demands no more of you than, what he thinks, justice. (TMS 260)

As the next chapter will explain, this passage suggests that the proud person's "impartial spectator" is not doing its job. The proud person fails to see him- or herself from a disinterested distance and esteems him- or herself not as a sympathetic stranger would, but with a strong bias in his or her own favor. The proud person sincerely believes that he or she is superior to the norm and fully expects you to share his belief and behave accordingly. Smith continues: "If you appear not to respect him as he respects himself, he is more offended than mortified, and feels the

[7] Kenneth Moler remarks that Mary Bennet's comments are a "warmed over" version of Smith's account of pride and vanity in the *Theory*. Her schoolbook delivery of the complex theory, Moler argues, indicates Mary's "intellectual sterility." Elizabeth's allusion to Smith, by contrast, is "light and deft" (Moler 1967, 567). Moler's astute observations about the connections between Adam Smith's moral theory and *Pride and Prejudice* have received little attention. Among the few relatively recent authors to mention Moler and build on his insights are Peter Know-Shaw (2004) and Christel Fricke, who argues that the relationship between Darcy and Elizabeth exemplifies the sympathetic process Smith describes in the *Theory* (Fricke 2014).

same indignant resentment as if he had suffered a real injury" (TMS 260). The proud person can be offended, but not mortified. Elizabeth Bennet said that Darcy had mortified her pride, but according to Smith mortification is a feeling experienced primarily by the vain.

At the dance where Mr. Darcy is first introduced he "soon drew the attention of the room by his fine, tall person, handsome features, noble mien, and the report which was in general circulation within five minutes after his entrance, of his having ten thousand a year" (Austen 2004, 6). The ladies present declared that he was "much handsomer than Mr. Bingley," his friend and soon to be love-interest of Jane, the oldest of the Bennet sisters. Mr. Bingley only has "four or five thousand" pounds a year and this makes him less attractive than his friend Darcy (Austen 2004, 1). The public estimation of Mr. Darcy quickly changes, however:

> He was looked at with great admiration for about half the evening, till his manners gave a disgust which turned the tide of his popularity; for he was discovered to be proud; to be above his company, and above being pleased; and not all his large estate in Derbyshire could then save him from having a most forbidding, disagreeable countenance, and being unworthy to be compared with his friend. (Austen 2004, 6)

In a matter of hours "his character was decided. He was the proudest, most disagreeable man in the world, and everybody hoped that he would never come there again" (Austen 2004, 7). Smith explains that the proud person does not care to explain or justify his superiority to anyone. If you do not recognize his greatness, he is not going to try to prove it to you. He does not "court your esteem" like the vain person does but regards you with disdain – if he can be bothered with you at all it is to crush *your* self-esteem: "He seems to wish, not so much to excite your esteem for *himself*, as to mortify *that* for *yourself*" (TMS 260).

When Darcy first proposes marriage to Elizabeth about midway through the novel, he makes it clear that the proposal goes against his better judgment. He sincerely believes her family to be far beneath his dignity and talks to Elizabeth as if this is an obvious fact. After telling Elizabeth how ardently he admires and loves her, Darcy continues in a different vein. "His sense of her inferiority— of its being a degradation— of the family obstacles which judgment had always opposed to inclination, were dwelt on with a warmth which seemed due to the consequence he was wounding, but was very unlikely to recommend his suit" (Austen 2004, 145). Despite his disparaging remarks about her inferiority, Darcy has no doubt that his proposal will be accepted and he is astonished at Elizabeth's rejection. From his reaction to her refusal, however, it can be deduced that his description of her inferiority (mostly because of her family) was not meant to wound but simply a statement of fact for Darcy. This means that his character, at least at this point in the story, aligns with only part of Smith's description: Darcy is sincerely convinced of his own superiority but does not feel the need to convince Elizabeth of her "meanness" – he simply states her family's inferiority as an obvious fact.[8]

---

[8] Robert C. Fox, argues that Elizabeth is neither prejudiced nor proud but vain, especially about her family. She knows how her family comes across and is hurt by Darcy's judgment of fact (1962).

A comparison between Mr. Darcy and VF's Mr. Osborne, George's father, shows the difference between the former's "genuine" pride (on Smith's account) and the latter's vanity masquerading as pride. Mr. Osborne is a successful businessman in large part because of the financial assistance of Mr. Sedley, Amelia's father. The Sedleys and the Osbornes have long been friends and George and Amelia have grown up together. When Mr. Sedley is ruined and loses his fortune, Mr. Osborne forbids George to continue his courtship of Amelia and instead wants him to focus on Miss Schwartz, a mixed-race heiress from the West Indies. The narrator's remarks about people like the Osbornes were referred to in the Introduction: "their affections rush out to meet and welcome money." He continues:

> I know some respectable people who don't consider themselves at liberty to indulge in friendship for any individual who has not a certain competency, or place in society. They give a loose to their feelings on proper occasions. And the proof is, that the major part of the Osborne family, who had not, in fifteen years, been able to get up a hearty regard for Amelia Sedley, became as fond of Miss Swartz in the course of a single evening as the most romantic advocate of friendship at first sight could desire. (VF 249)

Dobbin, aware of Amelia's distress at the prospect of losing George for good, implores George to keep his word and marry her before the army leaves for the continent. Mr. Osborne, meanwhile, is eager to break off his son's engagement to Amelia not only because of Miss Schwartz's money but also because he cannot abide the thought of his family being in any way allied to his former benefactor's:

> Then Osborne had the intolerable sense of former benefits to goad and irritate him: these are always a cause of hostility aggravated. Finally, he had to break off the match between Sedley's daughter and his son; and as it had gone very far indeed, and as the poor girl's happiness and perhaps character were compromised, it was necessary to show the strongest reasons for the rupture, and for John Osborne to prove John Sedley to be a very bad character indeed (VF 216).

Osborne's sullenness makes him appear proud but he really is as vain as his son. He is the one supplying George with funds to court members of the upper classes and arranging a match with Miss Schwartz. His vanity is such that it even overcomes his racism. It shows itself equally strongly in his need to cut Mr. Sedley from his acquaintance altogether. He cannot bear to think of the debt of friendship (or even of common decency) he owes Mr. Sedley who in his ruin could use a return of the favors he once bestowed on Osborne. But "one of the great conditions of anger and hatred is, that you must tell and believe lies against the hated object, in order … to be consistent" (VF 216). "He was proud of his hatred as of everything else. Always to be right, always to trample forward, and never to doubt, are not these the great qualities with which dullness takes the lead in the world?" (VF 444).

Smith opens his account of vanity with a remark about sincerity just like he did in his description of pride: "The vain man is not sincere, and, in the bottom of his heart, is very seldom convinced of that superiority which he wishes you to ascribe to him." The vain person suffers from an insecurity unknown to the proud person and "wishes you to view him in much more splendid colours than those in which, when he places himself in your situation, and supposes you to know all that he knows, he can really view himself" (TMS 260). This is why Smith suggests that there is more hope for the vain person than for the proud person in terms of moral development: the vain person knows, deep down, that the image she wishes to project and wants you to praise does not correspond to who she really is – she wants your esteem but knows that her praiseworthiness falls short of the praise received.

When you appear to see the vain person "in his proper colours," this person is "more mortified than offended." The proud person takes offense at your lack of respect and admiration, but the vain person is mortified. This is because the vain person does everything in his or her power to convince you of the reasons you should be praising him or her. He or she puts his "good qualities" on display, boasts of accomplishments that may be partially true but are likely exaggerated. The vain person is likely to lie to gain your esteem which he or she "courts with the most anxious assiduity." The vain person does not wish to "mortify your self-estimation," but is in fact "happy to cherish it, in hopes that in return you will cherish his own. He flatters in order to be flattered." He will do anything to make you think well of him or her and may actually perform "real and essential good offices, though often displayed, perhaps, with unnecessary ostentation" (TMS 260).

It would be too generous to ascribe to George any "real and essential good offices," but he does give up the prospect of a large fortune when he marries Amelia. Yet he likely would not have refused his father's command to break off his engagement had not Dobbin appealed to George's sense of honor. Not out of love for Amelia but because he wants to think of himself as really belonging to that class of men he has bought his way into, and because honor is the defining gentlemanly trait, he thwarts his father's wishes. Later, in Brussels, he announces to Amelia: "Curse the whole pack of money-grubbing vulgarians! I fall asleep at their great heavy dinners. I feel ashamed in my father's great stupid parties. I've been accustomed to live with gentlemen, and men of the world and fashion, Emmy, not with a parcel of turtle-fed tradesmen" (VF 246). As he prepares to leave for battle and sees Amelia's forlornness, "This prostration and sweet unrepining obedience exquisitely touched and flattered George Osborne. He saw a slave before him in that simple yielding faithful creature, and his soul within him thrilled secretly somehow at the knowledge of his power" (VF 236). George has done the proper thing in marrying Amelia but his motives were vain, not virtuous. He tried to raise himself above his father (which, ironically, is exactly what Osborne always wanted for his son: to gain social status) who wanted him to marry for money. Once married he starts a flirtation with Becky, ignoring Amelia except for when he rejoices in his power over her, his slave.

Becky's Mixed Disposition

Self-estimation is virtuous only when it is a proper reflection of one's worth. "The man who esteems himself as he ought, and no more than he ought, seldom fails to obtain from other people all the esteem that he himself thinks due" (TMS 265). This (very rare) person is completely satisfied, as opposed to the vain and proud people who regard themselves too highly. Proud people are prone to feelings of indignation at the sight of others taking up positions of superiority they do not deserve. Vain people, on the other hand, live in fear of the shame of exposure and can never be at ease. If Becky esteems herself as she ought, she is an exception to Smith's rule that the person with proper self-esteem "seldom" fails to obtain "all the esteem" that she thinks herself due. Leaving aside the question whether or not Becky is correct in esteeming herself very highly, she clearly esteems herself more highly than is reflected in her station and fortune. And even if her self-estimation is excessive, it looks more like pride than like vanity.

Becky Sharp is not vain, or at least not in the sense that George and Jos are vain, each in their own way. She clearly does not suffer from low self-esteem but neither does she appear to esteem herself excessively. She is well aware of her intelligence and attractions and confident in her ability to turn other people's vanity to her advantage, but she is not proud like Mr. Darcy: she lacks the sincerity that, for Smith, is an essential part of pride. She thinks highly of herself and takes offense when others do not recognize her superiority but unlike the proud person as described by Smith she takes great pains to make her (mostly rich, mostly male) targets think well of her. However, from the perspective of those she does not care to impress Becky *appears* proud, and she is sincere in her disdain of them. Becky, it appears at first glance, is more proud than vain even if she chooses to sacrifice sincerity when it furthers her goals as a social climber. But Smith's account of vanity and pride goes deeper than a list of easily defined traits and behaviors: he holds that in most cases, both the proud and the vain are justified in their sense of self-worth *up to a point*. They are worthy of esteem but want the people around them to esteem them more highly than is reasonable.

Smith writes: "the falsehoods of the vain man are all innocent falsehoods, meant to raise himself, not to lower other people" (TMS 262). In line with his earlier comments on the sincerity of the proud person, he adds: "To do the proud man justice, he very seldom stoops to the baseness of falsehoods" (TMS 262). Elizabeth estimates Mr. Darcy accordingly when she says to Mr. Wickham: "I wonder that the very pride of this Mr. Darcy has not made him just to you! If from no better motive, that he should not have been too proud to be dishonest—for dishonesty I must call it" (PP 61). But Mr. Darcy does not tell lies either to flatter Elizabeth or to raise himself in her opinion. On the contrary, he points out a number of painful truths about the Bennet family. In doing so he is not strategic or tactful; rather, he appears to think that he is merely stating the obvious.[9] While Darcy is proudly sincere, Becky's pride is accompanied by falsehoods – but not the innocent untruths of vanity: "The worst falsehoods of vanity are all what we call white lies: those of pride, whenever it condescends to falsehood, are all of the opposite complexion" (TMS 262).

In our dislike of pride and vanity, we tend to rank people who have these vices "below the common level" but in this we are frequently mistaken: "both the proud

[9]And Elizabeth, though hurt, cannot help but agree with his assessment: "When she came to that part of the letter in which her family were mentioned in terms of such mortifying, yet merited reproach, her sense of shame was severe" (Austen 2004, 160).

and the vain man are often (perhaps for the most part) a good deal above it; though not near so much as either the one really thinks himself, or as the other wishes to you think him." This is instructive because it shows that it is really only the proud person's self-estimation that is excessive; the vain person's self-estimation merely appears that way. The vain person wishes you to think of him as far superior to the norm but lacks the conviction of the proud person. Both the vain and the proud fall short of "their own pretensions" but "when we compare them with what the greater part of their rivals and competitors really are, they may appear quite otherwise, and very much above the common level" (TMS 262). Proud people who, like Mr. Darcy, have "real superiority," often possess "many respectable virtues" like truth, integrity, a sense of honor, and the capacity for "steady friendship." They have an "inflexible firmness and resolution." Mr. Darcy possesses all these traits: he is a loyal friend to Bingley, inflexible in his dislike of Wickham, loyal to his sister, unwavering in his love for Elizabeth. Vanity, by contrast, is often associated with a range of "amiable" virtues: humanity, politeness, "a desire to oblige in all little matters, and sometimes with a real generosity in great ones" (TMS 262).

"The words *vain* and *vanity* are never taken in a good sense," even when we use the term good-humoredly, "we still consider it as a foible and a ridicule" in someone's character (TMS 303). "The words *proud* and *pride*, on the contrary, are sometimes taken in a good sense," like when we say of someone that his pride kept him from doing something base. In the latter case we confound pride with magnanimity, a virtue Smith adopts from Aristotle.[10] As opposed to the magnanimous person, the proud man is too conceited for self-improvement: "The proud man is commonly too well contented with himself to think that his character requires any amendment. The man who feels himself all-perfect, naturally enough despises all further improvement. His self-sufficiency and absurd conceit of his own superiority, commonly attend him from his youth to his most advanced age." (TMS 263) Compare the following exchange between Elizabeth and Darcy in *Pride and Prejudice*:

> "I am perfectly convinced by it that Mr. Darcy has no defect. He owns it himself without disguise."
>
> "No," said Darcy, "I have made no such pretension. I have faults enough, but they are not, I hope, of understanding. My temper I dare not vouch for. It is, I believe, too little yielding—certainly too little for the convenience of the world. I cannot forget the follies and vices of others so soon as I ought, nor their offenses against myself. My feelings are not puffed about with every attempt to move them. My temper would perhaps be called resentful. My good opinion once lost, is lost forever."
>
> "That is a failing indeed!" cried Elizabeth. "Implacable resentment is a shade in a character. But you have chosen your fault well. I really cannot laugh at it. You are safe from me." (PP 43)

[10] Smith remarks that the magnanimous man as Aristotle described him has "many features… commonly ascribed to the Spanish character." "It was said… that he was deliberate in all his resolutions; slow, and even tardy, in all his actions; that his voice was grave, his speech deliberate, his step and motion slow; that he appeared indolent and even slothful, not at all disposed to bustle about little matters, but to act with the most determined and vigorous resolution upon all great and illustrious occasions" (TMS 263; see Aristotle, *Nicomachean Ethics* 4.3: 1124b6–9).

Mr. Darcy, of course, eventually recognizes his own presumption in his dealings with Elizabeth and, to an extent, his actions regarding Bingley and Jane. He is proud, even by his own admission, but he both has the virtues commonly associated with pride and a self-knowledge that allows him to eventually move past his own prejudices. Most importantly perhaps, he is open to criticism: Elizabeth's rejection of his first proposal and her words on that occasion do not only give offense but cause him to eventually reconsider his own actions and presumptions. This sets him apart from Becky, who throughout the course of *Vanity Fair* never once is disturbed by somebody else's opinion of her.

Considering Becky within the framework of Smith's remarks on pride and vanity, she appears to be of a "mixed disposition." Smith does not tell us much about people who have traits of both the vain and the proud person but indicates that it is a common phenomenon. Becky does not believe her character needs amendment and takes offense when people do not esteem her accordingly. She bears grudges against her offenders and is implacable in her resentment. But she is often insincere and hides her resentment and envy, so much so that she appears to have the "amiable" virtues commonly associated with vanity. Women like Mrs. Bute, sister in law to Sir Pitt and instigator of trouble between Becky and rich Miss Crawley, think Becky is giving herself airs and suspect her of the worst motives. But most men consider Becky perfectly charming and artless, and would not call her self-estimation excessive. If anything, Becky comes across as modest and unassuming, at least when she wants to. Because she delights in mimicry, her behavior can hardly be taken as an indication of her sense of self-worth. As readers, however, we know that Becky is not amiable but artful, not modest and unassuming but "a great conqueror." The next section discusses self-command, a virtue which, especially when combined with pride, can lead to greatness but can also be exceedingly dangerous.

Self-command for Ladies

Becky's artlessness takes great self-command, a "virtue" common to "the best of women," as we know from Chaps. 3 and 4. The manager of the performance in Vanity Fair links this virtue to hypocrisy: "the best of women" are watchful "when they seem most artless and confidential" (VF 208). For Smith, self-command is both a virtue in its own right and a condition for other virtues: "Self-command is not only itself a great virtue, but from it all the other virtues seem to derive their principal lustre" (TMS 250). Smith praises it both as a separate character trait and as a necessary condition for other virtues: self-command is part of all the other virtues because every virtue requires us to check our self-love at least to an extent. But though self-command is in the main a laudable character trait, it can also be very dangerous. Smith does not share the narrator's lighthearted tone but the two are in agreement that self-command can make people appear "artless and confidential" when in fact they are hypocrites.

Smith posits that we use our self-command to restrain two kinds of passions. Anger and fear are difficult to restrain even for a moment and demand that our self-command is strong when it matters most; our love of pleasure and ease is a near constant seduction and calls for steadiness rather than force. Socrates' composure in the face of death serves Smith as an illustration of the first way in which self-command is exercised. The kind of fortitude required in his situation is characteristic of "manhood" and can be acquired in the "school of war." It is the nobility of soldiers. "The love of ease, of pleasure, of applause, and of many other selfish gratifications" are easier to restrain in the short term than fear or anger, but because of the nature of these passions they call for a long-term steadiness in the face of constant temptation. Fear and anger are difficult to restrain even for a moment, while "the continual and almost incessant solicitations" of the selfish gratifications call for steadiness. These "are in the course of a life, very apt to mislead into great deviations" (TMS 247). These passions do not drive but rather *seduce* us from our duties. Self-command over these gratifications is commonly called prudence, a virtue that overlaps with self-command and that has security as its principle object. But prudence makes one cautious and risk-averse – traits that do not describe Becky. Becky is interested in her security but her steadiness is not her principal defining trait. Her self-command shows in her ability to defer gratification of the seductive passions but it is her strength especially in the face of anger that makes her a mighty conqueror and, one could argue, a dangerous person.

Amiably vain people like Jos and George have little self-command and keep industry in motion by giving in to the seductive passions Becky is able to resist without much effort. Like all vain characters in *Vanity Fair*, both Jos and George are sensitive to Becky's manipulations; her self-command enables her to control others in turn. Caesar and Alexander both eventually let their excessive self-estimation overrule their self-command and fell prey to insanity and folly. This does not happen to Becky, perhaps because she, though widely admired, is never surrounded only by people who foolishly admire her but always has enemies close by. She is proud, and meets with many insults, but she commands her anger. Smith recognizes that command over anger is not always dignified. "Amidst great provocations, apparent tranquillity and good-humour may sometimes conceal the most determined and cruel resolution to revenge" (TMS 250). He mentions Catharine of Medicis as and example, and Homer's Ulysses.

> This character of dark and deep dissimulation occurs most commonly in times of great public disorder; amidst the violence of faction and civil war. ... This false character, too, is frequently accompanied with the coolest and most determined courage. The proper exercise of it supposes that courage, as death is commonly the certain consequence of detection. It may be employed indifferently, either to exasperate or to allay those furious animosities of adverse factions which impose the necessity of assuming it; and though it may sometimes be useful, it is at least equally liable to be excessively pernicious" (TMS 250).

Becky's self-command is that of the warrior and conqueror, masculine and awe-inspiring. She mimics "temperance, decency, modesty, and moderation," which "are always amiable, and can seldom be directed to any bad end." These "gentler exertions of self-command" have a "sober lustre" as expressed in "chastity... industry...

frugality." Becky operates under cover of these modest and feminine virtues while she is in Sir Pitt's employment, giving the impression that she is "contented to walk in the humble paths of private and peaceable life" (TMS 250).

Shame, Prudence, and Security

It has already been remarked that unlike the vain person Smith describes, Becky rarely feels ashamed or mortified. A scene from *Pride and Prejudice* helps illuminate Smith's notion of spectatorship and its relation to shame. Whereas the vain person (excepting extreme cases like George Osborne) is always in suspense, fearing that he or she may be discovered to be less praiseworthy than they wish themselves to be believed, Becky's high self-esteem makes her unafraid of her spectators. She does not feel herself to be a fraud and so does not fear discovery. She knows that not everybody is fooled by her performance but she does not try to flatter them into liking her. Becky recognizes early on that Dobbin is impervious to her charms so she avoids him – not because she is ashamed of herself in his company but because she knows she stands nothing to gain from him. Becky is ever aware of her spectators but not with the anxiety that marks the vain person, who wants people to like him to bolster the image he wishes to build up and preserve. But Becky is impervious to another kind of shame as well: she never feels ashamed for somebody else. Because she does not sympathize with others and only "enters into" their situations in order to understand and exploit them but not to reach a "harmony of sentiments," she does not share their resentment, sorrow, or shame either. Becky has the keen observational skills of a vain person, aware of every glance and signal that may indicate approval or disapproval, but without the actual vanity. This enables her to observe her surroundings with a degree of detachment, coolly evaluating people's strengths and weaknesses. Elizabeth Bennet is as keen a spectator as Becky, but in contrast with VF's heroine Elizabeth's capacity for sympathy is highly developed. She cannot help but enter into the situations her family members create for themselves and watch with mortification the spectacle they stage for everyone to see.

At supper during the ball at Netherfield, Elizabeth Bennet observes Mr. Darcy's as he overhears her mother talking about Jane's prospects of marrying the eligible Mr. Bingley, Mr. Darcy's friend. Mrs. Bennet is loudly telling her friend Lady Lucas that the match is all but certain and that "Jane's marrying so greatly must throw [her sisters] in the way of other rich men" (Austen 2004, 76). Elizabeth tries to persuade her mother "to describe her felicity in a less audible whisper" because she witnesses Mr. Darcy's stony-faced disapproval. "Elizabeth blushed and blushed again with shame and vexation." Looking at Mr. Darcy, she finds confirmation of what she dreads: "The expression of his face changed gradually from indignant contempt to a composed and steady gravity" (Austen 2004, 76). Elizabeth's vexation, dread and shame result from her awareness of her mother's impropriety on the one hand, and the awareness of Mr. Darcy's witnessing the situation on the other. She is not detached because she is too emotionally invested in the situation that is evolving.

But she has the sense of propriety and prudence that her mother lacks and knows how her mother must come across to someone as proud as Mr. Darcy. Becky would likely reach the same conclusion as does Elizabeth if Becky found herself in a similar situation: she, too, would recognize the mother's blunder and Mr. Darcy's judgment. But unlike Elizabeth she would not be moved by her insight because there is nobody in Becky's life who receives her fellow-feeling the way Elizabeth's mother receives her daughter's sympathy.

Mrs. Bennet is not the only family member causing Elizabeth to feel mortified; her younger sister Mary, too, breaks the rules of propriety and decorum. "When supper was over, singing was talked of, and she had the mortification of seeing Mary, after very little entreaty, preparing to oblige the company." Her "significant looks and silent entreaties" have no effect on Mary whose "powers were by no means fitted for such a display; her voice was weak, and her manner affected. Elizabeth was in agonies." Elizabeth looks at the other spectators of the scene to see how they respond. She is a spectator of other spectators: "She looked at Jane, to see how she bore it; but Jane was very composedly talking to Bingley. She looked at his two sisters, and saw them making signs of derision at each other, and at Darcy, who continued, however, imperturbably grave" (Austen 2004, 77). As a highly sensitive (and sensible) spectator, Elizabeth is able to enter into the feelings not only of those near and dear to her, but also of the people who sneer at her loved ones. She understands their derision and their judgment and so finds herself prey to a mixture of feelings ranging from pain on her family's behalf, to a degree of sympathy with the judgments of the onlookers, to pain on her own behalf for her misfortune in belonging to so imprudent and improper a family. "To Elizabeth it appeared that, had her family made an agreement to expose themselves as much as they could during the evening, it would have been impossible for them to play their parts with more spirit or finer success" (Austen 2004, 78).

Elizabeth's own vanity as well as her awareness of the vanity of her family members and its visibility to all spectators make her a keen observer. Becky appears to enjoy the same keenness but without the sensitivity to praise and derision that usually accompanies vanity. This gives her a great advantage because she can detect vanity in other people and use it to her advantage without herself suffering the shame and embarrassment that would be her part if she herself were vain. Similarly, Becky understands the benefits of prudence without feeling the necessity of it the way a vain person does. To the vain person, prudence is an important virtue because it provides security. Prudence often falls by the wayside once the vain person meets with great success, like in the cases of Caesar and Alexander the Great, but for vain people in the humbler walks of life prudence is an achievable virtue that helps them avoid shame.

"Security," writes Smith, "is the first and principal object of prudence," and this applies to both our finances and our (moral) conduct. The prudent person has "real knowledge and skill in [her] trade or profession, assiduity and industry in the exercise of it, frugality, and even some degree of parsimony, in all [her] expenses" (TMS 227). The prudent man is earnest and though he may not be brilliant in his talents he is genuinely artless and without cunning, arrogance, pretense, or ostentation. The prudent person's conversation is simple and modest and "he is averse to all the quackish arts by which other people so frequently thrust themselves into public notice and reputation." His reputation relies on real knowledge and he keeps himself far from "little clubs and cabals" and the "clamours," whispers and intrigues of the vain parts of society (TMS 227). Though Becky knows when to appear prudent (i.e. when she plays the part of the dutiful wife and mother for Rawdon's brother's benefit, making a show of mending her little son's shirt and talking about her modest means), she is unlike the prudent person Smith describes here. Like the prudent person, Becky has "real knowledge and skill in [her] trade" but security is not her primary goal. She exercises prudence as a means but not as an end in itself.

Becky's prudence is best understood in contrast with the virtue of self-command discussed above. While self-command is a virtue developed on the battle field or in other life and death situations, prudence is important at times of peace when our love of pleasure poses a greater threat to our security. Prudence keeps us from giving into the temptations that may damage our health, moral character and financial stability. The prudent person is content to be secure and "in the bottom of his heart he would prefer the undisturbed enjoyment of secure tranquility, not only to all the vain splendour of successful ambition, but to the real and solid glory of performing the greatest and most magnanimous actions" (TMS 229). Prudence is respectable but not glamorous or particularly admirable. "It commands a certain cold esteem, but seems not entitled to any very ardent love or admiration."[11] Just like vanity is always a "folly" but pernicious only when joined with more serious vices, prudence is truly admirable only when combined with other, greater, virtues. Similarly, imprudence is only really disgraceful when combined with other vices. "As prudence combined with other virtues constitutes the noblest; so imprudence combined with other vices, constitutes the vilest of all characters" (TMS 230). Prudence narrowly construed, considered apart from the possible presence of other more lovable virtues and sympathy, is narrow, calculating, and self-centered.[12] It requires a kind of self-command, especially where it concerns our desire for instant gratification, and this is why Becky looks prudent at times: she has the self-command to withstand temptation when doing so increases her chances of "bettering her condition."[13] The prudent person cares about fortune and reputation but is not rash, minds her

[11] Smith discerns a spectrum of prudence ranging from a "narrow" kind of cleverness to a superior form of prudence that concerns itself with issues that transcend individual concerns like health and reputation. This superior kind of prudence joins "the best head… to the best heart. It is the most perfect wisdom combined with the most perfect virtue. It constitutes very nearly the character of the Academical or Peripatetic sage" (TMS 229). It appears that this superior prudence depends almost entirely on the presence of other, greater virtues.

[12] As Griswold points out, it is this narrow or "ordinary" prudence which helps us "better our condition" and is therefore both a moral and an economic virtue, linking TMS to WN. "All in all this kind of prudence is an achievable virtue suited to commercial society" (Griswold 1999, 204).

[13] The fact that he calls this kind of limited prudence a virtue shows that Smith does not condemn a character trait just because it is self-interested. He holds that it is praiseworthy to (desire to) better our condition, as long as our motives and actions are of the right kind and accompanied by the right emotions.

own business, inspires confidence, mild esteem and goodwill – if not warm admiration and praise.

Humanity and Generosity

The prudent person as Smith describes him is content in his station and unambitious. Since the desire to be seen and acknowledged is universal, this must mean that the prudent person feels like he is sufficiently regarded in his current condition. If he feels the need to better his condition it is only within the bounds of what is deemed proper. As the prudent person prefers to stay away from cabals and pursuits that would push him into public notice, his self-estimation must be about average or at least not high enough to encourage any great undertakings. Prudence serves as a restraint on the seductive temptations of pleasure and ease and so essentially is a peacetime virtue. We know from previous chapters that according to Smith, societies tend to lose their martial spirit at times of peace and prosperity. No longer faced with great and immediate danger, people can allow themselves to develop their "humanity." Chapter 4 discussed this virtue in the context of civilized societies where people can afford the luxury of friendship and the display of emotions. Smith opposed these societies with the "barbarous" ones where "savages" are forced to treat everyone with the reserve of strangers, hiding their feelings and never showing weakness. This takes great self-command and breeds the kind of martial spirit Smith talks about elsewhere (in the context of education/courage). The description Smith offers of the virtue of humanity reveals a larger, gendered frame operating in the background of Smith's thinking on self-command and related traits.

Though humanity is sometimes confused with generosity, Smith argues that they should be seen as separate virtues. By means of explanation he states "humanity is the virtue of a woman, generosity of a man" (TMS 208). Women (or as Smith puts it, the "fair sex") "have commonly much more tenderness than ours" but they "have seldom so much generosity." As evidence of the second point Smith simply observes "that women rarely make considerable donations." Smith does not mention any further evidence for his description of humanity as a typically female virtue comprising "tenderness." He goes on to offer the following definition: "Humanity consists merely in the exquisite fellow-feeling which the spectator entertains with the sentiments of the persons principally concerned, so as to grieve for their sufferings, to resent their injuries, and to rejoice at their good fortune" (TMS 208). The word "merely" is important here because it emphasizes that humanity requires little effort from those to whom it comes naturally, i.e. women. But this definition of humanity is almost identical to Smith's account of sympathy which he describes as the ability to "bring home to oneself" and "enter into" someone else's sorrow or joy. That humanity can be regarded as a particularly fine-tuned form of sympathy is confirmed in what Smith writes next: "The most humane actions require no self-denial, no self-command, no great exertion of the sense of propriety. They consist only in doing what this exquisite sympathy would of its own accord prompt us to do" (TMS

209). Humane actions therefore require no great effort, especially not from women who are naturally humane. Sympathy in the form of humanity may be "exquisite" but it is not a trait that had to be developed, let alone acquired with great difficulty like the manly virtue of generosity.

While humanity only asks of women that they act the way they are naturally inclined to, "it is otherwise with generosity." Humanity is achieved by simply following the current of our sympathy, but generosity asks that we make a sacrifice: "We never are generous except when in some respect we prefer some other person to ourselves, and sacrifice some great and important interest of our own to an equal interest of a friend or of a superior" (TMS 209). Smith follows this statement with a long list of increasingly dramatic examples. The first concerns a man who gives up a position he had aspired to because he knows that somebody else is more suited for the job. Second is the man who risks his own life to save that of a friend, not because he does not value his own life or because "humanity" prompts him to act in this way, but because he knows that "to any third person" his friend's life must appear more valuable than his own. While the first example concerned the sacrifice of ambition and the second the sacrifice of one's life for a friend's, the third goes a step further and concerns a soldier sacrificing his life for his officer. Though the sacrifice is the same in absolute terms, it is greater in terms of the interests concerned: in Smith's example, the soldier would have been "but little affected" if his officer had died "without any fault of his own." The soldier does not care for his officer the way the man from the second example cares for his friend and so the soldier can rightly be said to sacrifice a very great interest (his self-love and desire to stay alive) for a much smaller one (his wish for his officer to stay alive). Smith continues along the same lines, finding ever more "generous" actions illustrating masculine virtue. "When a young officer exposes his life to acquire some *inconsiderable* addition to the dominions of his sovereign," he does not consider that to himself the preservation of his own life is far more important than "the conquest of a whole kingdom" (emphasis added). Instead, he considers what is more important to "the nation he fights for" and judges that to the people of this nation, "the success of the war is of the highest importance; the life of a private person of scarce any consequence" (TMS 209). Though most Englishmen would in their day to day life be "more seriously disturbed by the loss of a guinea, than by the national loss of Minorca," these same men would have sacrificed their lives "a thousand times rather than … have let it fall into the hands of the enemy" had it been in their power to defend it. Smith's final and most "heroic" example of generosity is "the first Brutus," who "led forth his own sons to a capital punishment, because they had conspired against the rising liberty of Rome." Even though Rome stands to benefit very little from their deaths, Brutus adopts the perspective of "a Roman citizen" and realizes that even "the smallest interest of Rome" is more important than his fatherly love for his sons. Our admiration for actions such as these "is not so much founded upon the utility, as upon the unexpected, and on that account the great, the noble, and exalted propriety of such actions" (TMS 210). Whereas humanity is merely a natural extension of the feeling of sympathy and requires very little effort, generosity is heroic because it consists in “thwarting, from a sense of duty and propriety, the strongest of all natural propensities” (TMS 209).

Smith’s examples make clear why self-command is a precondition for generosity. Self-command is what enables us to act with propriety in the face of great danger and even death and so it is no coincidence that the majority of Smith’s examples involve battle of some kind. We also know that self-command tends to weaken in civilized societies which tend to incline more toward humanity. And humanity, as a virtue based in “tenderness,” is distinctly feminine, suited to a society prone to the indulgence of luxury and that corruption of sympathy, vanity.

A Character of Dark and Deep Dissimulation

Two extremes emerge from the connections Smith sees between the traits, virtues and vices discussed in this and the previous chapters. A Spartan, savage society requires great self-command and a martial spirit from its members. There is no room or opportunity for humanity because people have to be on their guard to survive, controlling their feelings and expecting to neither give nor receive sympathy. These people have an ability to stay calm under torture that is scarcely conceivable for the members of the society on the opposite end of the spectrum. There we find civilized people who live in peace and freely enter into the feelings of others like they expect others to enter into their own feelings. Tenderness and affection can flourish because people are not preoccupied with survival or even the “necessaries” of life; their focus is on bettering their condition and gaining esteem and recognition. This opens them up to the corruption of their moral sentiments and the folly of vanity.

Since generosity depends on self-command, it at first glance appears to be a virtue belonging to savage, Spartan societies. But it is unclear that the savages as Smith describes them have a sufficiently developed awareness of the spectator’s point of view. Smith’s examples of generosity all rely on the perspective of a third person, or even an entire nation. We need to consider our own and any other relevant interests from this (imagined) third person perspective and act in accordance with the judgment of this supposedly impartial spectator. Smith does not mention generosity in his description of savage societies, nor does he include examples that parallel the ones listed earlier in this chapter. Since generous acts are rare in an effeminate society reigned by vanity and an excess of humanity, generosity must belong to a more “mixed” society somewhere on the spectrum between the two extremes described here. But this mixed society, like Smith’s society at the time, can hardly be in a stable state: in times of peace and security, vanity, effeminacy, corruption and cowardice will spread; in times of war, humanity will decrease. Smith speaks with such obvious admiration about masculine generosity, self-command, and the martial spirit that it is clear where his sympathies lie.[14]

[14] See Marshall (1984) for a nuanced account of Smith’s “clearly masculine” impartial spectator *as* spectator (and only secondarily as impartial). Edith Kuiper suggests that Smith constructs an

Becky is emphatically ungenerous and she clearly lacks the "exquisite" sympathy of humanity. But her self-command is unparalleled in Vanity Fair and makes her a formidable opponent. Like the savage Smith describes, she hides her cruel intentions until she finds an opportune moment to strike back at those who thwarted her. Her apparent good humor and artlessness are the result of her own "school of war" and like the savage from TMS she is exceedingly dangerous. She feels resentment and indignation like the proud person does, never under-rating herself like the "idiots" Smith describes. While they doubt their "fitness" even for those offices they could reasonably obtain, Becky's ambition makes her consider herself fit for the highest ranks in society. She is not held back by shame or embarrassment and never suffers the mortification experienced by the vain. Becky is difficult to pin down or categorize within the confines of Smith's gendered moral framework and most closely resembles the "character of dissimulation," marked by self-command and a great ability to deceive, which, "flourishes in times of disorder." Becky uses the vanity-based order of society to her advantage while she disrupts the traditional relationships between men and women. Her powers of dissimulation are such that she can convincingly mimic the "feminine" virtues of humanity and prudence while taking advantage of the "effeminate" vice of vanity in the men she uses to further her upward mobility.

References

Aristotle. 1985. *Nicomachean ethics*. Trans. T. Irwin. Indianapolis: Hackett.

Austen, Jane. 2004. *Pride and Prejudice*. Oxford: Oxford University Press.

Fox, Robert C. 1962. Elizabeth Bennet: Prejudice or Vanity? *Nineteenth-Century Fiction* 17 (2): 185–187.

Fricke, Christel. 2014. The Challenges of Pride and Prejudice: Adam Smith and Jane Austen on Moral Education. *Revue Internationale de Philosophie* 269 (3): 343–372.

Griswold, Charles. 1999. *Adam Smith and the Virtues of Enlightenment*. Cambridge: Cambridge University Press.

Know-Shaw, Peter. 2004. *Jane Austen and the Enlightenment*. Cambridge: Cambridge University Press.

Kuiper, Edith. 2003. The Construction of Masculine Identity in Adam Smith's Theory of Moral Sentiments. In *Toward a Feminist Philosophy of Economics*, ed. D. Barker and E. Kuiper, 145–160. New York: Routledge.

Marshall, D. 1984. Adam Smith and the Theatricality of Moral Sentiments. *Critical Inquiry* 10 (4): 592–613.

Moler, Kenneth. 1967. The Bennet Girls and Adam Smith on Vanity and Pride. *Philological Quarterly* 46: 4.

Smith, Adam. 1981. An inquiry into the nature and causes of the wealth of nations. In *Vol. 2 of the Glasgow Edition of the Works and Correspondence of Adam Smith*, ed. R.H. Campbell and A.S. Skinner. Indianapolis: Liberty Fund.

explicitly masculine identity for the impartial spectator based on the virtues of generosity, self-command, and humanity. I am in agreement with her general claims but argue that humanity, on Smith's account, is only of secondary importance to the masculine ideal Smith creates (2003).

———. 1982a. *The theory of moral sentiments*. In *Vol. 1 of the Glasgow Edition of the Works and Correspondence of Adam Smith*, ed. D.D. Raphael and A.L. Macfie. Indianapolis: Liberty Fund.

———. 1982b. *Lectures on Jurisprudence*. In *Vol. 5 of the Glasgow Edition of the Works and Correspondence of Adam Smith*, ed. R.L. Meek, D.D. Raphael, and P.G. Stein. Indianapolis: Liberty Fund.

Thackeray, William Makepeace. 1983. In *Vanity fair: A novel without a hero*, ed. John Sutherland. New York: Oxford UP.

Chapter 7
Partial and Impartial Spectators in Vanity Fair

Abstract Adam Smith encourages us to regard our actions in an impartial light and to look at ourselves the way we imagine a fair-minded third person would. Society holds up a mirror for us and we can infer from other people's reactions to our behavior whether we are acting appropriately or inappropriately. Over time, we learn to restrain our natural self-love and come to judge ourselves the way an impartial spectator would. Partial spectators are a threat to this learning process because with their flattery they encourage us to think more highly of ourselves than we should. *Vanity Fair* is full of partial spectators who encourage the vanity of the already vain for personal gain. They are the opposite of the person Smith describes who is forced to develop a sense of impartiality and strong self-command because he lives with strangers who care nothing for him. Becky Sharp and Jane Eyre both develop strong self-command under difficult circumstances, living with partial spectators who never let them forget their inferior place in society. Their stories raise questions about the mirror society provides to women and about the impartiality of Smith's impartial spectator.

A Siren with a Clear Conscience

Rawdon has lost his aunt's favor and with it his prospects of a great fortune, but he has a knack for living well "on nothing a year" (VF 452). His and Becky's talents combined make them a formidable couple. They move from London to Brussels to Paris and back to London, leaving their debts behind with every change of location. Becky sets and follows her own rules where it comes to household economics and life in general. The narrator depicts her as a Siren, beautiful and angelic above the water line and depraved and monstrous below. Her deceit is in large part necessary because of the society she lives in: she is supposed to play the part of dutiful wife and society lady but few (if any) women can or want to fully identify with this role. Becky delights in her various performances and personas because they remain poses she adopts at will, leaving her self-esteem and confidence unperturbed – she cannot be humiliated or be made to feel ashamed about either her conduct or her motives.

R. Slegers, *Adam Smith's Moral Sentiments in Vanity Fair*, Issues in Business Ethics 49, https://doi.org/10.1007/978-3-319-98731-6_7

In almost everything Becky does there is a sense of joy and playfulness. She enjoys operating the machinery that keeps industry in motion; not because she cares about industry, let alone the good of humankind, but because she delights in mastery. She plays with the mores of the time, her pleasure trumping her prudence and even her economic self-interest. When she serves as Miss Crawley's companion and tends her during her illness, she amuses the dowager with her wit and mimicry like she did her father's friends in the Artists' Quarter. Becky is smart enough to know that her wicked humor must also make her protectress wary – Miss Crawley witnesses how Becky can appear perfectly docile and sweet one moment only to engage in relentless mockery the next. And naturally Miss Crawley understands that she herself could well become the object of Becky's wit once the old lady is out of earshot.

This chapter considers Smith's notions of sympathy and impartiality in the context of Becky's unsentimental conduct and judgment. The impartial spectator, a theoretical entity similar to what we today would call our conscience, regards our own and other people's behavior with the appropriate degree of sympathy, unencumbered by sentiments that could bias his judgment. Becky's internal spectator, constantly at work evaluating and monitoring herself and her surroundings, quite obviously is not the kind of impartial spectator Smith had in mind. Yet Becky's internal spectator bears an interesting resemblance to Smith's account of the "great inmate of the breast" (TMS 165). Furthermore, VF's narrator tells us that Becky's conscience is clear – but how can a Siren have a clear conscience? This is one of the questions addressed in this chapter, which compares Becky Sharp to Jane Eyre, another famous fictional Victorian governess.[1]

Looking at Oneself Through the Eyes of Others

In Part III of TMS, Smith discuses "the Foundation of our Judgments Concerning Our Own Sentiments and Conduct, and of the Sense of Duty." The first chapter of this part deals with "the Principle of Self-Approbation and of Self-disapprobation and includes information about the virtue of generosity. Generosity requires us to overcome our self-love and regard our own interests from the perspective of a third person. As we already know from the previous chapter, Smith holds that we naturally feel like our own interests are most important until we take on an "impartial" point of view that shows us that the interests of others trump our own. Exercising

[1] Charlotte Brontë was a great admirer of Thackeray and dedicated the second edition of *Jane Eyre* to him: "There is a man in our own days whose words are not framed to tickle delicate ears.... Why have I alluded to this man? I have alluded to him, Reader, because I think I see in him an intellect profounder and more unique than his contemporaries have yet recognised; because I regard him as the first social regenerator of the day, as the very master of that working corps who would restore to rectitude the warped system of things; because I think no commentator on his writings has yet found the comparison that suits him, the terms which rightly characterise his talent" (Brontë 2016, 149).

self-command to overcome our desire to benefit ourselves, we act in accordance with what we imagine a third person would expect of us. This is the mechanism underlying Smith's theory of impartial spectatorship. The examples of heroic, generous actions listed at the end of the previous chapter illustrate the kind of behavior that a third person spectator could "go along with" and "enter into," but they also raise questions about the impartiality Smith ascribes to these third persons. For Smith, our actions are judged on three levels and of increasing impartiality: first there are the outside spectators of our behavior, the actual people witnessing our actions and judging them according to their standards of right and wrong. These people are often partial in one way or another: they may have a stake in the outcome of our actions or be biased in their judgment because of their upbringing or background. Second, there is the impartial spectator, "the man within the breast" or our "divine inmate." Smith also calls this entity our conscience, but prefers the term "impartial spectator" because it captures the way this theoretical judge inside ourselves observes and evaluates our own behavior and that of others. The third and highest level of judgment is the domain of religion, the "still higher tribunal," God (TMS 162).

In order to judge "our own sentiments and motives," we have "endeavour to view them as at a certain distance from us." This means that we have "to view them with the eyes of other people," referring "either to what are, or to what ... would be, or to what, we imagine, ought to be the judgment of others." In short, "we endeavour to examine our own conduct as we imagine any other fair and impartial spectator would examine it." Looking at ourselves from this detached point of view, we gauge if this imagined spectator could enter into our sentiments and motives with approbation. In this exercise we sympathize not with ourselves, but with the impartial spectator. If the impartial spectator approves of our behavior, our sympathy with him causes us to approve of ourselves. If the impartial spectator disapproves of our behavior, our sympathy with him causes us to disapprove of ourselves. Smith sums up the function of the impartial spectator: "We suppose ourselves the spectators of our own behaviour, and endeavour to imagine what effect it would, in this light, produce upon us. This is the only looking-glass by which we can, in some measure, with the eyes of other people, scrutinize the propriety of our own conduct" (TMS 149–50).

The mirror or looking glass will be a motif in the present chapter as it is of major importance to both Smith and the heroines in *Vanity Fair* and *Jane Eyre*. When we look in a mirror we look at ourselves the way we imagine other people see us, and this holds true for real and imagined mirrors alike. We judge our physical and moral beauty or deformity through the eyes of our (imagined) spectators, always dividing ourselves into judge and person judged. As part of his spectator metaphor, Smith repeatedly talks about regarding ourselves and others in a certain "light." He asks us to consider what others would think of us if they saw us in the light in which we "ought to appear" if our companions knew the truth about our situation. If we regard our behavior in the "light in which the impartial spectator would view it" and view it with "pleasure and approbation," we may be content. Moral judgment, like aesthetic judgment, is all about seeing and being seen – and just like for the physical eye, our mental eye's sight depends on the quality of the light. The impartial spectator judges by a light that reveals everything there is to know and so forms fair judgments. But "a weak man," eager for praise and ignoring the perspective of the impartial spectator, "is often much delighted with viewing himself in [a] false and delusive light" (TMS 157).

Returning to the acts of generosity mentioned in the previous chapter, we may wonder how the virtuous men Smith describes as sacrificing their lives know that the third person perspective they adopt is in fact fair and impartial. How does the man risking his life for an insignificant expansion of the kingdom know that this is what the impartial spectator asks of him? Does this person regard his own behavior from the perspective of a fair and impartial spectator or from the perspective of a partial expansionist warmonger? Smith's theory of the impartial spectator is appealing because we know from experience that we are more likely to judge ourselves fairly if we try to look at our own motives and behavior through the eyes of others. But as this chapter will show, the mirror motif, key to Smith's understanding of (impartial) spectatorship, introduces a number of difficulties especially if we take into account the way women in particular look at themselves and they way they are looked at. Smith's dismissive treatment of humanity as an easy, soft virtue primarily belonging to women and generosity as a heroic and masculine virtue leads us to suspect that the "impartial" spectator has a decidedly male perspective on things. A discussion of obviously partial spectatorship will help set the stage for a discussion of Smith's masculine impartial spectator.

Miss Crawley's Partial Spectators

While Becky is still a governess in Sir Pitt's household, Miss Crawley falls ill after indulging in too much food and drink: "The causes which had led to the deplorable illness of Miss Crawley, and her departure from her brother's house in the country, were of such an unromantic nature that they are hardly fit to be explained in this genteel and sentimental novel" (VF 162). Becky keeps her company and watches her: "how peevish a patient was the jovial old lady; how angry; how sleepless; in what horrors of death." Like the poor man's son discussed in Chap. 5, Miss Crawley only considers the vanity of her lifestyle when she is subject to spleen: "during what long nights she lay moaning, and in almost delirious agonies respecting that future world which she quite ignored when she was in good health." The narrator holds up this instructive picture to his "fair young reader" of "a worldly, selfish, graceless, thankless, religionless old woman, writhing in pain and fear, and without her wig. Picture her to yourself, and ere you be old, learn to love and pray!" (VF 164) Of the three "tribunals" of judgment to which our sentiments and actions are subjected according to Smith, Miss Crawley only has experience with the lowest one: she does not believe in God (at least not when she is healthy), nor does she heed the voice of the impartial spectator (an entity we suspect is so weak in her case it may not even have a voice) and so she is left with the partial judgments of the people around her.

Smith echoes the narrator's admonition cited above (though without the irony marking the narrator's account in VF) in a passage from TMS that deals with the poor man's son. The son spends his life in pursuit of frivolous trinkets but "in the languor of disease and the weariness of old age, the pleasures of the vain and empty distinctions of greatness disappear." The poor man's son, "reduced either by spleen or disease to observe with attention his own situation," regrets his choices and "toilsome pursuits" and recognizes that they have brought him no real happiness. While the poor man's son is interested in the "trifling conveniencies" (e.g. coaches) that accompany power and riches, the "enormous and operose machines," Miss Crawley's primary enjoyment consists in the food and drink that her great wealth affords her (TMS 202). Unlike the poor man's son, Miss Crawley did not spend her life gathering her fortune; rather, she is the kind of person driving around in coaches who inspired the poor man's son ambition in the first place. But when diseased and subject to spleen, Miss Crawley, too, realizes that her wealth cannot protect her from "the severer inclemencies of the season" and that because of her habits she is exposed "to anxiety, to fear, and to sorrow; to diseases, to danger, and to death." (TMS 202). She has neither prudence nor self-command and cannot withstand either the temptations of ease and pleasure nor act calmly in the face of death. Like Jos Sedley who will be discussed below, Miss Crawley is an example of the kind of person typically found in a luxurious, vain society devoid of martial spirit.

When we are sick, Smith observes, we are likely to endorse a "splenetic philosophy" while the imagination "seems to be confined and cooped up within our own persons." But once we regain our health, the imagination again "expands itself to every thing around us" and we are "charmed with the beauty of that accommodation which reigns in the palaces and oeconomy of the great" (TMS 202). Miss Crawley accordingly prays only when she is ill and cultivates neither love nor friendship when she is well again. Her brushes with disease and death do not make her see her lifestyle by a different light or regard her choices from a more detached point of view. Her impartial spectator, if indeed she has one, does not make himself heard. Becky, on the other hand, observes Miss Crawley with detached attention, entering into her situation only in so far as it helps her gather intelligence:

> Sharp watched this graceless bedside with indomitable patience. Nothing escaped her; and, like a prudent steward, she found a use for everything. She told many a good story about Miss Crawley's illness in after days— stories which made the lady blush through her artificial carnations. During the illness she was never out of temper; always alert; she slept light, having a perfectly clear conscience; and could take that refreshment at almost any minute's warning. (VF 164)

Becky is patient and prudent, gathering information for future use but never making Miss Crawley feel like she is being judged. Regrets do not trouble her like they do Miss Crawley and she can sleep at a moment's notice while Miss Crawley is described as "sleepless." The contrast between the worldly old woman and Becky is clear: Miss Crawley has a life with all the trappings that Becky desires for herself, but she lacks Becky's indomitable spirit and "clear conscience." Spleen never bothers Becky and we know from Chap. 5 that she is unlike the poor man's son in her ambition: while he is part of the machinery and therefore at risk of being crushed by it, Becky operates the machine (and joyfully so). Her manner of tending the sick Miss Crawley is in line with Becky's usual modus operandi: she observes, interprets, and never loses her good humor. Everything Becky sees and hears during this time is potentially useful, or at least potentially entertaining "in after days."

> And I am not sure that, in spite of Rebecca's simplicity and activity, and gentleness and untiring good humour, the shrewd old London lady, upon whom these treasures of friendship were lavished, had not a lurking suspicion all the while of her affectionate nurse and friend. It must have often crossed Miss Crawley's mind that nobody does anything for nothing. If she measured her own feeling towards the world, she must have been pretty well able to gauge those of the world towards herself; and perhaps she reflected that it is the ordinary lot of people to have no friends if they themselves care for nobody. (VF 167)

Becky is not one to do anything for nothing but her motives are not purely or perhaps even primarily mercenary. She is interested in Miss Crawley's fortune but she is also gathering ammunition for mockery and mimicry. Becky takes pleasure in imitation and caricature, as we know from her early days at Chiswick Hall when Miss Pinkerton was her main target. Miss Crawley knows about Becky's talents, having enjoyed her satire and cruel wit at the expense of her own companions and family: "Meanwhile Becky was the greatest comfort and convenience to her, and she gave her a couple of new gowns, and an old necklace and shawl, and showed her friendship by abusing all her intimate acquaintances to her new confidante (than which there can't be a more touching proof of regard)." Miss Crawley also "meditated vaguely some great future benefit— to marry her perhaps to Clump, the apothecary, or to settle her in some advantageous way of life; or at any rate, to send her back to Queen's Crawley when she had done with her, and the full London season had begun" (VF 167). Miss Crawley is not deceived by Becky, nor Becky by Miss Crawley. They both get something out of the relationship, or believe that they might. For Miss Crawley it is comfort and amusement, for Becky it is the prospect of future gains but also the joy of mockery and performance. And yet, Becky's conscience is clear while Miss Crawley's is not.

Miss Crawley freely gives vent to her fears, pains and anxieties. She does not adjust the "pitch" of her emotions for the benefit of those around her because she does not have to: Becky (and other, less artful sycophants surrounding the old lady) indulge her and do not require that she exercise any prudence or self-command. Miss Crawley desires sympathy, as do most sufferers, but she is not in the habit of toning down the display of her emotions in order to find better reception with her audience. This of course is a result of her "balance at the banker's" (VF 103). She is surrounded by flatterers who uncritically tend to her every whim.

After Becky has eloped with Rawdon, Miss Crawley rages against her former nurse and companion, demanding that everyone she meets shares in her resentment. When Miss Crawley later receives a letter from a Paris acquaintance praising Becky (who spends some time in Paris society after the British victory over Bonaparte), she cannot abide the unfairness of the situation and paints Becky in the darkest colors[2] - intending to show her, Smith might say, in a different light than the light by

[2] But she does so in a letter written in English, which the Paris lady does not understand. Miss Crawley's attempt to hurt Becky's reputation fails.

which her acquaintance sees Becky. Smith comments on our need for "that relief which nothing can afford … but the entire concord of the affections of the spectators with [our] own" (TMS 72). We want others to sympathize with our joy, but it is even more important that "the emotions of their hearts" reflect our "violent and disagreeable passions." Most of us, however, can only obtain this sympathy by "lowering" our passions "to that pitch, in which the spectators are capable of going along with" us. The people surrounding Miss Crawley do not, for the most part, feel real sympathy for her pain but merely pretend to it. The narrator suggests that Miss Crawley suspects as much and understands that since she has never cultivated real loves or friendships she cannot trust the apparent sympathy people show her. But because of her riches she has never learned to "flatten … the sharpness of [her passion's] natural tone, in order to reduce it to harmony and concord with the emotions of those who are about" her (TMS 72).[3]

Because we desire a harmony of sentiments with people around us, we are led to imagine what our situation looks like from the outside. We understand that if we want others to sympathize with our pain we have to (in most cases) take some pains to make our situation accessible and understood. We know from experience what it is like to try to understand someone's suffering. Conversely, we try to imagine what our situation looks like to someone on the outside when we are ourselves the sufferer. About the sufferer and his spectators, Smith writes:

> As their sympathy makes them look at [his suffering], in some measure, with his eyes, so his sympathy makes him look at it, in some measure, with theirs, especially when in their presence and acting under their observation: and as the reflected passion, which he thus conceives, is much weaker than the original one, it necessarily abates the violence of what he felt before he came into their presence, before he began to recollect in what manner they would be affected by it, and to view his situation in this candid and impartial light. (TMS 72)

The presence of spectators to our suffering is beneficial because it helps us detach from our own situation – unless of course our spectators are partial like the ones surrounding Miss Crawley. Looking at our own suffering through the eyes of a spectator who is not trying to flatter us, we gain a distance from the passions that before threatened to cloud our judgment and impair our decision-making processes. It is natural for us to care about ourselves first and foremost and we need to learn to "humble the arrogance of [our] self-love, and bring it down to something which other men can go along with" if we wish to be receive sympathy from others (pp. 69–70). Our own experience teaches us that we are willing to indulge other people's self-love only up to a point. Miss Crawley's relatives and "friends" are willing to venture beyond this point only because they hope for a monetary reward.

[3] Smith holds that a perfect union of sentiments may be impossible but we can reach a "concord" and that is enough to make society harmonious (TMS 72).

Dorothea Brooke's Sympathy

One of Smith's starting assumptions in TMS is that everybody longs for sympathy. "Nothing pleases us more than to observe in other men a fellow-feeling with all the emotions of our own breast; nor are we ever so much shocked as by the appearance of the contrary" (TMS 64). Our desire for sympathy can slide into vanity when we become more interested in receiving praise than in being praiseworthy. What we really want is for people to know us and sympathize with our emotions, but since we know that outward appearances are more readily and easily judged than our inner workings, we are tempted to focus on how we come across, not on our character. Vanity is thus a degraded desire for sympathy. Becky exploits this mechanism and makes George and Jos (and many others besides) feel like she not only admires their appearance but also sympathizes with their emotions while in fact she is not experiencing any admiration or fellow-feeling whatsoever. This caricature of sympathy contrasts with the real fellow-feeling Smith has in mind in TMS. A brief excursion to George Eliot's *Middlemarch* will enrich his account.

Lydgate, the ambitious young doctor who marries Rosamond, his "basil plant" and very much not the passive angel he had in view for this position, suffers a severe blow to his reputation when he is implicated in the death of Raffles. Raffles is an old acquaintance of Bulstrode's, the town banker known for his pompous Christian morality. Fearing that Raffles will reveal information about Bulstrode's unsavory past, the latter hastens the former's demise by allowing him to drink alcohol against Lydgate's orders. Because Lydgate is in debt and has just received a large sum from Bulstrode to tide him over, the doctor does not investigate the situation even though Raffles' death strikes him as suspicious. When the story comes out, Lydgate is too proud to defend his actions even against his friends. Dorothea, widowed now that Casaubon is dead, and in possession of his fortune, is the only one who openly addresses the issue with Lydgate. She believes he has been treated unfairly and "the idea of some active good within her reach, haunted her like a passion." She is hopeful that she may be able to benefit Lydgate and break through his proud reserve, "never heeding that she was a very young woman. Nothing could have seemed more irrelevant to Dorothea than insistence on her youth and sex when she was moved to show her human fellowship" (Eliot 716). Visiting her, Lydgate immediately experiences the beneficial effects of Dorothea's sympathy. The narrator remarks:

> The presence of a noble nature, generous in its wishes, ardent in its charity, changes the lights for us: we begin to see things again in their larger, quieter masses, and to believe that we too can be seen and judged in the wholeness of our character. That influence was beginning to act on Lydgate, who had for many days been seeing all life as one who is dragged and struggling amid the throng. He sat down again, and felt that he was recovering his old self in the consciousness that he was with one who believed in it. (Eliot 717)

Lydgate feels that Dorothea acknowledges and sees him the way he wants to see himself. Her sympathy encourages him to give "himself up, for the first time in his life, to the exquisite sense of leaning entirely on a generous sympathy, without any check of proud reserve." He tells her the whole story of Raffles and Bulstrode and his doubt about his own conduct, "feeling that here he had found room for the full meaning of his grief (Eliot 718). One can imagine Becky in Dorothea's role, artfully playing the part of the earnest young widow. But where Dorothea is authentic, Becky would be putting on a show. This does not mean that Becky could not achieve the same effect, because as we know her powers of mimicry are significant especially when she is faced with a male audience. Dorothea, on the other hand, is in no way flirtatious and Lydgate says to himself, as he rides away: "She seems to have what I never saw in any woman before— a fountain of friendship towards men— a man can make a friend of her" (Eliot 723).[4]

The sympathy Lydgate experiences with Dorothea can be placed on a spectrum described by Smith. On the one end there is the happy feeling of we get when we read "a book or poem … to a companion" and find that they share our appreciation. Even though we know the text too well to any longer enjoy it by ourselves, "We are amused by sympathy with his amusement which thus enlivens our own." On the other end are the more complex and profound feelings of grief and joy. "This correspondence of the sentiments of others with our own appears to be a cause of pleasure, and the want of it a cause of pain." Sympathy in both its simple and more complex forms "enlivens joy and alleviates grief. It enlivens joy by presenting another source of satisfaction; and it alleviates grief by insinuating into the heart almost the only agreeable sensation which it is at that time capable of receiving" (TMS 64). Lydgate experiences sympathy of the latter kind in the presence of Dorothea who allows him to "recover his old self" when he feels most misunderstood and alone.

Becky is of course aware of the importance of appearing sympathetic and practices what Smith preaches: "To seem not to be affected with the joy of our companions is but want of politeness; but not to wear a serious countenance when they tell us their afflictions, is real and gross inhumanity" (TMS 65). Though she does not in fact enter into the afflicted feelings of Miss Crawley to the extent that she experiences any fellow-feeling with her whatsoever (except, perhaps, their mutual enjoyment of mockery), she makes sure to appear as if she does. Dorothea on the other hand intuitively understands that it is most important to Lydgate that his injuries are seen and understood and she does not have to fake the appropriate sentiments. Smith notes:

> Love is an agreeable; resentment, a disagreeable passion; and accordingly we are not half so anxious that our friends should adopt our friendships, as that they should enter into our resentments. We can forgive them though they seem to be little affected with the favours which we may have received, but lose all patience if they seem indifferent about the injuries which may have been done to us. (TMS 65)

Dorothea realizes that Lydgate wants recognition for his suffering and in recognizing him allows him to feel himself once again. She is able to "enter into" his

---

[4] It is more difficult to imagine Becky sharing in Dorothea's generosity: "Think how much money I have; it would be like taking a burthen from me if you took some of it every year till you got free from this fettering want of income. Why should not people do these things? It is so difficult to make shares at all even. This is one way" (Eliot 1996, 722).

emotions and, by sharing them, make them more bearable to him. Part of the reason she is able to do so is that she knows what it is like to desire to perform great offices but fail because of unexpected circumstances and constraints. But her rational understanding of Lydgate's situation is only one of the conditions of her sympathy. She recognizes his emotions, not as a mere observer but as someone who shares the experience from within.

Smith explains that we are likely to be annoyed when someone laughs longer or louder at a joke than we think the joke merited. This is a small but telling example of the extent to which it displeases us *not* to be able to enter into someone else's emotions: we measure those emotions by our own and call them silly or overblown when there is no match. When we sympathize we approve, but when we find ourselves unable to sympathize with another person's feelings we call them improper, unjust, or ridiculous. "The man who resents the injuries that have been done to me, and observes that I resent them precisely as he does, necessarily approves of my resentment." To him it is "reasonable" for me to feel this way: "Upon all occasions his own sentiments are the standards and measures by which he judges of mine" (TMS 66). If this is true for Becky as well, this means that almost everybody in Vanity Fair must appear ridiculous to her. Since she is not herself vain, but almost everyone around her is, she does not sympathize but merely registers and judges according to her own standards. As Smith points out: "Every faculty in one man is the measure by which he judges of the like faculty in another. I judge of your sight by my sight, of your ear by my ear, of your reason by my reason, of your resentment by my resentment, of your love by my love. I neither have, nor can have, any other way of judging about them." (TMS 69).

Becky is less interested in forming (moral) judgments than in finding out what makes people tick. It takes her barely any time at all to figure out George Osborne when she catches him admiring himself in the mirror when he should have been looking at his fiancée Amelia (VF 57). She does not judge of his vanity as folly, or if she does it is not what matters most to her. Rather, she is content to know which levers to pull should she ever wish to use George for her own purposes – and subsequent events bear out that she does not overestimate her abilities in this respect.

Personal and Moral Beauty in the Mirror

To explain the principle of impartial spectatorship in his chapter on self-approbation and self-disapprobation, Smith refers to our use of a mirror to judge our appearance. Society is a mirror, Smith holds, and "our first ideas of personal beauty and deformity are drawn from the shape and appearance of others, not from our own" (TMS 149). Realizing that others look at us just like we look at them, we "become anxious to know" whether they approve or disapprove of our appearance. We find a mirror and try to look at ourselves the way we imagine other people look at us. If we come to the conclusion that we are "tolerably handsome," we do not mind someone laughing at a "little irregularity" in our appearance. If, on the other hand, our "limb by limb" examination of ourselves has shown us that we are "really deformed," we cannot bear other people's mockery. "It is evident ... that we are anxious about our own beauty and deformity, *only* upon account of its effect upon others" (emphasis added 149).

Smith holds that our moral judgments of ourselves develop along the same lines, and he again uses the word "anxious" to describe our receptiveness to the way other people regard us. Just like a handsome man can shrug off taunts concerning his appearance, the person convinced of their moral probity is not much moved by either applause or "censure." But this reveals a curious feature of our self-estimation: it is based on the way other people look at us, yet in some cases it is unperturbed by the way other people look at us – provided our self-estimation first was allowed to grow sufficiently strong. Something similar must be true of the impartial spectator who gains in impartiality the more we look at ourselves through the eyes of strangers and who can withstand the "cabal" of partial spectators only if he has first been firmly establish "within the breast." Just like a mirror can encourage our vanity if we see in it only those features our flatterers have praised, society can make us forget to consider ourselves with impartiality if we are surrounded by partial spectators as is Miss Crawley.

Becky uses her mirror impartially - as an instrument and without vanity. She considers herself "limb by limb" the way Smith describes, evaluating her strengths and weaknesses according to the fashion of her society and the tastes of the people she seeks to impress. We already observed that when Lord Steyne visits her, she makes sure to be "seated in some artless and agreeable posture ready to receive him," though "whenever she was surprised, of course, she had to fly to her apartment to take a rapid survey of matters in the glass, and to trip down again to wait upon the great peer" (VF 606). The mirror is a useful instrument, not a means to indulge her vanity. Jos, by contrast, uses his mirror to feed his vanity and to help him appear a certain way not to anyone in particular but to "the public." When he hears rumors about the defeat of the British army, Jos wants to leave Brussels before the French reach the city. Grabbing his hat, Jos sees himself reflected in the mirror at which he "used to coquet" before the regiment marched out. "Such is the force of habit, that even in the midst of his terror he began mechanically to twiddle with his hair, and arrange the cock of his hat." Jos is going through the motions, caught up in his usual ritual, before he really sees his reflection in light of current events. "Then he looked amazed at the pale face in the glass before him, and especially at his mustachios, which had attained a rich growth in the course of near seven weeks, since they had come into the world. They *will* mistake me for a military man, thought he" (VF 391–2). He orders his valet to shave his moustache so he may once again pass for a civilian.

Blurring the distinction between Smith's aesthetic and moral mirrors, Jos regards his moral character as an extension of his looks. He fancies himself a military man because he has grown a moustache, and a great seducer because of his Hessian boots. "When I endeavor to examine my own conduct," Smith argues,

> I divide myself, as it were, into two persons.... The first is the spectator, whose sentiments with regard to my own conduct I endeavour to enter into, by placing myself in his situation, and by considering how it would appear to me, when seen from that particular point of view. The second is the agent, the person whom I properly call myself, and of whose conduct, under the character of a spectator, I was endeavouring to form some opinion. (TMS 150)

For Smith, the self-approbation resulting from this division of the self is an essential ingredient of virtue. Jos, too, divides himself, all be it only briefly and never with the intention to scrutinize his moral character. Looking at himself in the mirror, Jos snaps out of his self-absorption and realizes that "they" will think he is a soldier. He does not on this occasion or any other try to imagine what spectators of his appearance and conduct might think of his assuming a military appearance – when he suspects somebody is mocking his motives or sentiments he quickly retreats and pushes away the thought. When Smith claims that "no action can properly be called virtuous, which is not accompanied with the sentiment of self-approbation," he clearly has in mind something different from George and Jos's self-satisfied and self-serving glances in the mirror (TMS 198). Theirs is not the approbation of the impartial spectator but the vanity of men who are content to regard themselves in a flattering light and look no further.

George and Jos's imperfect self-scrutiny is explained by our natural inclination "to be more or less pleased" when people around us approve of our conduct, and "to be more or less hurt when they disapprove of it" (TMS 161). We are surrounded by our "immediate" judges but they form only the imperfect and flawed representation of "a much higher tribunal" namely our "own consciences," "the supposed impartial and well-informed spectator," "the man within the breast, the great judge and arbiter of their conduct" (TMS 161). George and Jos (and the majority of VF's denizens) care only about "the man without" and "actual praise" and "actual blame." If they look at themselves from the point of view of a spectator, it is not the "impartial man within the breast" but a partial onlooker. For George these partial spectators could be Dobbin, Amelia, his father, or any one of his many admirers. Jos's partial spectators are primarily the products of his imagination as nobody appears to truly admire him. George and Jos do not consider "the jurisdiction of the man within" concerned with "the desire of praise-worthiness, and ... the aversion to blame-worthiness" (TMS 161). The "demi-god within the breast" is not making itself felt or heard to either of these men. Even the strongest impartial spectator can be shaken by loud praise or blame, and since this entity was never really developed in either George or Jos it might as well not have existed at all.

Smith's description of our self-evaluation in the mirror already showed that if, after dividing ourselves, we are pleased with what we see, we can be more indifferent to applause and criticism from others. But if we are "doubtful" about what we see, we become more anxious to receive praise. Thoughts of "censure" strike us with "double severity." The wise person discussed in the previous chapter, esteeming him- or herself neither more nor less than is warranted, has a well developed impartial spectator. When we feel that the impartial spectator would approve of our actions, we sense that we are deserving of praise, i.e. that we are praiseworthy. In Smith's words, a person "desires, not only praise, but praiseworthiness; or to be that thing which, though it should be praised by nobody, is, however, the natural and proper object of praise. He dreads, not only blame, but blameworthiness or to be that thing which, though it should be blamed by nobody, is, however, the natural and proper object of blame" (TMS 151).

We only know what is praiseworthy and what is blameworthy because we live among people who have made us feel the difference. We look at ourselves through the eyes of others and distill a sense of impartiality from all the different judgments out there. This process can easily go awry because "praise and blame express what actually are; praise-worthiness and blameworthiness, what naturally ought to be the sentiments of other people with regard to our character and conduct" (TMS 160). A lot of praise is unmerited and the same is true for blame. So how does this impartial judge emerge from the muddle of worldly judgments? How do we learn to distinguish blameworthiness from blame, praiseworthiness from praise? George Osborne never learns to make the distinction, nor do most of VF's inhabitants. "The love of praise is the desire of obtaining the favorable sentiments of our brethren," Smith writes, and where Dobbin and Amelia are concerned George can fulfill this desire. Becky's case, once again, is different: she knows the kind of things that are praised and also recognizes that they are frequently not identical with the things considered praiseworthy. But for Becky there is no real difference between praise and praiseworthiness. Praise can be bestowed genuinely or it may be flattery; but even when it is bestowed genuinely this does not mean that the praised person is praiseworthy. "The love of praiseworthiness is the desire of rendering ourselves the proper objects of those [favorable] sentiments," writes Smith, but as the examples of generosity made clear, what is defined as praiseworthy is contingent on culture, time, place and a host of other factors influencing a spectator's perspective (TMS 160).

Sentimentality is more common than authentic sentiment in VF. Becky generally regards other people's sentiments with a degree of skepticism. She keenly detects affectation and recognizes when people indulge or exaggerate their feelings. All these sentiments, moral or otherwise, provide Becky with information. She is not without sentiments herself but she is rarely swept away on a tide of feeling and she never grows sentimental. She experiences resentment, anger, and regret, but her active nature does not dwell on these negative emotions – nor does she expect sympathy for them. Becky rarely stagnates but is almost always dynamic and forward-looking. The next section compares the sentiments and actions of Becky, Amelia and Jane Eyre in order to better understand the connection between sentimentality, sympathy, and impartiality.

Sentimentality and Useless Regrets

Becky, Amelia and their husbands are stationed in Brussels with the rest of the regiment when the call to arms comes. The narrator does not follow Captain Crawley and George Osborne into war but claims his place is with the "non-combatants" (VF 361). (Yet who more combative than Becky?) Rawdon, in what may be the first non-selfish moment of his life, is concerned about Becky's welfare should he perish on the battlefield. He scolds himself for not being more prudent in money matters in the past and when Becky responds with her usual sense of satire and irony, Rawdon's feelings are hurt. "'Dearest love,' she said, 'do you suppose I feel nothing?' and hastily dashing something from her eyes, she looked up in her husband's face with a smile." Rawdon rides off to war wearing "his oldest and shabbiest uniform and epaulets," and "a kit as modest as that of a sergeant, and with something like a prayer on his lips for the woman he was leaving" (VF 367). He leaves behind everything of value so that his wife will be provided for should she become a widow. Between Rawdon's possessions and the gifts she has received from other male admirers unbeknownst to Rawdon, Becky calculates that she has at least eight hundred pounds at her disposal should her husband die in the war.

"Knowing how useless regrets are, and how the indulgence of sentiment only serves to make people more miserable, Mrs. Rebecca wisely determined to give way to no vain feelings of sorrow, and bore the parting from her husband with quite a Spartan equanimity" (VF 363). And again: "Rebecca, as we have said, wisely determined not to give way to unavailing sentimentality on her husband's departure. She waved him an adieu from the window, and stood there for a moment looking out after he was gone" (VF 368). Compare the Crawleys' farewell to the Osbornes': Amelia's face on the morning of George's departure is "white, so wild and despair-stricken," and "wrapped in a white morning dress, her hair falling on her shoulders, and her large eyes fixed and without light," she mutely follows her husband around the room holding one of his sashes "against her bosom, from which the heavy net of crimson dropped like a large stain of blood" (VF 372). After the regiment's departure, "Amelia remained for hours, silent, motionless, and haggard, by the windows in which she had placed herself to watch the last bayonets of the column as it marched away" (VF 367). She is "a great deal too ill" to come down to breakfast to "cut the tartines that Mr. Jos liked" (VF 374).

While Amelia sits by the windows for hours, Becky only wastes a moment after Rawdon has disappeared from sight.

> There had been no rest for her that night. She was still in her pretty ball-dress, her fair hair hanging somewhat out of curl on her neck, and the circles round her eyes dark with watching. "What a fright I seem," she said, examining herself in the glass, "and how pale this pink makes one look!" So she divested herself of this pink raiment; in doing which a note fell out from her corsage, which she picked up with a smile, and locked into her dressing-box. And then she put her bouquet of the ball into a glass of water, and went to bed, and slept very comfortably. The town was quite quiet when she woke up at ten o'clock, and partook of coffee, very requisite and comforting after the exhaustion and grief of the morning's occurrences. (VF 368)

The note is from George and contains his proposal to run away with Becky, abandoning Amelia.[5] Becky is content in the knowledge that she took her revenge on George who snubbed her in the early days of their acquaintance and prevented her

---

[5] Many years later Becky shows this note to Amelia to prove to her that her revered dead husband was never worthy of her devotion.

marriage to Jos. Since she never intended to run away with George but only wanted to establish her power over him, his riding off to war is a convenience. While "the exhaustion and grief of the morning's occurrences" have left Amelia a nervous wreck, sitting by the window and foregoing breakfast, Becky's attitude and mindset are more practical and wholly unsentimental. She is, as the narrator puts is, "indomitable:" "If this is a novel without a hero, at least let us lay claim to a heroine. No man in the British army which has marched away, not the great Duke himself, could be more cool or collected in the presence of doubts and difficulties, than the indomitable little aide de camp's wife" (VF 369). Looking in the mirror, Becky becomes her own spectator. She observes that she looks "a fright," but the observation is almost cheerfully detached, much like when she later takes "a rapid survey of matters" (VF 606) in the mirror before Lord Steyne visits. She does not dwell on either her victory over George or her fatigue but decides that she needs sleep and (as she did at Miss Crawley's bedside) she has no trouble finding this refreshment. Once again it appears that Becky's conscience is clear.

While Amelia is prey to sentimentality (hypocritical in its own way as George is so clearly unworthy of devotion, and it is Amelia's own vanity that prevents her from recognizing this), Becky's attitude is pragmatic. The difference between Becky and Jane Eyre is of a different nature. As we will see later in this chapter, Jane chides herself for sentiments she should not have indulged and so can be said to share Becky's impatience with "sentimentality." But Becky does not have to fight her sentiments because they always already point her in the direction she wants to go. Becky does not sacrifice her sentiments to a "higher tribunal," because her internal spectator and her sentiments are for the most part perfectly aligned. She lightheartedly takes a survey of her physical and mental state and acts in the manner most conducive to her sense of well-being. Does this mean that her impartial spectator is malfunctioning or wholly absent, like he is for George, Jos and Miss Crawley? Or is Becky like the rare person Smith describes who can be wholly content with his motivations and behavior because the "man within the breast" can enter into his situation with nothing but approval and sympathy? If the latter, then Becky's impartial spectator uses a different set of standards for fairness and impartiality than does Smith's.

Becky Sharp and Jane Eyre Care for themselves

Jane Eyre is an orphan living with relatives, her aunt Mrs. Reed and her children, who make her feel inferior to them. When one day she is attacked by her oldest cousin and fights back, her aunt refuses to believe that it was not Jane who started the fight. The incident sets in motion a chain of events that leads to Jane moving away to Lowood school. The headmaster there, Mr. Brocklehurst, comes to visit and hears Mrs. Reed's account of the events:

> 'Deceit is, indeed, a sad fault in a child,' said Mr Brocklehurst; 'it is akin to falsehood, and all liars will have their portion in the lake burning with fire and brimstone; she shall, however, be watched, Mrs Reed. I will speak to Miss Temple and the teachers.'
>
> 'I should wish her to be brought up in a manner suiting her prospects,' continued my benefactress; 'to be made useful, to be kept humble.
>
> 'Humility is a Christian grace, and one peculiarly appropriate to the pupils of Lowood; I, therefore, direct that special care shall be bestowed on its cultivation amongst them. I have studied how best to mortify in them the worldly sentiment of pride, and, only the other day, I had a pleasing proof of my success. My second daughter, Augusta, went with her mamma to visit the school, and on her return she exclaimed, "Oh, dear papa, how quiet and plain all the girls at Lowood look; with their hair combed behind their ears, and their long pinafores, and those little holland pockets outside their frocks, they are almost like poor people's children! and," said she, "they looked at my dress, and mamma's, as if they had never seen a silk gown before."' (Brontë 789)

The girls at Lowood are being prepared for a life as teacher or governess, the only two options open to middle class women lacking the money and family to sustain the unemployed lifestyle prescribed by the Victorian ideal. The only other "career" open to the Lowood pupils is marriage, but given their situation as orphaned daughters (or daughters of parents unable to sustain them) their prospects in this regard are bleak. They therefore are to prepare for a life of humility and dependence, signified by plain dress and modest behavior, suited to governesses who, though they live and work at the heart of moneyed families, must always be made to feel inferior to their employers and their employers' children.[6] Jane worries that Mr. Brocklehurst's public shaming of her once she is at Lowood has ruined her reputation with her new friend Helen and with Miss Temple, the admired head teacher. Jane is angry and feels powerless in the face of the unfair treatment she receives from the authorities controlling her life.

Becky Sharp, too, is angry at the unfairness of her position. She considers herself prettier than most and smarter than all the girls at Miss Pinkerton's school and yet she is expected to be not only content with but grateful for her position as "articled pupil." But while Jane's passionate anger is a response to injustice and encourages her to distinguish herself from the perpetrators of moral outrage by living a principled life, Becky recognizes very early on that it is more prudent to hide her anger and exact vengeance under the guise of docility and propriety. Working as a governess for Sir Pitt, her behavior is "exceedingly modest and affable" (VF 110). Becky's "after-history," of course, proves that it may have been Becky's heart that dictated this behavior, but that it in no way follows that she experienced a "sincere desire of amendment" (VF 111). The narrator makes clear that Becky is a hypocrite, and a clever one at that. How can an orphaned young woman with no family or money move up, economically speaking? The only way for a governess to get a "promotion"

[6] In a 1859 piece in the *Saturday Review* titled "Queen bees or worker bees," an anonymous author observes: "Married life is a woman's profession; and to this life her training – that of dependence – is modeled. Of course by not getting a husband, or losing him, she may find that she is without resources. All hat can be said of her is, she has failed in business; and no social reform can prevent such failures. The mischance of the distressed governess and the unprovided widow, is that of every insolvent tradesmen" (Hollis 2013, 11).

is for her to marry her employer or a relation of her employer. This is exactly what Becky proposes to do by secretly marrying Rawdon Crawley, Sir Pitt's nephew. Jane Eyre, too, marries her employer, though not for economic gain. From an ethical perspective, the two strong-willed governesses appear very different: while Jane is principled throughout, time and again scrutinizing her own sentiments and behavior through the eyes of the impartial spectator, Becky is driven by a will to power and status. She, too, is constantly monitoring her own feelings and actions, subjecting herself to an inner judge. But Becky's internal spectator is unconcerned with morality for its own sake, while Jane's internal spectator is completely preoccupied with it.

A closer look at Jane reveals that her impartial spectator abides by a strict and traditional set of rules. When her employer Mr. Rochester begs Jane to stay with him after she has found out that he already has a wife, insane and living in the attic, she is firm in her response:

> Still indomitable was the reply: 'I care for myself. The more solitary, the more friendless, the more unsustained I am, the more I will respect myself. I will keep the law given by God; sanctioned by man. I will hold to the principles received by me when I was sane, and not mad – as I am now. Laws and principles are not for the times when there is no temptation: they are for such moments as this, when body and soul rise in mutiny against their rigour; stringent are they; inviolate they shall be. If at my individual convenience I might break them, what would be their worth? They have a worth – so I have always believed; and if I cannot believe it now, it is because I am insane – quite insane, with my veins running fire, and my heart beating faster than I can count its throbs. Preconceived opinions, foregone determinations, are all I have at this hour to stand by: there I plant my foot.' (Brontë 6904)

Jane recognizes that she is overcome with emotion and needs to take firm measures to divide herself into judge and person judged. For her to look at herself the way an impartial spectator would, she has to detach and distance herself from her own situation. Only then can she measure her own case against the impartial standard – or at least the standard comprised by the "laws and principles" mentioned in the excerpt above. Jane knows she could not live with herself if she ignored the voice of her internal spectator because she knows that its judgment is correct. But are these laws and principles impartial and fair merely because they are "preconceived" and "foregone?" Becky the hypocrite appears to scrupulously live by the laws and principles regulating Victorian society but does not take them to heart like Jane does. She understands that to get ahead she needs to use the "preconceived opinions" and "foregone determinations" of her time to her advantage and act the part of the angelic woman. Jane's laws and principles mark her strong sense of right and wrong: overwhelming as her feelings for Rochester may be, it would be wrong to give in to temptation and violate her self-respect which is based on principles. She holds herself to a high standard even if it is to her material disadvantage to act according to her sense of duty.

Becky, too, has a high standard and we can imagine her saying, like Jane: "I care for myself. The more solitary, the more friendless, the more unsustained I am, the more I will respect myself." Both Becky and Jane care for themselves but obviously in very different ways. Both heroines defy social convention but while Jane's defiance tends to be open and uncalculating, respecting a higher or even a divine law, Becky's defiance secretly subverts convention from within. She has no interest in openly going against the rules dictating proper womanly behavior; rather, she is sincerely unbothered by the very notion of morality and right and wrong. She has no patience for sentimentality because it gets in the way of decisive action and dampens her apparently innate vivacity. Just as importantly, sentimentality clouds one's judgment because it impedes one's impartiality. A sentimental person cannot judge what he or she sees in the mirror, be it a real looking glass or the gaze of the spectator. The next section considers the way Jane and Becky use their mirrors.

Portrait of a Two Governesses, Disconnected, Poor, and Plain

After Rawdon's departure, Becky examines herself in the mirror and takes stock. The circles round her eyes are "dark with watching" and she looks tired (VF 368). She observes that the pretty pink dress emphasizes her paleness. Her attitude is matter of fact and practical: the pretty, innocent dress that the night before helped her conquer George and inspire selfless affection in Rawdon has served its purpose; now it is time for restorative sleep so that she will be ready to exploit her new status as the brave wife of a husband away at war. Becky's use of her mirror is instructive: the mirror is an instrument that enables her to take inventory of her assets. She is self-confident and aware of her powers: she may look pale now, but she is aware that this is merely the result of a night spent exerting her powers to great effect. The only thing she needs is sleep (and coffee) to recharge. She is, as the narrator points out, indomitable. There may be difficulties ahead but she does not seem to be prey to insecurity or, for that matter, vanity. She is aware of her power and confident in her abilities.

After Jane saves Mr. Rochester from a fiery death one night (Jane suspects that the mysterious and scary servant Grace Poole had something to do with Mr. Rochester's bed curtains catching flame), she finds that her employer has left Thornfield to visit friends. Mrs. Fairfax informs Jane that among these friends is a beautiful woman, Miss Blanche Ingram, who seems to possess every possible female charm and furthermore comes from a good family. Alone in her room, Jane scolds herself for thinking that Rochester was ever interested in her: "'You,' I said, 'a favourite with Mr Rochester? You gifted with the power of pleasing him? You of importance to him in any way? Go! your folly sickens me'" (Brontë 3521). Jane goes on to rail at herself with a contempt we never see in Becky:

> "Poor stupid dupe! – Could not even self-interest make you wiser? You repeated to yourself this morning the brief scene of last night? – Cover your face and be ashamed! He said something in praise of your eyes, did he? Blind puppy! Open their bleared lids and look on your own accursed senselessness! It does good to no woman to be flattered by her superior, who cannot possibly intend to marry her. … 'Listen, then, Jane Eyre, to your sentence: to-morrow, place the glass before you, and draw in chalk your own picture, faithfully, without

> softening one defect; omit no harsh line, smooth away no displeasing irregularity; write under it, "Portrait of a Governess, disconnected, poor, and plain." (Brontë 3519)

Jane is "sickened by her own folly" and proposes to punish herself for her "accursed senselessness." Flattery from a superior cannot possibly lead to anything good, or so it seems at this moment of shame and embarrassment. The self-portrait Jane proposes will be "faithful" and honest because she will use a mirror ("glass") to unflinchingly register every detail. Like Becky, she proposes to take stock. But while Becky looks at herself with a lighthearted, detached practicality, Jane scorns her own "bleared lids" and ridicules herself for ever thinking that her appearance could appeal to a man of rank like Rochester. One key difference between Jane and Becky is that Jane genuinely cares for Rochester and wants him to love her because she loves him. Becky is unencumbered by sentiments of this sort and appears as self-sufficient as ever. Her self-esteem and sense of purpose prevent her from ever feeling ashamed, silly, or embarrassed. Jane indulges her shame and prolongs and deepens her self-mortification by not only sketching her self-portrait in chalk but also painting a picture of what she believes Miss Ingram must look like. She gives it the title "Blanche, an accomplished lady of rank" to further increase the contrast with her "Portrait of a Governess, disconnected, poor, and plain." "'Whenever, in future, you should chance to fancy Mr Rochester thinks well of you, take out these two pictures and compare them: say, "Mr Rochester might probably win that noble lady's love, if he chose to strive for it; is it likely he would waste a serious thought on this indigent and insignificant plebeian?"' (Brontë 3530).

Jane spends two hours on her own portrait in chalk and two weeks on an oil painting of Blanche Ingram. Having finished both, she is better prepared to face a visit from the Ingrams and company to Thornfield. Jane's exercise in self-humiliation is obviously not impartial, or at least it does not lead her to look at herself the way an "indifferent spectator" or an "impartial judge" would (TMS 71). In fact, Jane's self-imposed punishment bears a close resemblance to the kind of treatment Mr. Brocklehurst boasted of in his description of the girls at Lowood. He, too, believed that pride had to be humbled in "insignificant plebeians" while he indulged the vanity of ladies of rank like his own wife and daughters. Smith holds that we practice our impartial abilities when "we bring home to ourselves the case of another" (TMS 363) or when, in judging our own situation and actions, we bring home to ourselves our own case the way somebody else would. When, for example, we look back on our own acts of generosity, we sympathize with ourselves through the eyes of society and feel like we are in harmony with all humankind. This gives us a sense of serenity and cheerfulness. We are conscious "of our own merit, or of deserved reward" (TMS 128). Jane's harsh self-mockery ("Blind puppy!") result from her bringing home to herself certain societal rules: "It does good to no woman to be flattered by her superior, who cannot possibly intend to marry her" (Brontë 3525). She forces herself to look in the mirror and see what she believes the rest of society would see: a plain governess who should not flatter herself to think that she could be of interest to a rich man like Rochester.

Jane disapproves of her own conduct because, in Smith's words, she cannot "enter into and sympathize with the sentiments and motives which influenced" her behavior when regarding her situation from a supposedly impartial distance. She chastises herself for indulging her feelings for Rochester and allowing herself to believe that he reciprocated them. Now that he has left without a word, she forces herself to look at her situation and actions the way an "impartial spectator" would. "But we can do this in no other way than by endeavouring to view them with the eyes of other people, or as other people are likely to view them … We endeavour to examine our own conduct as we imagine any other fair and impartial spectator would examine it" (TMS 148). Yet the spectatorial stance taken up by Jane seems hardly fair or impartial; it rather feels like an exercise in self-loathing. And yet: the judgment she issues on her own behavior is perfectly in line with the mores and morality of the time. Jane is only a governess, after all, and has been raised (first at the Reeds, and later at Lowood) to accept the humility of her station. Plainness, prudence, and humility are expected from her in every respect, inside and out.[7]

The reader already has a sense of Jane's appearance, or at least about her own estimation of it. She describes herself as "plain" but "neat" and explains that though she regrets that she is "not handsomer," "I ever wished to look as well as I could, and to please as much as my want of beauty would permit." She has only a few outfits and usually wears her black frock which, though "Quaker-like," fits "to a nicety" (Brontë 2176). When Rochester has called for Jane early on during her stay at Thornfield, she ascertains "that I was myself in my usual Quaker trim, where there was nothing to retouch – all being too close and plain, braided locks included, to admit of disarrangement (Brontë 2857). When Rochester later confesses his love for Jane and she agrees to marry him, he proposes to cover her in jewels. Jane rejects the idea: "Jewels for Jane Eyre sounds unnatural and strange: I would rather not have them" (Brontë 5648). She adds: "Don't address me as if I were a beauty; I am your plain, Quakerish governess" (Brontë 5652). Rochester ignores Jane's objections and continues outlining his plans to dress her in "satin and lace" and put roses in her hair. "And then you won't know me, sir; and I shall not be your Jane Eyre any longer, but an ape in a harlequin's jacket – a jay in borrowed plumes." Rochester appears lost in his own ideals and daydreams as he continues to describe a future for his Mrs. Rochester: "young Mrs. Rochester – Fairfax Rochester's girl-bride" (Brontë 5639). Jane will be his "angel" (Brontë 5668).

Unlike Becky, Jane declines the clothes and "gimcracks" her lover wants to bestow on her together with the childlike, angelic role they imply. Her principles forbid it and she insists on thinking of herself as a plain governess, even calling herself an ape and a harlequin. Part of her resistance appears to be aimed at the infantilization inherent in Rochester's admiration and plans for her. Being addressed "as if" she were a beauty bothers Jane, as does the idea of the clothes and jewels that

[7] In her analysis of Jane's self-portrait of a "disconnected, poor, and plain" governess, Millicent Bell points out that "the first two attributes are social and economic, and the third prohibits the hope of any escape from such disadvantages…. her lack of the requisite beauty of such a heroine is stressed continually" (Bell 1996, 263).

Rochester wants to buy for her. Becky not only welcomes all gifts from her lovers (like the watches she receives from George and General Tufto) as tokens of her power over them, she also appreciates them for their monetary value and as status symbols. She is unbothered by the moral implications of the gifts (e.g. the disloyalty to lawful spouses they represent) and pragmatic about their future uses. Becky regards her natural beauty and all the artifice at her disposal to enhance it as useful assets. She is pleased with her appearance and knows how to dress herself to great advantage. Her self-esteem is such that she does not need others to confirm her beauty – she enjoys their flattery but inwardly regards it as her due. While Jane repeatedly emphasizes her own Quakerish plainness and contrasts it with Blanche Ingram's supposed beauty, Becky is never inclined to self-mortification. Miss Pinkerton of Chiswick Hall was only the first to try to put her in her proper place and instill in Becky a desire to be plain and proper in both her appearance and ambition. Jane and her fellow boarders at Lowood are subjected to much mortification, doled out primarily by headmaster Brocklehurst:

> 'Miss Temple, Miss Temple, what – what is that girl with curled hair? Red hair, ma'am, curled – curled all over?' And extending his cane he pointed to the awful object, his hand shaking as he did so. 'It is Julia Severn,' replied Miss Temple very quietly. 'Julia Severn, ma'am! And why has she, or any other, curled hair? Why, in defiance of every precept and principle of this house, does she conform to the world so openly – here in an evangelical, charitable establishment – as to wear her hair one mass of curls?' 'Julia's hair curls naturally,' returned Miss Temple.
>
> 'Naturally! Yes, but we are not to conform to nature. I wish these girls to be the children of Grace: and why that abundance? I have again and again intimated that I desire the hair to be arranged closely, modestly, plainly (Brontë 1437).

The future governesses are supposed to be modest and plain, even if nature did not form them on those lines. Indicating that all girls should have their "top-knots" cut off, Brocklehurst explains:

> "'I have a Master to serve whose kingdom is not of this world: my mission is to mortify in these girls the lusts of the flesh, to teach them to clothe themselves with shamefacedness and sobriety, not with braided hair and costly apparel; and each of the young persons before us has a string of hair twisted in plaits which vanity itself might have woven: these, I repeat, must be cut off; think of the time wasted, of—' Mr Brocklehurst was here interrupted: three other visitors, ladies, now entered the room. They ought to have come a little sooner to have heard his lecture on dress, for they were splendidly attired in velvet, silk, and furs" (Brontë 1446).

The ladies interrupting Mr. Brocklehurst's speech are his wife and daughters, women for whom plainness is obviously not a personal goal.[8] But while the richly attired fellow-boarders at Chiswick inspire in Becky a frustration and sense of unfairness because she feels that she deserves their outfits more than they do, Jane

[8] Esther Godfrey observes: "Brocklehurst's position expressed a middle-class interest in preserving the economic status quo, and that position required clearer divisions between the classes themselves. Bronte carefully portrays Brocklehurst as one who, like the owners of the mines, sees femininity as a construct afforded by middle-class luxury and working-class androgyny as a necessary, though clearly distinct, part of the hierarchical social order" (Godfrey 2005, 857).

Eyre never comes to aspire to wealth and in fact feels burdened by it when much later she inherits a fortune. Perhaps it is no coincidence that Jane Eyre keeps for herself only five thousand pounds to last her for the rest of her life, exactly the amount Becky has in mind when she muses that she could be a "good woman" if she had "five thousand a year" (VF 532).[9] Like Becky, Jane has plenty of opportunity to practice her self-command but the two women exercise it to different ends: Jane out of respect for what she herself (and likely her readership, too) thinks of as high moral standards, Becky out of respect for her own ambition for power and status. Furthermore, as women forced to hide their pains and resentments from a young age and to perform a part imposed on them by society, both Becky and Jane have lived under circumstances that by Smith standards are ideal for the cultivation of a strong impartial spectator.

Live with Strangers

In an aside to his treatment of the battle at Waterloo, the narrator of VF remarks: "Time out of mind strength and courage have been the theme of bards and romances; and from the story of Troy down to to-day, poetry has always chosen a soldier for a hero. I wonder is it because men are cowards in heart that they admire bravery so much, and place military valour so far beyond every other quality for reward and worship?" (VF 372) Smith emphasizes war as a school not only for the martial spirit and masculine virtues like generosity and courage but also for the development of the impartial spectator. "Hardships, dangers, injuries, misfortunes, are the only masters under whom we can learn the exercise of" the self-command needed to regard ourselves with the detachment required for sound moral judgment. "But these are all masters to whom nobody willingly puts himself to school" (TMS 177).

Though they have not literally gone to war, both Becky and Jane Eyre have been subject to all these masters from a young age. They have had to learn self-command out of self-preservation and self-respect, not having had much opportunity to cultivate the "gentle virtue of humanity" more appropriate to women. Humanity is cultivated under very different circumstances: in the "mild sunshine of undisturbed

[9] Richard A. Kaye describes the difficult relationship between Thackeray and Brontë. Though the two admired each other's work, they did not get along on the few occasions they met in person. Kaye detects a stab at Brontë's Jane Eyre in the passage that describes Becky's musing about being a country gentleman's wife: "Thackeray clearly had Jane's inheritance in mind when he assigned Becky her soon-to-become-infamous remark on an ideal income. He was writing chapter 41 of Vanity Fair in the very weeks in which he had completed his reading of the novel he soon championed." Furthermore, "What for Bronte's highly ethical heroine is a figure denoting financial freedom for life becomes, for her fictional counterpart, merely a reasonable prerequisite for ethical action, provided it is multiplied annually in perpetuity" (Kaye 1995, 723). The relevant passage in *JE* reads: "It would please and benefit me to have five thousands pounds… it would torment and oppress me to have twenty thousand; which, moreover, could never be mine in justice, though it might be in law"(Brontë, 8387).

tranquility, in the calm retirement of undissipated and philosophical leisure" (TMS 178).

This quintessentially feminine tenderness is a spectator virtue, a trait belonging to the sympathetic witness to pain. The feeling of sympathy comes naturally to most of us and, as we know from the previous chapter, humanity comes naturally to women. This is not true of self-command, which is a virtue belonging not primarily to the spectator but to the sufferer – the soldier about to give up his life for his country, the father about to kill his son to set a heroic example. Self-command is an actor virtue and requires a much greater effort. For the spectator to enter into the emotions of the sufferer, he or she has to heighten his or her own emotion in order to achieve harmony with the sufferer. This sympathetic adjustment suits the feminine character, naturally disposed to show tender affection. When exercising self-command, on the other hand, we have to restrain our great pain and fear, which according to Smith is much more difficult. We can only learn self-command in the presence of others who "awaken" in us "the man within the breast, the abstract and ideal spectator of our sentiments and conduct" (TMS 178).

Real spectators, the ones "from whom we can expect the least sympathy and indulgence," are required for us to learn "the most complete lesson of self-command" (TMS 178). These people do not indulge us or sympathize with our pain and they teach us to look at ourselves in a way opposed to any self-love we might have been feeling. For Jane, these "real spectators" include the Reed family, Brocklehurst, and later the Ingrams. For Becky, the list is much longer still – she is disliked by women across England and the continent and is aware of their judgment on her. Both Jane and Becky have lived by Smith's prescription (be it not by choice):

> Are you in adversity? Do not mourn in the darkness of solitude, do not regulate your sorrow according to the indulgent sympathy of your intimate friends; return, as soon as possible, to the day-light of the world and of society. Live with strangers, with those who know nothing, or care nothing about your misfortune; do not even shun the company of enemies; but give yourself the pleasure of mortifying their malignant joy, by making them feel how little you are affected by your calamity, and how much you are above it. (TMS 178)

We have seen Becky's application of the last part of this rule in her exchange with George Osborne when she routs him completely by offering him only a finger. She knows the pleasure of mortifying the malignant joy of others. Smith further urges us to spend time with people who in no way depend on your fortune or who dislike you for now being their equal or even their superior. Their contempt for you may make them disagreeable company but at least they are not partial to you like your flatterers.

The greatest danger to the impartial spectator is the partial spectator close by. George Osborne, raised as an extension of his father's vanity and pride to think far more highly of himself than is warranted, presents a caricature of Smith's thesis. George's impartial spectator presumably never had the chance to develop because its voice was always already overpowered by the clamor of the people surrounding him. George never lived among strangers, never experienced solitude and always received the "indulgent sympathy" of intimate friends and family. It is ironic that in the eyes of vain society, George is considered the quintessential soldier: dashing in his uniform and perfectly mustachioed, even though he has never experienced the "hardships, dangers, injuries, misfortunes" that help build the self-command Smith considers essential to the martial character. On Smith's account, George perhaps cannot be blamed for his vanity and self-indulgence given that he has never had occasion to look at himself critically. Smith observes that society provides us with a mirror: "It is placed in the countenance and behaviour of those he lives with, which always mark when they enter into, and when they disapprove of his sentiments; and it is here that he first views the propriety and impropriety of his own passions, the beauty and deformity of his own mind" (TMS 149). Since George has met with flattery and praise all his life, and rarely experienced any disapproval, it is unsurprising that he considers himself proper and beautiful in both body and mind.

As opposed to Becky and Jane, George has never been forced to "scrutinize the propriety" of his own conduct or give much thought to the effect of his behavior on others. Because he has never met with humiliation or severe criticism, he has not learned to use "the only looking-glass by which we can, in some measure, with the eyes of other people, scrutinize the propriety of our own conduct" (TMS 150). George's vanity thus clearly stands in the way of his impartiality because he rarely experiences anything other than self-satisfaction. He is surrounded by partial spectators and does not need to adjust the pitch of his selfish passions to harmonize with those around him. In fact, he *is* in harmony with the people around him because their sentiments are in accord with his: everyone close to George admires him. The young aristocrats who take advantage of George at the gambling table and who let him wine and dine them look down on him but George does not notice; he is impervious to their condescension because he only regards himself in the mirror of partial spectatorship. A sense of moral self-awareness needs to be acquired over time and George's moral consciousness does not function properly because it has never been habituated. This explains why George rarely feels remorse or guilt. Even when he leaves for battle on the night of the ball, the thought that he has done wrong in betraying Amelia and proposing to run off with Becky is a fleeting one.

Becky's Impartial Spectator

When we regard our own sentiments and behavior through the eyes of the impartial spectator, we divide ourselves into judge and judged. It is possible, however, to habituate ourselves to the impartial spectator's perspective to the extent that we almost become one with him. About the man of "constancy and firmness," Smith writes: "He does not merely affect the sentiments of the impartial spectator. He really adopts them. He almost identifies himself with, he almost becomes himself that impartial spectator, and scarce even feels but as that great arbiter of his conduct directs him to feel" (TMS 173). Becky monitors her own behavior and her feelings carefully, using her reflection in the mirror and the feedback she gets from people around her as information to guide her through the complicated maze of society. She regards herself with the detachment of a third person and corrects flaws in her physical appearance the same way she changes her conduct to strike the right pitch in any company. She makes it easy for people, especially men, to "enter into" her situation and go along with her sentiments, showing her mastery of the actor virtue of self-command: she rarely abandons herself to "paroxysms" of emotion but instead tones down the expression of her feelings to make it easy for people to sympathize with her. Except when she can barely hide her contempt (one of Becky's strongest emotions and a topic of Chap. 8) Becky has no difficulty feeling "as that great arbiter of [her] conduct directs [her] to feel" (TMS 173). But Becky's "great arbiter" and "tribunal inside the breast" resembles Smith's impartial spectator only up to a point. Her third person perspective is detached but, on Smith's account, both immoral and unnatural.

"For one man to deprive another unjustly of any thing, or unjustly to promote his own advantage by the loss or disadvantage of another, is more contrary to nature, than death, than poverty, than pain, than all the misfortunes which can affect him, either in his body, or in his external circumstances" (TMS 167). We may try to fool ourselves into thinking that our actions are exempt from this judgment, but we can never long succeed in this self-deceit, "this fatal weakness of mankind" which "is the source of half the disorders of human life" (TMS 182). Yet we know that Smith also recognizes our desire for power, rank, and status and holds that if one person rises, another must fall. Becky is keenly aware of this and knows that for her to gain in status she must promote her own advantage "by the loss or disadvantage of another." We are left with a tension between Smith's idea that the desire to subjugate and dominate is a part of human psychology, and the position cited above that to "deprive another unjustly of any thing … is more contrary to nature than death" (TMS 167). Becky, both in her outlook on herself and her perspective on the world, clearly demonstrates the first idea, but not the second. Her lust for domination appears perfectly natural but she operates according to a set of rules that contrast with the rules Smith advocates.

Though the impartial spectator is the highest tribunal of our actions (excepting God), we also use "general rules" to judge conduct. These rules are based in our experience of the actions and judgments of others. We naturally approve of some actions and condemn others, finding that "our natural sentiments" are confirmed by other people's reactions to these actions. Over time, general rules are formed because experience shows "that all actions of a certain kind, or circumstanced in a certain manner, are approved or disapproved of" (TMS 183). In the interplay of our own "natural" reactions with the reactions we see in others around us, we learn to judge appropriately. Provided that we are surrounded by prudent and proper people, we get used to regarding ourselves and others from a third person perspective and identify whenever possible with this "impartial spectator within the breast." When we deceive ourselves, we refuse to see ourselves "in the light in which others see us, or in which they would see us if they knew all." Were we to look at ourselves in this light, "a reformation would generally be unavoidable. We could not otherwise endure the sight" (TMS 182). Becky is not deceived about the way in which others see her and is perfectly aware of what people would think "if they knew all." She is not prone to self-deceit on this account, yet she does not feel the need for reformation.

In fact, she more closely resembles the man of constancy and firmness who has become one with the impartial spectator than she does the person who on Smith's account can live with himself only because he is deceiving himself.

Becky's conscience is clear and, in Smith's words, "Misery and wretchedness can never enter the breast in which dwells complete self-satisfaction" (TMS 173). True, undeceiving self-satisfaction is a sign, for Smith, that we are living in accordance with the rules we set for ourselves. These rules, in turn, result from our experience with the approval and detestation others have expressed about our own actions and the actions of others. As discussed in Chaps. 3 and 4, the "sacred regard" that the "second best kind of wife" feels for the rules prescribing her conduct toward the husband she does not love is an example of the importance Smith ascribes to the general rules derived from experience. Though they are derived from and therefore secondary to the verdict of the impartial spectator, they function as important guidelines. Jane Eyre clings to the general rules when she realizes that she is "mad" and cannot rely on her impartial spectator. She knows that she can feel self-approbation only when she abides by the rules she knows to be just. Misery and wretchedness would be her part if she let her emotions overrule her respect for the rules. Becky experiences no such divided self: she acts opportunistically not against her better judgment, but in line with it. The next chapter discusses how Becky's performance and success put her at odds with other women.

References

Bell, Millicent. 1996. Jane Eyre: The tale of the governess. *The American Scholar* 65 (2): 263–269.

Brontë, Charlotte. 2016. *Jane Eyre*. Kindle Edition. New York: W.W. Norton.

Eliot, George. 1996. *Middlemarch*. Oxford: Oxford University Press.

Godfrey, Esther. 2005. Jane Eyre, from Governess to Girl Bride. *Studies in English Literature, 1500–1900* 45 (4): 853–871.

Hollis, Patricia. 2013. *Women in public, 1850–1900: Documents of the Victorian Women's movement*. New York: Routledge.

Kaye, Richard A. 1995. A good woman on five thousand pounds: Jane Eyre, vanity fair, and literary rivalry. *Studies in English Literature, 1500–1900* 35 (4): 723–739.

Smith, Adam. 1981. An inquiry into the nature and causes of the wealth of nations. In *Vol. 2 of the Glasgow Edition of the Works and Correspondence of Adam Smith*, ed. R.H. Campbell and A.S. Skinner. Indianapolis: Liberty Fund.

———. 1982a. The theory of moral sentiments. In *Vol. 1 of the Glasgow Edition of the Works and Correspondence of Adam Smith*, ed. D.D. Raphael and A.L. Macfie. Indianapolis: Liberty Fund.

———. 1982b. Lectures on Jurisprudence. In *Vol. 5 of the Glasgow Edition of the Works and Correspondence of Adam Smith*, ed. R.L. Meek, D.D. Raphael, and P.G. Stein. Indianapolis: Liberty Fund.

Thackeray, William Makepeace. 1983. In *Vanity fair: A novel without a hero*, ed. John Sutherland. New York: Oxford UP.

Chapter 8
An Industrious Knave Becomes Respectable

Abstract On Adam Smith's account in the *Theory of Moral Sentiments,* humanity is a soft, feminine virtue that flourishes at times of peace. It is a natural extension of the sentiment of sympathy and the actions it inspires require little self-command. Becky Sharp in *Vanity Fair* feels little sympathy even for the people she, as a woman, should care about most: her child and her husband. She is an unnatural woman not only because she lacks the appropriate tender sentiments but also because she excels in the typically masculine virtue of self-command. Becky uses her self-command to act in accordance with the decrees of Smith's impartial spectator but only if and when actual spectators are present; she feels no remorse about her lack of sympathy for her child, her husband, or anyone else. Her successes rouse the envy of other women who, like Becky, desire status and superiority over others. Lady Jane, Becky's sister-in-law, is one of the few people in VF who experiences sympathy and acts on it, befriending Becky's husband and son. It is no coincidence that Lady Jane, a true, sympathetic woman, is the ultimate cause of Becky's downfall. According to Smith, industrious knaves like Becky are "naturally" rewarded with success in business even if they are morally condemned by their peers. How, then, are we to evaluate Becky if we regard her in what Smith would call an "impartial light"?

Becky Sharp, Unnatural Woman

The previous chapters raised questions about the impartiality of Smith's impartial spectator. Marked by self-command and generosity, virtues Smith extols as particularly masculine, the impartial spectator has its reservations about behavior guided primarily by the sentiment of humanity. To be sure, humanity is a virtue, but one that can easily slide into weakness and effeminacy. Smith mocks the "man of humanity" who would be unable to sleep if he knew he would "lose his little finger tomorrow" yet "snores over the ruin of a hundred million" when he hears that "the great empire of China" has been "swallowed up by an earthquake" (TMS 166). Humanity makes us feel more acutely the pain of others close by and hence is a virtue we expect to see in women who naturally care most for their husbands and children. But as we can tell from Smith's mocking description of the "man of

R. Slegers, *Adam Smith's Moral Sentiments in Vanity Fair*, Issues in Business Ethics 49, https://doi.org/10.1007/978-3-319-98731-6_8

humanity," this "natural" virtue is often accompanied by weakness in the face of adversity.

In the humane person, the sympathy that is naturally extended to kin and loved ones is often a mere extension of self-love. We imagine what we would feel if we were the sufferer and enter into his or her situation because we recognize the possibility for the same kind of suffering in ourselves. Humanity in the absence of self-command is weak and can result in behavior the impartial spectator would not approve of. Self-command, in turn, can be acquired only under warlike circumstances not accessible to women, which means that on Smith's account women (and men made effeminate by the peaceful and luxurious society they live in) can develop neither self-command nor generosity. It is not "the love of mankind" but "the love of what is honourable and noble, of the grandeur, and dignity, and superiority of our own characters" that can conquer self-love and make us act with generosity (TMS 166). Women are in a peculiar position because on the one hand they are expected to act in accordance with the humanity and tenderness that characterize their gender, while on the other their impartial spectator (assuming this to be the same entity in men and women alike) presumably encourages them to act in accordance with the virtues of self-command and generosity. Is the impartial spectator as manly in women as it is in men? Or do women have a different impartial spectator – but then does it still make sense to call the entity "impartial"?

One way to approach this complex issue is to consider Becky's version of the "impartial" spectator. Like Smith's theoretical "man inside the breast," Becky's internal spectator has been formed over time. Looking at her own behavior through the eyes of others, Becky has learned how to please and how to act "appropriately." She has learned (but does not judge herself by) society's rules and knows that women are supposed to show their humanity foremost while keeping their self-command hidden. Becky has experienced poverty and adversity and learned how to adjust the pitch of her emotions, recognizing that some emotions (like her resentment) should be entirely invisible from much of the world. She has lived among strangers and enemies and knows how friends and foes regard her. But humanity, a virtue so easy according to Smith that it barely deserves the name, does not come naturally to Becky. She knows how to perform *acts* of sympathy and humanity but they are for the benefit of the external spectator. In other words, Becky acts in accordance with the decrees of the impartial spectator but only if and when actual spectators are present.

Women in general, supposedly too sympathetic and humane to be capable of the self-command that characterizes martial men, can never quite obtain the full approval of the man inside the breast. Becky, who lacks the sympathy which prevents most women from developing self-command, is unnatural, strange. A man without (much) humanity, like one of the "savages" described in Chap. 4, still deserves praise from both third parties and the man within the breast because of his great self-command and courage. But a woman lacking humanity is hardly a woman at all. This makes her dangerous and unnatural.

Smith holds that when we do not act in accordance with the judgments of the impartial spectator, we are haunted by shame and remorse. We have already established that Becky's conscience is clear despite the fact that Smith's impartial spectator would not approve of her actions. Among the people openly confronting Becky about her behavior (and intentions) are Amelia Sedley and Lady Jane. Both women have witnessed Becky's (largely successful) attempts to win over their husbands, but it is only Lady Jane who besides envy and resentment also feels genuine sympathy for Rawdon Senior and Junior, Becky's husband and son. Lady Jane's capacity for sympathy sets her apart from all the other women envious of Becky's successes, and she is the only woman Becky not only scorns but hates. Becky cannot beat Lady Jane at her own game because Lady Jane is neither ambitious or vain but judges Becky for being an unloving wife and mother. All the other women in VF are rivals who can be defeated because they seek status just like Becky does and are driven primarily by vanity, not by sympathy in its uncorrupted form. Lady Jane's genuine sympathy for Rawdon Sr. leads to Becky's fall from grace - that is to say, Lord Steyne's grace and with it the good graces of high society. This provides an opportunity for Becky's many female enemies to finally crush their main rival. Once again invoking the image of a serpent, VF's narrator observes:

> And so— guiltless very likely— she was writhing and pushing onward towards what they call "a position in society," and the servants were pointing at her as lost and ruined. So you see Molly, the housemaid, of a morning, watching a spider in the doorpost lay his thread and laboriously crawl up it, until, tired of the sport, she raises her broom and sweeps away the thread and the artificer (VF 563).

The Avenging Furies of Shame and Remorse

Self-deceit, Smith holds, is at the root of "half the disorders of human life" (TMS 182). We can deceive ourselves only if we willfully ignore the impartial spectator and the perspective of any actual person approaching the perspective of the impartial spectator. Surrounding ourselves with partial spectators or paying attention only to those selective judgments which reflect positively on our behavior and sentiments, we can fool ourselves into thinking that we are praiseworthy when we are not.

Mrs. Reed, Jane Eyre's cruel aunt who regards Jane's actions as proof of her unworthiness and base moral nature, does not believe her niece when she claims to have been assaulted by Mrs. Reed's son. Much to Mrs. Reed's shock and surprise, Jane vents her anger at being called a liar: "I am not deceitful: if I were, I should say I loved you; but I declare I do not love you: I dislike you the worst of anybody in the world except John Reed" (Brontë 838). In reply to Mrs. Reed's indignation, she adds: "How dare I? Because it is the truth.... People think you are a good woman but you are bad, hard-hearted. You are deceitful!" Mrs. Reed is afraid of Jane's unchildlike outburst: "Mrs. Reed looked frightened: her work had slipped from her knee; she was lifting up her hands, rocking herself to and fro, and even twisting her face as if she would cry" (Brontë 844). After her aunt leaves the room, defeated and upset, Jane enjoys her "conqueror's solitude" but soon the "fierce pleasure" subsides:

"A child cannot quarrel with its elders, as I had done – cannot give its furious feelings uncontrolled play, as I had given mine – without experiencing afterwards the pang of remorse and the chill of reaction." "Half an hour's silence and reflection" shows Jane "the madness of my conduct, and the dreariness of my hated and hating position." She has tasted vengeance but finds "its after-flavour metallic and corroding." It gives her the feeling she has been "poisoned" (Brontë 861).

After Jane's anger and her sense of vengeful triumph subside, her internal spectator asserts itself and she feels miserable. And yet Jane has only spoken the truth – Mrs. Reed did in fact treat her cruelly and unjustly called her a liar. So is it really an *impartial* spectator that judges Jane, or rather the internalized version of the "elders" Jane mentions, with whom a child cannot quarrel without feeling remorse? What standards are represented by the "man within" Jane's breast? To the reader, entering into her situation and bringing her case home to herself, Jane's outrage is justified. But Jane has no sympathetic spectators to turn to and her solitude makes her miserable. No matter how justified her sentiments and their expression, they do not change the fact that she is lonely and feels unloved. Like George Osborne, Jane is surrounded by partial spectators – but unlike George's spectators, Jane's spectators make her feel alien, unloved, and miserable. If we cultivate our impartial spectator over time by internalizing the judgments of others, can Jane's sense of remorse (shaped as it is by her unloving surroundings) be trusted? Jane's greatest desire is to be loved, and be worthy of love, and in her loneliness her remorse only increases her misery and the distance between herself and the people she lives with.

Becky is generally not susceptible to feelings of remorse though she betrays a faint trace of the sentiment in the chapter following the regiment's departure from Brussels. Becky goes to visit Jos Sedley and Amelia and after securing a seat in Jos's carriage (should she decide to flee), she enters Amelia's room. At the sight of Becky, Amelia is reminded of her jealousy and gets angry with her friend for the first time since they have known each other, refusing to take Becky's hand. Becky is "somewhat abashed" at this unexpected behavior. "You don't love your husband," Amelia tells Becky. "Why did you come between my love and me? … His love was everything to me. You knew it, and wanted to rob me of it. For shame, Rebecca; bad and wicked woman— false friend and false wife" (VF 382). To this uncharacteristically honest and direct accusation, Amelia adds: "Have you done me no wrong, Rebecca? You did not succeed, but you tried. Ask your heart if you did not." Amelia asks Becky to consult her impartial spectator and judge her actions from the point of view of an informed and reasonable third party. Becky, who had been wondering whether Amelia knew about George's note and his intention to run away with her, concludes: "She knows nothing" (VF 383). Having established Amelia's ignorance, Becky is "touched in spite of herself," but on the whole she is unconcerned. "Rebecca was of a good-natured and obliging disposition; and she liked Amelia rather than otherwise. Even her hard words, reproachful as they were, were complimentary— the groans of a person stinging under defeat" (VF 384). After being abashed for just a moment at Amelia's anger, Becky congratulates herself on her triumph.

Smith states that the person who committed wrongs on the way to achieve his or her goals is haunted by the "avenging furies of shame and remorse" (TMS 110).

These painful sentiments ruin the happiness this person had hoped to attain by his misdeeds. He cannot forget his crimes and has the nagging sense that though in his ambition he really wanted "honor," he took the wrong way to get there. "While glory seems to surround him on all sides, he himself, in his own imagination, sees black and foul infamy fast pursuing him, and every moment ready to overtake him from behind" (TMS 110). If Becky is not troubled by any avenging furies of this kind, it is perhaps because she is not interested in virtue and honor but in what she calls "respectability," a trait entirely in the eye of the beholder as this chapter will explain. Without Amelia knowing about the note there is no evidence to prove that Becky's behavior has been anything less than proper. In her pursuit of respectability, Becky does not hesitate to use all means at her disposal and it is clear that to her mind, none of these means taint (the desirability of) her goal. She has no regard for the rules Amelia invokes other than for the sake of keeping up appearances – and then only for the benefit of those people she considers important.

The Vilest and Most Abject of All States

Smith writes: "The violator of the more sacred laws of justice can never reflect on the sentiments which mankind must entertain with regard to him, without feeling all the agonies of shame, and horror, and consternation" (TMS 127). Though this clearly does not apply to Becky, Jane Eyre is acutely aware of these sentiments. The Reeds, a group of partial spectators representing humankind in Jane Eyre's small world, make her feel miserable about her rage, no matter how justified in the eyes of the reader. A virtuously educated person, Smith argues, sympathizes with the "hatred and abhorrence" others feel toward him and changes his behavior because he does not want to hate and abhor himself. Realizing how we would judge ourselves if we were to look at our actions from the perspective modeled by the actual onlookers who express their horror at our conduct, we start to pity the person we hurt and we feel regret. We are haunted by the thought that we are a proper object of resentment, vengeance and punishment.

Jane has the good fortune to make friends and Lowood who with their sympathy restore her to herself, at least to a degree. But those of us who have violated what Smith calls "the more sacred laws of justice" cannot find solace in sympathy. They "dare not look society in the face" and so they seek solitude. But even that does not help them because when they are alone, they are haunted by their own thoughts. After a while they return to society to appear before their judges "as a supplicant," aware of their guilt. This is why remorse is "the most dreadful" of all the sentiments: it combines shame at the wrong we committed, grief for the way we have affected other people, pity for our victims, "and of the dread and terror of punishment from the consciousness of the justly provoked resentment of all rational creatures" (TMS 128). Even more ominously:

> These natural pangs of an affrighted conscience are the daemons, the avenging furies, which, in this life, haunt the guilty, which allow them neither quiet nor repose, which often drive them to despair and distraction, from which no assurance of secrecy can protect them, from which no principles of irreligion can entirely deliver them, and from which nothing can free them but the vilest and most abject of all states, a complete insensibility to honour and infamy, to vice and virtue (TMS 154).

As Becky's conscience is clear (or so the Manager of VF tells us) and she either has no daemons or is unbothered by them, she must be in what Smith here calls "the vilest and most abject of all states." And in a sense it is true that Becky is indifferent to honor and virtue on the one hand and infamy and vice on the other: she does not pursue the one or avoid the other out of a desire to be praiseworthy on Smith's definition of praiseworthiness. Becky judges how her various behaviors will be regarded by the spectators instrumental to her ambition and acts accordingly. If they praise her, she is contented and confirmed in her sense of the proper order of things. If they fail to praise her, they do not detract from her self-estimation and self-approbation.

Becky's confrontation with Amelia after George has marched off to war is paralleled much later in the story when the usually calm Lady Jane has finally had enough of her sister in law's behavior. After Rawdon has discovered Becky's affair with Lord Steyne and leaves her, Becky goes to Sir Pitt, Rawdon's brother, to ask him for help. Lady Jane, Sir Pitt's wife, is the one who unwittingly caused the discovery by bailing out Rawdon from the "spunge house" earlier than Becky had foreseen. Lady Jane, who has often felt herself bested by Becky and who sympathizes with Rawdon, does not want her husband to help Becky. Sir Pitt, who has always felt flattered by Becky's attention, suggests that his wife is doing Becky an injustice. To this, Lady Jane responds with uncharacteristic anger, saying she believes Becky "to be a wicked woman— a heartless mother, a false wife."

> She never loved her dear little boy, who used to fly here and tell me of her cruelty to him. She never came into a family but she strove to bring misery with her and to weaken the most sacred affections with her wicked flattery and falsehoods. She has deceived her husband, as she has deceived everybody; her soul is black with vanity, worldliness, and all sorts of crime. I tremble when I touch her. I keep my children out of her sight" (VF 696-7).

Lady Jane, usually silent and never boasting of her own qualities, adds:

> "I have been a true and faithful wife to you, Sir Pitt," Lady Jane continued, intrepidly; "I have kept my marriage vow as I made it to God and have been obedient and gentle as a wife should. But righteous obedience has its limits, and I declare that I will not bear that— that woman again under my roof; if she enters it, I and my children will leave it. She is not worthy to sit down with Christian people. You— you must choose, sir, between her and me" (VF 697).

Lady Jane shows that, unlike her husband, she has taken Becky's measure. And expressing her opinion of Becky in Becky's presence, she allows Becky the opportunity to see herself in the light a third person sees her. As Lady Jane's description of both Becky's intentions and her conduct are largely accurate, Becky on Smith's account should not be able to "bear the sight" of the picture Lady Jane paints of her. This is not how Lady Jane's speech affects Becky, however. After

Lady Jane departs, the narrator observes that Becky "was not hurt; nay, she was pleased. 'It was the diamond clasp you gave me,' she said to Sir Pitt" (VF 697). After hearing all Lady Jane's accusations, Becky does not try to defend herself or express regret about anything. All she does is observe to Sir Pitt that Lady Jane lashed out simply because of a piece of jewelry he had given Becky to complement the dress she wore when he presented her at court. With one simple sentence Becky dismisses Lady Jane's tirade as motivated not my moral rectitude but by envy.

The narrator of VF wonders if it ever struck Becky "that to have been honest and humble, to have done her duty, and to have marched straightforward on her way, would have brought her as near happiness as that path by which she was striving to attain it." But "if ever Becky had these thoughts," she was used to disregarding them.

> She eluded them and despised them—or at least she was committed to the other path from which retreat was now impossible. And for my part I believe that remorse is the least active of all a man's moral senses—the very easiest to be deadened when wakened, and in some never wakened at all. We grieve at being found out and at the idea of shame or punishment, but the mere sense of wrong makes very few people unhappy in Vanity Fair. (VF 534)

"The most dreadful" of all the sentiments to Smith is "the least active" in Vanity Fair. Jane Eyre's impartial spectator is very active – so active we may wonder about his impartiality. Her "sense of wrong" makes her unhappy but as we have seen we have reason to believe that the "man inside the breast" is not impartial because Jane has been surrounded by detractors her whole life. She has learned to look at herself through the eyes of people who dislike her and internalized this point of view. Becky, on the other hand, experiences only the faintest trace of remorse in her confrontation with Amelia, and no remorse at all at Lady Jane's harsh words. It appears that for a person to be impervious to remorse, they have to either have a very weak impartial spectator who is easily ignored or a strong impartial spectator who allows them to ignore the clamor from the partial spectators without. The narrator of VF appears to have in mind something like the former in the passage cited above, which suggests that remorse is not very active in VF because people ignore their "sense of wrong." They know they have done wrong but they do not care as long as they are not found out. Becky, too, is primarily concerned with being found out and is relieved when she realizes that Amelia knows nothing, and that Lady Jane can be dismissed with a comment about Sir Pitt's gift of jewelry. But more importantly, she does not appear to have the sense that she has done wrong. Is this because her impartial spectator is so weak that she can ignore its judgment, or because her impartial spectator is strong but differently constituted than the "divine spark" Smith describes in TMS? To answer this question, the desire "to be loved, and lovely" deserves closer attention as it is a requirement for the impartial spectator to develop.

To Be Loved, and Lovely

Living with her aunt Mrs. Reed and her cruel children, young Jane Eyre realizes that it is "useless to try to win anyone's favor" (Brontë 367) and that her attempts to live in harmony with those around her are bound to fail no matter how hard she tries. She knows herself to be a "heterogeneous thing" unable to evoke any "fellow-feeling" because of her difference from the Reed children: she calls herself an "uncongenial alien." It is not just her lowly status as an orphaned foster child but also her appearance that works against her. Jane overhears the servants saying that they could have sympathized with her had she been pretty "but one really cannot care for such a little toad as that" (Brontë 615).

"What so great happiness as to be loved," asks Smith, "and to know that we deserve to be loved? What so great misery as to be hated, and to know that we deserve to be hated?" Once she is at Lowood, the boarding school under direction of Mr. Brocklehurst, Jane makes her first friend, Helen. Jane tells her: "I should think well of myself; but that is not enough: if others don't love me, I would rather die than live – I cannot bear to be solitary and hated, Helen" (Brontë 1564). Jane explains that she cannot help but dislike the people who dislike her no matter how hard she tries to please them. Helen speaks of patience, love, forgetting wrongs – as a Christian, she believes that life is too short for animosity.[1]

Both Helen and the head teacher at Lowood, Miss Temple, help Jane cultivate her impartial spectator. Miss Temple allows Jane to defend herself against the unfair accusations from Mr. Brocklehurst who calls Jane a liar in front of the assembled students. Inspired by Helen, who warned Jane against "the indulgence of resentment," Jane knows she must take the opportunity provided her by Miss Temple to be "moderate" and "correct." Accordingly, her account to Miss Temple includes less "gall and wormwood than ordinary:" Jane tells Miss Temple in straightforward terms about the Reeds and the conversation between her aunt and Mr. Brocklehurst from which Jane emerged as a liar. "Thus restrained and simplified," her narrative "sounded more credible" (Brontë 1601). Invited by Miss Temple's kindness, Jane manages to adjust her pitch and tone down her emotions so that her interlocutor can enter into them. The promise of sympathy helps her exercise self-command.

Mutual sympathy can occur only when the actor tones down his or her emotions enough for the spectator to enter into them. These actor virtues are more difficult to achieve than the spectator virtues because they call for a high degree of self-command: in order to receive the spectator's sympathy, I have to recognize that he or she cannot (and likely does not want to) share in the full force of my emotions (Griswold 1999). The spectator virtues are, overall, easier than the actor virtues because they call on us to heighten our emotions. We cannot feel the actor's emotions first-hand, but with the help of the imagination and the pleasure we naturally take in the harmony of sentiments we can heighten our own emotions and so enter into the actor's situation. This is easier to do where it concerns pleasurable emotions than

[1] And a good thing, too, since she dies young.

painful ones because we naturally seek pleasure and avoid pain. Our desire to be loved is an important motivation to tone down our emotions when we are in pain. Chapter 7 painted a picture of Miss Crawley who never bothered to adjust the pitch of her fear and resentment, both because she never learned how and because her money insured feigned sympathy from her partial spectators no matter what she did. Miss Crawley models the opposite of the "majestic" bearing of grief Smith admires. When we exercise self-command under the most difficult circumstances and bear our grief majestically we can reach a harmony of sentiments with our spectators. "As to love our neighbour as we love ourselves is the great law of Christianity, so it is the great precept of nature to love ourselves only as we love our neighbour, or what comes to the same thing, as our neighbour is capable of loving us" (TMS 75).

In this passage Smith distinguishes between the "amiable" virtues belonging to the spectator and consisting in sensibility, delicacy, tenderness on the one hand and "the awful and respectable" virtues which require a "degree of self-command which astonishes by its amazing superiority over the most ungovernable passions of human nature" (TMS 75). Chapter 6 discussed the contrast Smith sees between the typically female virtues related to "humanity" and the male virtues of generosity and self-command and linked these virtues to the conduct literature of the late 18th and early nineteenth century (Gilbert and Gubar 1980, Armstrong 1990). Becky has almost perfected her self-command and we are reminded of the fact when she is called upon to give "a narrative of her own life" when she meets with Jos after years of estrangement. The contrast with Jane Eyre explaining herself to Miss Temple is clear: Becky, who has been living a life so vile that the narrator dares only to hint at its details, "began, forthwith, to tell her story – a tale so neat, simple, and artless that it was quite evident from hearing her that if ever there was a white-robed angel escaped from heaven to be subject to the infernal machinations and villainy of fiends here below, that spotless being – that unsullied martyr, was present on the bed before Jos – on the bed, sitting on the brandy bottle" (VF 834).

Becky exercises self-command and mimics authenticity, fooling Jos into once again believing her to be a perfect angel. In *Jane Eyre,* Miss Temple believes Jane's story and gives her a fresh start by clearing her name at Lowood. For once Jane's success is in proportion to her efforts and for the first time her desire to be seen and to be sympathized with has been fulfilled. She had never before experienced the serenity that results from sympathy. She even internalizes some of her friends' even-tempered qualities: "I had imbibed from [Miss Temple] something of her nature and much of her habits; more harmonious thoughts… better regulated feelings" (Brontë 1873). But Helen dies and Miss Temple eventually leaves Lowood to get married. Miss Temple's "refined propriety… precluded deviation into the ardent, the excited, the eager" and lowered the pitch of those emotions that according to Smith affect the impartiality of our judgment. Jane had "appeared a disciplined and subdued character" while in Miss Temple's presence but now that she is gone Jane becomes restless. She is gripped by a desire for liberty. She soon realizes that liberty is "too sweet" and unrealistic a goal but that a "new servitude" is attainable: "it is of no use wanting anything better" (Brontë 1912). She applies for a position as governess and finds employment at Thornfield where she meets her master and future lover Mr. Rochester.

Once she has learned to tone down her emotions so that her friends can "bring home" her case to themselves and "enter into" her situation, Jane experiences what it is like to be loved. But her ardent, eager nature is essentially unchanged even though she has learned to exercise self-command. On this point Jane and Becky resemble each other. But Jane's feelings of remorse and shame (as also apparent from her self-portrait in contrast with the portrait she made of Miss Blanche Ingram) show that her "impartial" spectator is differently constituted than Becky's, raising questions about the notion of impartiality. We have reason to believe that Jane's impartial spectator was severely warped by the partial spectators surrounding her in her childhood, while Becky's impartial spectator seems to be largely unconcerned with matters of morality other than for appearance's sake. Jane's impartial spectator bears significant resemblance to the entity Smith describes: a stern, masculine judge of propriety who reminds Jane of her place as a "governess, poor, disconnected and plain" (Brontë 3530). Becky's impartial spectator on the other hand is calculating, goal-oriented and above the fray of unproductive emotions like shame and remorse. This entity serves as her compass and points her in the direction most conducive to the fulfillment of her ambition.

While Jane wants nothing more than "to be loved, and lovely," Becky wants to be "respectable." Smith holds that we can consider ourselves "lovely," i.e. worthy of love, even when others do not love us. If we know that we did the right thing and have been true to the judgment of the "great inmate within the breast," we can withstand the negative judgments of others at least for a while. The more self-command we have and the stronger we are as a person, the more we will be able to bear negative judgments from partial spectators – as long as we know ourselves to be blameless and perhaps even praiseworthy. This is what forces Jane to leave Rochester when she finds out he already has a wife. Even though her passions pull her towards him, her sense of right and her self-command force her to leave. She knows that Rochester loves her, but that she would not be able to live with herself if she gave in to his desire: she would know herself to be unlovely, to have violated the sacred rules dictated by her impartial spectator. In Becky's desire for respectability, the distinction between the external and internal spectator's point of view collapses. On Becky's definition of respectability, one cannot consider oneself respectable without experiencing the respect of others. Respectability is in the eye of the beholder, that is to say, society. To be respected *is* to be respectable.

Becky Sharp Becomes Respectable

According to Smith, "Man naturally desires, not only to be loved, but to be lovely; or to be that thing which is the natural and proper object of love." But what is the natural and proper object of love? In the same passage from TMS, Smith writes that we desire "not only praise, but praiseworthiness" (TMS 151). The lovely, praiseworthy person is virtuous and enjoys the approval of the impartial spectator, the "man within the breast." We want to be sympathized with, to be appreciated for who we really are. Low self-esteem may cause us to adopt airs meant to make others think more highly of us than we secretly think is our due. Vanity leads us to focus on appearances that we think will gain us praise and love. Smith believes that concerned as we may be with appearances, we "naturally" "dread not just to be hated, but to be hateful, "or to be that thing which is the natural and proper object of hatred" (TMS 151). It follows from Smith's account of the impartial spectator that our "divine inmate" discerns the proper object of hatred as well as the proper object of love.

For those of us without properly developed impartial spectators, the dread of being hateful may be no more than an indefinable nagging sense that we are doing something wrong. George Osborne's conscience only plays up when he is about to leave for battle and realizes that he has wronged Amelia, but his remorse only lasts for a few hours; he hurries off to meet the rest of the regiment ashamed to have been delayed by his feelings for his wife. George's vanity is such that there is no room for impartial consideration of his feelings and motivations. For George, there appears to be little difference between the desire to be loved and the desire to be lovely because his whole life the partial spectators of his behavior have helped him believe that the two desires are one and the same thing. George rarely reflects on his feelings or his conduct, nor do his father or Jos Sedley who are alike caught up in their respective pride and vanity.

Becky does not appear to have the desire to be lovely in the sense of being virtuous. But "if she did not wish to lead a virtuous life, at least she desired to enjoy a character for virtue," the narrator tells us. "And we know that no lady in the genteel world can possess this desideratum, until she has put on a train and feathers and has been presented to her Sovereign at Court. From that august interview they come out stamped as honest women" (VF 598). Becky does not experience the desire to be lovely even though Smith describes it as "natural." What she wants is a good reputation, "a certificate of virtue," given out by the Lord Chamberlain on the occasion of a lady's presentation to the King. "And as dubious goods or letters are passed through an oven at quarantine, sprinkled with aromatic vinegar, and then pronounced clean, many a lady, whose reputation would be doubtful otherwise and liable to give infection, passes through the wholesome ordeal of the Royal presence and issues from it free from all taint" (VF 598).

We may have been slow to perceive it, the narrator observes, but "to be, and to be thought, a respectable woman was Becky's aim in life, and she got up the genteel with amazing assiduity, readiness, and success" (VF 600). Yet if Becky "did not wish to lead a virtuous life," how are we to understand her desire to be respectable? It appears that respectability is entirely in the eye of the beholder, a trait bestowed on the agent by his or her spectators and not related to inner qualities. This might be why "there were times when she believed herself to be a fine lady and forgot that there was no money in the chest at home— duns round the gate, tradesmen to coax and wheedle— no ground to walk upon, in a word" (VF 600). If to be considered respectable is the same as being respectable, Becky's forgetfulness is understandable.

On one of the rare occasions that Becky "forgets herself," she goes to Court adopting "a demeanour so grand, self-satisfied, deliberate, and imposing that it made even Lady Jane laugh. She walked into the royal apartments with a toss of the head which would have befitted an empress, and I have no doubt had she been one, she would have become the character perfectly" (VF 601). Everything depends on Becky's context and society. Smith might observe that had she been living "alone in a desolate island it might be a matter of doubt, perhaps, whether a palace, or a collection of such small conveniencies as are commonly contained in a tweezer-case, would contribute most to [her] happiness and enjoyment." But in London the spectator is everything. Smith observes: "If he is to live in society, indeed, there can be no comparison, because in this, as in all other cases, we constantly pay more regard to the sentiments of the spectator, than to those of the person principally concerned, and consider rather how his situation will appear to other people, than how it will appear to himself" (TMS 201). Becky's high self-esteem and her frustration with people who fail to acknowledge what she considers to be her true worth show that there is a discrepancy between how her situation appears to (some) others and the way she herself sees it. Her desire to appear (and hence to be) respectable aims to align the spectator's view with her own.

As in the case of wealth, we are interested in respectability because of our social, not because of our "necessitous animal nature." "If it was possible, therefore, that a person should grow up to manhood without any communication with society, his own actions might, notwithstanding, be agreeable or disagreeable to him on account of their tendency to his happiness or disadvantage." But "bring him into society, and all his own passions will immediately become the causes of new passions. He will observe that mankind approve of some of them, and are disgusted by others." We know from experience that people are more likely to sympathize "with our joy than with our sorrow, that we make parade of our riches, and conceal our poverty." This in turn fuels the ambition of people like the poor man's son who sees others parade their riches and aspires to become like them. Conversely "nothing is so mortifying as to be obliged to expose our distress to the view of the public." We hide our poverty because we feel that people cannot and do not sympathize with it the way they sympathize with our wealth and status. When our poverty is in plain view, "no mortal conceives for us the half of what we suffer." Because we desire love and sympathy, and know from experience that "the sentiments of mankind" run one way and not the other, "we pursue riches and avoid poverty" (TMS 99).[2]

Becky wants to be approved of, not because she doubts her self-worth and needs outside affirmation but because she believes that her proper place in the natural order of things is at the very top. She exposes her poverty selectively: to the new Sir

---

[2] In *Vanity Fair*, Mrs. Bute is keenly aware of how society regards poverty and starves herself and her daughters so that they may save money to spend on outward appearances. The narrator comments: "I know no sort of lying which is more frequent in Vanity Fair than this, and it may be remarked how people who practise it take credit to themselves for their hypocrisy, and fancy that they are exceedingly virtuous and praiseworthy, because they are able to deceive the world with regard to the extent of their means" (VF 499).

Pitt when he has inherited Queen's Crawley and all of Miss Crawley's fortune, and to Lord Steyne when she makes a tearful confession of her debts. These confessions are part of her strategy, however, and make her feel triumphant rather than mortified. To the general public, on the other hand, she appears as one of the most fashionably dressed and dashing socialites, even if many people wonder about the financial situation of Mrs. Rawdon Crawley's household. Though Becky takes great care of her appearance, stealing lace from the closets of the deceased Lady Crawleys for the dress that she wears to Court, she is never mortified at the exposure of her actual poverty. And despite her preoccupation with appearing (and hence, to Becky's mind, being) respectable, she does not experience shame when people suspect her of baseness. Instead, Becky meets slights and doubts with indifference or mockery.

Becky knows that she can win over most men, even after she has mortified their vanity on more than once occasion. George, Jos, and Sir Pitt are all examples of men who were at one point humiliated by Becky but later come to admire her once again. Becky engages their vanity and they forget her past offenses or come to see them in a different light (i.e. the light by which Becky wants them to see her and her past actions). But Becky's strategy, so effective with men, fails with women. Having been educated in the same "school" as Becky and having learned to perform, flatter, and observe the way Becky has, women tend not to trust Becky. They see an "artful minx" who has perfected the skills they themselves posses to an imperfect degree (VF 58). Becky's success does not endear her to them the way it does their husbands; it marks her as their enemy and rival. They understand that Becky's ambition is dangerous to them because it threatens the position and status they have worked so hard to achieve.

Welcomed by Gentlemen, Cut by Their Wives

In his *A Father's Legacy to his Daughters,* Dr. Gregory comments on female rivalry: "Another great obstacle to the sincerity as well as steadiness of your friendship, is the great clashing of your interests in the pursuits of love, ambition or vanity" (Gregory 54–55). The Manager of the Performance agrees with this observation: "Who has not seen how women bully women? What tortures have men to endure, comparable to those daily repeated shafts of scorn and cruelty with which poor women are riddled by the tyrants of their sex?" (VF 407) Dr. Gregory tells his daughters that because of the great clashing of interests, "it would appear … more eligible for you to contract your friendships with the men" (Gregory 55). Becky much more easily makes friends with men than with women (if she can be said to make friends at all). In fact, she appears to be one of those "ladies, who may be called men's women, being welcomed entirely by all the gentlemen and cut or slighted by all their wives" (VF 468).

Becky's husband Rawdon, at this point still unsuspecting of his wife's infidelity, is frustrated at the way Becky is slighted by the ladies of high society. Becky tells him "You can't shoot me into society," and reminds him of their position:

"Remember, my dear, that I was but a governess, and you, you poor silly old man, have the worst reputation for debt, and dice, and all sorts of wickedness. We shall get quite as many friends as we want by and by, and in the meanwhile you must be a good boy, and obey your schoolmistress in everything she tells you to do" (VF 470). There is no point in being angry about their lack of money and social status, Becky continues. All Aunt Crawley's money has gone to Rawdon's brother, Sir Pitt, but this means she and her husband need to take pains to befriend them. Becky lightheartedly observes: "If we are ruined, you can carve and take charge of the stable, and I can be a governess to Lady Jane's children. Ruined! fiddlede-dee! I will get you a good place before that; or Pitt and his little boy will die, and we will be Sir Rawdon and my lady." Status and rank depend on a combination of craftiness and good fortune and Becky has the former in spades. She tells Rawdon: "'While there is life, there is hope, my dear, and I intend to make a man of you yet. Who sold your horses for you? Who paid your debts for you?' Rawdon was obliged to confess that he owed all these benefits to his wife, and to trust himself to her guidance for the future" (VF 470).

Becky calls herself Rawdon's "schoolmistress" and tells him to be "a good boy" so she can "make a man" of him. She has gone a few steps beyond Dr. Gregory's prescription that his daughters "soften and polish" their future husbands' hearts and manners (Gregory 12). Becky good-naturedly (or so it appears) shows herself to be Rawdon's superior and once she enters society he becomes negligible, Mrs. Rawdon's husband. In the meantime, Becky's rise depends almost entirely on her "friendships" with men of rank who admire her and sometimes manage to convince their wives to invite Becky to their parties. But as Lord Steyne warned her, Becky, a penniless "earthenware pipkin" is in danger of being crushed by the wealthy "copper kettles" bobbing around in the same stream (VF 607).[3] These women of rank and fortune will not accept her, Lord Steyne predicted, on the contrary: the more Becky rises, the more the envy of other women will throw obstacles in her way. When Becky finally obtains an invitation to a party at Gaunt House, attended by the finest selection of copper kettles and their aristocratic husbands, she knows that she is safe as long as the men are around:

> But it was when the ladies were alone that Becky knew the tug of war would come. And then indeed the little woman found herself in such a situation as made her acknowledge the correctness of Lord Steyne's caution to her to beware of the society of ladies above her own sphere. As they say, the persons who hate Irishmen most are Irishmen; so, assuredly, the greatest tyrants over women are women. When poor little Becky, alone with the ladies, went up to the fire-place whither the great ladies had repaired, the great ladies marched away and took possession of a table of drawings (VF 618).

Like Rawdon, these great ladies' husbands are taken in by Becky's charm. But the more successful Becky is in charming their husbands, the more she suffers the wrath of the great ladies themselves. These ladies understand that status is a positional good and that for some to rise, others must fall. The attention Becky receives goes at the expense of the women who used to be the recipients of that admiration.

[3] See Chap. 4.

Dr. Gregory was right to point out that this stands in the way of friendship between women. Corrupted sympathy turns into vanity, and vanity demands that we be observed and praised. Praise, in turn, is worthless if it is extended to everyone equally.

Though Dr. Gregory and VF's narrator point to rivalry among women as particular to their sex, Smith regards the striving for rank as a universal flaw in human psychology. We have a strong "love of domination" that can lead us to put others down even when it is not to our economic advantage to do so. In his *Lectures on Jurisprudence,* Smith explains that though the slave owners' "real interest would lead them to set free their slaves and cultivate their lands by free servants or tenents, yet the love of domination and authority and the pleasure men take in having every done by their express orders, ... this love of domination and tyrannizing, I say, will make it impossible for the slaves in a free country ever to recover their liberty" (Lectures 179). Chapter 5 discussed the "desire of real superiority, of leading and directing" (TMS 326). What emerges is a picture of human psychology that shows the power of corrupted sympathy: when unrestrained by wisdom or virtue, our desire to receive approval expresses itself in the wish to enslave others. What better way to feel regarded and "seen" than to be at the top of the pyramid, even if the position is economically disadvantageous?

Lord Steyne, Becky's aristocratic "mentor" and admirer, has no illusions about high society and the inherent worth the masses attribute to it. His relationship to Becky, and the contrast he provides with Rawdon, help frame Smith's pessimistic observations about the human desire to dominate and the applicability of these observations to the struggle for rank between women.

The Desire for Superiority

Becky meets with several personages who, like Rawdon's aunt Miss Crawley, enjoy Becky's wit and sarcasm at the expense of others while they accept Becky's attention and flattery as their due. Notable among them is Lord Steyne with whom Becky has a special understanding. Like Miss Crawley, Lord Steyne recognizes Becky's self-conscious mimicry: he knows that she is acting the part of the innocent, dutiful wife, the charming society lady, the "artless" object of the admiration of young officers who come over to play cards with Rawdon. We first encounter Lord Steyne "very late one night, as a party of gentlemen were seated round her crackling drawing-room fire (for the men came to her house to finish the night; and she had ice and coffee for them, the best in London)." Becky appears to be addressing Rawdon when she says: "I must have a sheep-dog," meaning she needs a lady companion who would enable her to move more freely. But in reality the comment is directed at Lord Steyne; Rawdon is playing cards and has no idea what she is talking about. "And so the shepherd is not enough," says Lord Steyne, talking about Rawdon, "to defend his lambkin?" "The shepherd is too fond of playing at cards and going to his clubs," answered Becky, laughing (VF 472).

Rawdon, once a proud dragoon, has been reduced to "Mrs. Crawley's husband" (VF 475). Lord Steyne is in the interesting position of feeling both flattered by Becky's attention (and hurt when she appears to withdraw it) and seeing through her performance of innocence and angelic womanhood. He sees her play the part of the dutiful wife to Rawdon while she makes it perfectly clear to Steyne that it is all just an act: she and Steyne are in on the joke together. Like Miss Crawley before him, Steyne is aware of Becky's powers and sees how she uses them to ridicule others, but he either represses the knowledge that he could himself one day become the butt of the joke or he feels that his position will always protect him against any such eventuality.

Among the men of VF, Dobbin provides the starkest contrast with Steyne. Like Steyne, Dobbin recognizes Becky's playacting for what it is but unlike Steyne, he is not enthralled by her art. When Becky is distracting George's (and everyone else's) attention from Amelia at the opera in Brussels, Dobbin says: "What a humbug that woman is!" Speaking to George, he adds: "She writhes and twists about like a snake. All the time she was here, didn't you see, George, how she was acting at the General over the way?" (VF 352).

To Dobbin, Becky is a dangerous siren, a deceitful, playacting serpent. Concerned with Amelia's well-being, he sees Becky's dangerous power over George, Amelia's husband. But though he does not admire her "arts," he recognizes them for what they are and witnesses their effects on the men she seeks to ensorcell. Dobbin sees the danger but does not share in the fascination. So among the men in Vanity Fair there is Dobbin, not vain, aware of Becky's powers and afraid of them for Amelia's sake; there is George, too vain to recognize Becky's act and to realize he is being played; and then there is Lord Steyne, also very vain and flattered by Becky's attentions yet aware of her powers. Of all the male inhabitants of VF, most fall into the same category as George and they make up the bulk of her admirers, flocking around her in Brussels, Paris, and London. Sooner or later, the wives of these men come to fear or resent Becky: as described earlier in this chapter, Amelia finally gives vent to her anger after the Brussels ball, and gentle Lady Jane eventually forces her husband to choose between her and Becky.

Becky's joyful ambition to "work" the machinery of society takes on another aspect here as it becomes clear that she knows that in order for her to climb, others must fall. In his *Lectures,* Smith claims that "every one" has "the naturall inclination … to persuade … even when the matter is of no consequence to them" (Lectures 306). Becky's "desire of real superiority, of leading and directing" is so great that, like the slave owners Smith discusses, she is willing to sacrifice her "real interests" in order to fulfill it. She might, for example, have benefited from Miss Crawley's fortune had she not shown the rich lady the full extent of her powers of mimicry and mockery. Had Becky refrained from mocking the rich and powerful Lady Bareacres when she was trying to flee Brussels, she would not have had to contend with her animosity once they were both back in London. In both cases Becky sacrificed her economic interests to her desire to humiliate ladies of rank.

Becky purposively charms all men from whom she stands to gain something, much to the dismay of the women who witness her act. Amelia shares neither

Becky's ambition nor her mercenary way of thinking but she has a similar effect on the men around her: "wherever she went she touched and charmed every one of the male sex," but unlike Becky she "invariably … awakened the scorn and incredulity of her own sisterhood." While Becky inspires envy, resentment and even fear, Amelia invites scorn. The narrator comments: "I think it was her weakness which was her principal charm" and, the readers of VF infer, the principal reason other women scorned her. Amelia has "a kind of sweet submission and softness, which seemed to appeal to each man she met for his sympathy and protection" (VF 489).[4] To these men, Dobbin first among them, Amelia represents quintessential womanhood – the kind of modest, mild softness that Becky successfully mimics but does not in fact possess. It can hardly be a coincidence that other women, aware of the angelic, childlike ideal and how it appears to be embodied in Amelia, find it difficult to respect these traits in another member of the "sisterhood."

The narrator confirms: "it IS the pretty face which creates sympathy in the hearts of men, those wicked rogues" (VF 491). No matter how hard a woman tries to conduct herself in accordance with the rules laid out by Dr. Gregory and his fellow authors, no degree of play-acting can compete with an appearance that promises the soft, weak, sweetness that attracts the "capricious" love of a man. As the narrator puts it:

> A woman may possess the wisdom and chastity of Minerva, and we give no heed to her, if she has a plain face. What folly will not a pair of bright eyes make pardonable? What dullness may not red lips and sweet accents render pleasant? And so, with their usual sense of justice, ladies argue that because a woman is handsome, therefore she is a fool. O ladies, ladies! there are some of you who are neither handsome nor wise (VF 491).

Again we find the opposition between men's and women's judgment on women, and it is clear that neither judgment is particularly fair. While men are likely to rate a pretty woman higher than she deserves (were all her traits taken into account), women tend to correlate beauty with stupidity – and, it appears, plainness with intelligence. Major Dobbin exemplifies this male tendency when he falls in love with Amelia the moment he sees her descend a staircase, singing. Her appearance that day set the tone for all his future judgments about her and as a result it was "very likely" that "Amelia was not like the portrait the Major had formed of her;

> there was a figure in a book of fashions which his sisters had in England, and with which William had made away privately, pasting it into the lid of his desk, and fancying he saw some resemblance to Mrs. Osborne in the print, whereas I have seen it, and can vouch that it is but the picture of a high-waisted gown with an impossible doll's face simpering over it— and, perhaps, Mr. Dobbin's sentimental Amelia was no more like the real one than this absurd little print which he cherished. But what man in love, of us, is better informed? (VF 549)

[4] The narrator himself, however, appears to more often share in Becky's scorn than in the men's admiration. Judith Law Fisher observes: "She purifies men by her very weakness … but her total vulnerability makes the Manager of the Performance impatient, even derisive at times" (Fisher 1985, 408).

Dobbin places Amelia on a pedestal and enslaves himself to her.[5] Becky establishes her superiority over Rawdon in a different way: she, too, relies on her looks and conduct (especially early on in their acquaintance) but also explicitly states her position as slave master/schoolmistress. Becky and Amelia both have many male admirers besides their husbands and are singled out as superior among women, though when they are together, Becky always wins in terms both of the number and the status of the men she manages to fascinate.

Against this backdrop it is of interest to consider Smith's claim in TMS that "the respect of *our equals*, our credit and rank in the society we live in" are of major importance to us (183, emphasis added). "The desire of becoming the proper objects of this respect, of deserving and obtaining this credit and rank *among our equals*, is, perhaps, the strongest of all our desires, and our anxiety to obtain the advantages of fortune is accordingly much more excited and irritated by this desire, than by that of supplying all the necessities and conveniencies of the body, which are always very easily supplied" (TMS 226, emphasis added). This passage was cited in Chap. 6 to emphasize the importance of status over "necessities and conveniencies" but here serves to highlight Smith's belief that the opinion of our equals is very important to us. We want to become the "proper" objects of the respect of our equals and we want to be deserving of it. Smith holds that anyone not completely lost to virtue and wisdom will prefer praiseworthiness to mere praise and posits that our equals most effectively bring out this desire: "Our rank and credit among our equals, too, depend very much upon, what, perhaps, a virtuous man would wish them to depend entirely, our character and conduct, or upon the confidence, esteem, and good-will, which these naturally excite in the people we live with" (TMS 226).

Becky and Amelia are respectively resented and scorned by their equals. How does this reflect on their character and conduct? They appear to "naturally excite" in their fellow women not esteem but these less flattering sentiments. Furthermore, though Becky desires respectability, she seeks to obtain it not among or from her equals but from the ranks above her. And even Amelia, whose vanity is invested entirely first in her husband and later in little Georgie and who seeks no social status for herself, meets with no goodwill from her equals except from a few maternal women like Mrs. O'Dowd. Smith holds that both real virtue and the corresponding real esteem are to be found in horizontal relationships among equals. But women evaluate Becky and Amelia based on their success with men. They do not care about Amelia's "real character" (whatever that may be) but about the fact that men fawn over her. The women around her do not inspire in Amelia wisdom or virtue but, it appears, only passivity. In Becky, the judgment of her equals fans the flames of her ambition, but not a desire to improve her moral character.

[5] Micael M. Clarke observes: "The most important reason for Amelia's hero worship, however, is Dobbin's insistence on the triple fiction that George had loved Amelia, that he had been a good and faithful husband, and that Amelia is too pure and innocent to know otherwise. These fictions satisfy Dobbin's need to idealize Amelia as an angelic, nonsexual being. To admit to an erotic component in her nature or in their relationship would render her unworthy of his love" (Clarke 1995, 109).

Becky's Triumph, Rawdon's Fear, and Lady Jane's Sympathy

After the "tug of war" in the drawing room where she is pointedly ignored by the great ladies, Becky gets her revenge. The men return and "whatever the previous portion of the evening had been, the rest of that night was a great triumph for Becky." She sings at the piano and all the men crowd round her; "the women, her enemies, were left quite alone" (VF 620). Lord Steyne, her greatest admirer and the party's host, applauds loudest of all. Becky accepts the flowers he throws at her, pressing them "to her heart with the air of a consummate comedian." All men are enraptured by Becky's performance and "Lord Steyne was frantic with delight" at the harmony of sentiments between his guests and himself. We know from Smith that joyful sentiments are pleasurable and that we rejoice in sharing these feelings when there is no envy. Unlike the great ladies present at the party, Lord Steyne's male guests are not envious of Becky – if they feel any envy, it is directed at the men who receive attention from her. The other women who participated in the charade have been "quite eclipsed" by Becky's brilliant performance. "All voices were for her" and the men agree "with good reason, very likely, that had she been an actress none on the stage could have surpassed her" (VF 652).

This particular bit of praise, "had she been an actress," shows the naiveté of the men's estimation of Becky's powers. We know her to *be* an actress, one so adept at her art that she can take on roles onstage in addition to the roles she plays offstage. Becky rejoices in her victory and she sees "fortune, fame, fashion before her. Lord Steyne was her slave, followed her everywhere, and scarcely spoke to any one in the room beside, and paid her the most marked compliments and attention" Not only are the "trinkets" marking the life of the great and powerful now within her reach, she also (and more importantly) has established her dominance in enslaving a great peer, Lord Steyne. In gaining his submission she has established her position at the top of the power pyramid. Becky makes the other women feel their defeat: "She passed by Lady Stunnington with a look of scorn. She patronized Lady Gaunt and her astonished and mortified sister-in-law— she *écrasé*'d all rival charmers" (VF 653). At supper she is placed at the same table as his Royal Highness and is "served on gold plate. She might have had pearls melted into her champagne if she liked— another Cleopatra." Meanwhile, "the ladies at the other tables, who supped off mere silver and marked Lord Steyne's constant attention to her, vowed it was a monstrous infatuation, a gross insult to ladies of rank. If sarcasm could have killed, Lady Stunnington would have slain her on the spot" (VF 653). Becky's ambition, art, and self-command have propelled her into the highest strata of society and she has taken her seat at the table.

Rawdon, once a proud military man ordering everyone about and thinking himself lucky for having found sweet Becky as a wife to run his household and manage his affairs, "was scared at these triumphs. They seemed to separate his wife farther than ever from him somehow. He thought with a feeling very like pain how immeasurably she was his superior" (VF 653). He is not among the men who are in ecstasy at her performance because he himself is becoming a mere afterthought:

Mrs. Rawdon Crawley's husband. Rawdon does not participate in her success but is the victim of it. In the last act of the charade for which Becky receives so much praise Rawdon plays the part of Agamemnon, murdered by his faithless wife Clytemnestra, played by Becky.[6] Becky does not regard him as her husband but "as her errand-man and humble slave." She no longer cares about his feelings, putting on a smile for his comfort as she used to do when she still needed him. When Rawdon is "depressed or sulky" Becky only sneers at his demeanor. "She was busy thinking about her position, or her pleasures, or her advancement in society; she ought to have held a great place in it, that is certain" (VF 659).

While Rawdon and Becky are growing further apart, Rawdon and Lady Jane (his brother Sir Pitt's wife) develop a certain affinity for each other because of Rawdon's love for his son. Both Rawdon and Rawdon Junior become frequent guests at Sir Pitt's and Lady Jane's home while Becky is working on her career. A pivotal moment in the relationship between the in-laws occurs when little Rawdon, kissed by Becky in a public performance of motherly affection, looks her "full in the face after the operation, trembling and turning very red, as his wont was when moved. 'You never kiss me at home, Mamma,' he said, at which there was a general silence and consternation and a by no means pleasant look in Becky's eyes" (VF 572). Becky has perfected her own persona but fails to effectively manage her child. While Becky's lack of motherly feelings estranges her from Lady Jane, Rawdon's genuine affection for his son endears him to her. He wins "her sincere regard" by showing in her presence the feelings "which he could not show to his own wife." In this way Lady Jane, because of the sincerity of her feelings and her appreciation of Rawdon's heartfelt love for his son, comes between Rawdon and Becky. Becky does not care about the estrangement. As the narrator observes, she "did not miss him or anybody" (VF 659).

Becky and Lady Jane avoid each other. Becky despises "Jane's feelings and softness; the other's kindly and gentle nature could not but revolt at her sister's callous behaviour" (VF 659). Becky feels scorn for Lady Jane's "goodness and simplicity," the same sentiment the narrator claims women commonly feel for Amelia. Lady Jane in turn feels uncomfortable in Becky's presence.

> Her husband talked constantly with Becky. Signs of intelligence seemed to pass between them, and Pitt spoke with her on subjects on which he never thought of discoursing with Lady Jane. The latter did not understand them, to be sure, but it was mortifying to remain silent; still more mortifying to know that you had nothing to say, and hear that little audacious Mrs. Rawdon dashing on from subject to subject, with a word for every man, and a joke always pat; and to sit in one's own house alone, by the fireside, and watching all the men round your rival (VF 575).

---

[6] The narrator does not comment on the significance of Becky's identification with Clytemnestra, presumably because the reader can form her own opinion of Becky's frighteningly admirable performance of this part. As Maria Dibattista points out, it is a significant and dark twist on Becky's often "comic" rise to power. "The scandalous identification of Becky... with the heroic figure of the most majestic female dissembler in the chronicles of myth and history marks the culmination of Becky's career in the world of vanity" (Dibattista 1980, 827).

Yet Becky cannot simply dismiss Lady Jane who, as her sister-in-law, has a unique insight into Becky's personal life. Lady Jane sees and knows too much and Becky's successes with the men that surround her do nothing to prevent Lady Jane from obtaining information that Becky would rather keep secret, especially about her relationship (or lack thereof) to Rawdon Junior. Becky knows that to be seen as a bad mother is a difficult judgment to overcome in other women. Lady Jane's "gentle thoughts and simple pleasures" annoy Becky, as when she finds her sister-in-law reading to and playing with the children. These seemingly innocent enjoyments are "odious" to Becky: "they discorded with her; she hated people for liking them; she spurned children and children-lovers" (VF 576). This is strong language for so harmless an interest, especially for Becky who tends to get angry only when she feels others are not treating her with the respect she deserves. And even then she hides her anger and uses it to fuel her ambition to win and gain her rightful position in society. Why this hatred for Lady Jane and her simple pursuits – a hatred Becky does not even care to fully hide from her sister-in-law?

Becky performs caricatures of Lady Jane for Lord Steyne, saying: "I have no taste for bread and butter" … "No more has a certain person for holy water," his lordship replied with a bow and a grin and a great jarring laugh afterwards (VF 576). Lord Steyne knows that Becky is a consummate actress and manager and this is not the only occasion on which he compares her to the devil.[7] Lord Steyne knows that Becky is not a good wife or mother; that, in short, she is not a good woman – not, at least, by common standards. Becky knows this, too. Lady Jane annoys Becky because she not only knows that Becky does not love her son but she also sincerely sympathizes with Rawdon Junior and Senior. Becky does not envy Lady Jane her capacity for sympathy but recognizes in her an attitude diametrically opposed to her own. Lady Jane fears Becky and is mortified at Sir Pitt's interest in her, but she does not share Becky's ambition. Lady Jane is happiest at home, playing with the children and sharing her innocent and sincere joy with like-minded people like Rawdon Senior. This sets Lady Jane apart from the women who jockey for place with Becky: Lady Jane genuinely cares more for her own son, and even for little Rawdon, than she does for a higher place in society. Lady Jane exemplifies Smith's observation that "except the frivolous pleasures of vanity and superiority, we may find, in the most humble station, where there is only personal liberty, every other which the most exalted can afford; and the pleasures of vanity and superiority are seldom consistent with perfect tranquillity, the principle and foundation of all real and satisfactory enjoyment" (TMS 175).

As she is married to a Baronet, Lady Jane's situation is by no means "the most humble." But she does find "real and satisfactory enjoyment" in her quiet domestic life, rather fearing the "glittering and exalted" occasions at which Becky tends to shine (TMS 175). Smith here argues that as long as we have "personal liberty," "real happiness" is at all times within our reach. We know from Smith's account of mutual sympathy that this happiness lies in the harmony of sentiments between others and ourselves. Becky achieves this harmony only in situations where her own sense of

[7] See Introduction, "Devil, actress, manager."

triumph is reflected in the praise of her admirers. Lady Jane's love for children makes for a very different kind of dynamic as (on Smith's account) parents are expected to love their children more than their children love them. We commonly expect parents to be a bit indulgent in the love for their children and consider a degree of coolness in a mother's or father's attitude strange and unnatural. But when children are too ostentatious in their grief at a parent's death, we are apt to get suspicious (TMS 168–9). We know that the love flowing from the older to the younger generation is naturally stronger than the current going the other way.[8]

Lady Jane's natural motherly love for her son and her nephew Rawdon Jr. is not a sentiment Becky can work with or exploit for her own purposes. There is no vanity in Lady Jane's love for children, nor is there any vanity in her sympathy for Rawdon. Lady Jane's affection for her brother-in-law and her nephew is genuine and makes Becky stand out as a fake by contrast. Very few people are aware of this contrast – it is likely that nobody besides Rawdon and Lady Jane sees the difference – but it enrages Becky not to be able to control the situation. She is powerless in the face of genuine affection, a very rare sentiment in VF.

Becky Sharp the Industrious Knave

Her lack of sympathy in general and her lack of motherly and wifely affection in particular make Becky false, unnatural, and even devilish. She acts the part, but the close observer notes that for all the effort she puts into the performance, Becky is relying on an act to achieve goals that have little to do with love, motherhood, or marital bliss. Smith wants to believe that virtue usually meets with its proper reward, claiming that "it requires a very extraordinary concurrence of circumstances entirely to disappoint" the expectation of success. But there is "virtue" in its full moral sense, i.e. a character trait that makes the bearer a good person, and "virtue" in the narrow sense of a trait that is good only if certain conditions are met. Smith states that nature encourages "industry, prudence, and circumspection" by rewarding it with "success in every sort of business." Smith asks: "Is it possible that in the whole of life these virtues should fail of attaining it?" Wealth and "external honours" are the proper reward for hard work and one who leads a life of industry rarely fails to acquire this "recompense" (TMS 188). But Smith also recognizes that "industry, prudence, and circumspection" can be used in the pursuit of any goals, no matter their moral worth. Hard work, diligence and caution can make a successful criminal. Industry, prudence and circumspection are truly virtuous only if these traits belong to a person who is also honest, magnanimous, generous, and humane. We commonly abhor the perpetrators of "fraud, falsehood, brutality, and violence" and are indignant when they reap the benefits of their immoral pursuits. But the fact remains that they

[8] Some kinds of affections are more natural than others: Piety to one's parents is looked at as too ostentatious and "the ostentatious sorrow of widows has, for a like reason, been suspected of insincerity" (TMS 169).

worked hard for these benefits even if their goals were blameworthy. Our "natural sentiments" rebel against the criminal's success but judging him or her on effort alone we cannot deny that they worked hard for it.

Becky is not, by Lady Jane's or Smith's standards, a good person. Her industry, prudence and circumspection are virtuous only in the narrow, qualified sense. This makes her what Smith calls an "industrious knave." Contrasting this figure with an otherwise morally good person who lacks the work ethic that marks people like Becky, Smith asks: "The industrious knave cultivates the soil; the indolent good man leaves it uncultivated. Who ought to reap the harvest?" Smith answers his own question: "The natural course of things decides it in favour of the knave: the natural sentiments of mankind in favour of the man of virtue" (TMS 189). And yet it is Nature that directs us "to correct, in some measure, that distribution of things which she herself would otherwise have made." Nature favors the industrious knave but also relies on the knave's virtuous peers to "correct" him. But what might this correction entail? Does Smith suggest that the virtuous help the knave to become a better person, and if so, what might this help look like? Does it consist in persuasion or imprisonment, fines and other punishments? Smith does not specify in the context of the passage dealing with the industrious knave. He only adds in a sweeping statement that both Nature and the "natural sentiments of man are calculated to promote the same great end, the order of the world, and the perfection and happiness of human nature" (TMS 190).

Further complicating the issue of Becky's "virtue" and her just deserts is Smith's claim that "no action can properly be called virtuous, which is not accompanied with the sentiment of self-approbation." It of course does not follow that all actions that are accompanied by self-approbation are therefore virtuous. But as Smith holds that true self-approbation depends on the impartial spectator and the impartial spectator's judgment is the highest tribunal the individual can know and follow, his statement does suggest that self-approbation is at least an indicator of virtuous behavior. Smith gives the example of a Quaker who, instead of turning the other cheek like his religion dictates, punches his assailant. This reaction, Smith suggests, may make us *like* the Quaker more but it makes us *esteem* him less because he did not act "from a just sense of what was proper to be done" (TMS 198). The Quaker violated the rules he set for himself and so presumably cannot approve of his own behavior. This anecdote shows that Smith believes it is important for us to act in accordance with our own rules, not only because it will increase our self-estimation but also because it will gain us the esteem of third party spectators.

Becky consistently acts in accordance with the principles she set for herself and so gains the admiration of VF's readers even if her story also makes us uncomfortable. Her system of conduct is coherent but in its execution threatens the moral rules Smith derives from the impartial spectator as he describes the entity. Becky is an industrious knave and she reaps the rewards of her efforts while she leaves the people around her to wonder how she can or should be "corrected."

References

Armstrong, Nancy. 1990. *Desire and domestic fiction: A political history of the novel*. Cary: Oxford University Press.

Brontë, Charlotte. 2016. *Jane Eyre*. Kindle Edition. New York: W.W. Norton.

Clarke, Micael M. 1995. *Thackeray and women*. Dekalb: Northern Illinois UP.

Dibattista, Maria. 1980. The Triumph of Clytemnestra: The Charades in Vanity Fair. *PMLA* 95 (5): 827–837.

Gilbert, Sandra M., and Susan Gubar. 1980. *The Madwoman in the attic: The woman writer and the nineteenth-century literary imagination*. New Haven: Yale University Press.

Fisher, Judith Law. 1985. Siren and Artist: Contradiction in Thackeray's Aesthetic Ideal. *Nineteenth-Century Fiction* 39 (4): 392–419.

Griswold, Charles. 1999. *Adam Smith and the Virtues of Enlightenment*. Cambridge: Cambridge University Press.

Smith, Adam. 1981. An inquiry into the nature and causes of the wealth of nations. In *Vol. 2 of the Glasgow Edition of the Works and Correspondence of Adam Smith*, ed. R. H. Campbell and A. S. Skinner. Indianapolis: Liberty Fund.

———. 1982a. The theory of moral sentiments. In *Vol. 1 of the Glasgow Edition of the Works and Correspondence of Adam Smith*, ed. D.D. Raphael and A.L. Macfie. Indianapolis: Liberty Fund.

———. 1982b. Lectures on Jurisprudence. In *Vol. 5 of the Glasgow Edition of the Works and Correspondence of Adam Smith*, ed. R.L. Meek, D.D. Raphael, and P.G. Stein. Indianapolis: Liberty Fund.

Thackeray, William Makepeace. 1983. In *Vanity fair: A novel without a hero*, ed. John Sutherland. New York: Oxford UP.

Chapter 9
Conclusion

Abstract We know that Becky Sharp is hardly morally praiseworthy, yet we root for her as her story unfolds. We sympathize with this anti-heroine who embodies some of the traits we fear in real-life others but would like for ourselves – at least to a degree. If we were more like Becky, we would not only be in a position to more effectively better our condition but we would also have much more fun in the process. If Becky is a heroine, then not in the way Smith appears to have in mind when he writes about the "heroes of tragedy and romance." We admire Becky not because she learns a moral lesson or exemplifies a particular virtue, but because of her irrepressible vivacity, resilience, joy and ruthlessness. Our readerly admiration for Becky the protagonist contrasts with the envy and hostility she inspires in the female population of VF. While we enjoy seeing Becky rise, her rivals in VF naturally resent her success. This concluding chapter discusses why we want Becky to win and why we are attracted to this deeply ambiguous role model.

We Want (Becky) to Win

There is no greater pleasure than (public) admiration, which is why most of us are susceptible to vanity: we seek to gain this admiration for ourselves using whatever means society holds up as most effective. The publicly admired person inspires both emulation and more admiration. In a snow balling effect, the more somebody is admired, the more people will take note of this person and their "system of happiness," and the more their relative status will increase. It is the "disposition of mankind to go along with all the passions of the rich and the powerful." Thus, Smith argues, the order of society is preserved:

> Our obsequiousness to our superiors more frequently arises from our admiration for the advantages of their situation, than from any private expectations of benefit from their good-will. Their benefits can extend but to a few, but their fortunes interest almost every body. We are eager to assist them in completing a system of happiness that approaches so near to perfection. (TMS 101; first quoted in Chapter 3)

R. Slegers, *Adam Smith's Moral Sentiments in Vanity Fair*, Issues in Business Ethics 49, https://doi.org/10.1007/978-3-319-98731-6_9

Chapter 5 discussed Smith's claim that we sympathize with the rich and powerful because we imagine ourselves in their position. We would like to be like them and, bringing their situation home to ourselves, we "go along with" their passions and want to contribute to their "system of happiness." It is an interesting feature of our moral psychology that we both want to be like the people we admire and preserve and increase their happiness because we sympathize with them. "Changing places in fancy" with the rich and famous, we imagine what it would be like to be them. We wish them the very best because we would want the best for ourselves in their position. This dynamic helps explain our response as readers to Becky Sharp.

Most of us bear a greater resemblance to the poor man's son than to Becky. Like the poor man's son, we wonder at the "conveniencies" of the rich and the clever "machines" of all kinds that make their life pleasant. We are aware of the great distance that separates them from us and yet we want to preserve their "system of happiness" because we enter into it through sympathy. But as we know from Smith's account in TMS, the poor man's son never achieves the happiness he imagines is part of the lifestyle he seeks to emulate. His ambition drives him to toil his entire life just to find that it was all vanity. In this he differs from Becky who derives enjoyment from the operation of the society machine. She takes pleasure in the "toil and bustle" of her art: her ability to manipulate and perform. Furthermore, Becky is exactly the kind of person with "spirit and ambition" who sees opportunities at times of dissent and confusion. And as we saw in Chap. 6, it is at these times that someone like Becky, who combines ambition with great skill and iron self-command, can be "exceedingly dangerous." Admiration for the rich and powerful generally preserves the order of society and motivates ambitious people like the poor man's son to submit to a life of relentless toil. But the "system of happiness" ascribed to the rich and powerful inspires in ambitious Becky both the desire to build a system of her own (not only in her imagination but in reality) and to disrupt it for others.

If Becky is a heroine, then not in the way Smith appears to have in mind when he writes about the "heroes of tragedy and romance." The tragedies Smith references in TMS allow the spectators to deepen their moral understanding in line with the judgments of Smith's impartial spectator.[1] We might admire Smith's heroes and sympathize with them, but these sentiments are of a different nature than the ones Becky inspires in us. We admire Becky not because she learns a moral lesson or exemplifies a particular virtue, but because of her irrepressible vivacity, resilience, and joy. Yet the way Becky's vivacity finds expression is hardly morally neutral, let alone morally praiseworthy – at least by conventional standards. The previous chapters include numerous examples of Becky's "love of dominion and authority," her joy at besting others, her taste for revenge and her delight in mockery and humiliation. Becky has a light touch and quickly and easily moves on after receiving slights and insults which would leave most of us mortified. Her conscience, as the narrator puts it, is clear – she is not haunted by the "avenging furies of shame and remorse"

[1] See, for example, Jean Racine's *Phèdre* (which allows us to "enter into" the feeling of remorse); Voltaire's *Mahomet* (which shows the dangers of religious fanaticism); and *L'Orphelin de la Chine* (offering the spectator insights into ambition, love, and character) (TMS 83, 198, 238).

that Smith claims are the inevitable and just desert of the immoral (TMS 110). Becky is an "industrious knave" and we like her the better for it (TMS 189).

Becky's story therefore resonates with us on a few different levels. We recognize how the people around Becky fawn over the wealthy and readily make great personal sacrifices to gain rank and status. We also see Becky use people's vanity to gain power, wealth and position for herself. And though we know Becky to be less than morally praiseworthy, we are rooting for her, wishing her to perfect her own "system of happiness." "Changing positions in fancy" with Becky, we want her to do well because we sympathize with this anti-heroine who embodies some of the traits we fear in others but would like for ourselves – at least to a degree. If we were more like Becky, we would not only be in a position to more effectively "better our condition" but we would also have much more fun in the process.

The Pursuit of Fashion under Difficulties & the Joy of Dominion

The pleasure Becky takes in embarrassing the great, even when it is not in her financial (i.e. "real") interest to do so, shows her to be a very different creature from the poor man's son and anyone else simply striving to be like their social superiors. Before Becky sells her horses to Jos Sedley for an astronomical amount, allowing him to flee Brussels in fear of the French army, she pretends to entertain an offer from Lady Bareacres who up to that point has consistently cut Becky and spoken ill of her. Never intending to sell her the horses, Becky makes the great Lady beg her to strike a deal only to have the opportunity to refuse her. After this humiliation,

> Rebecca had the pleasure of seeing her Ladyship in the horseless carriage, and keeping her eyes fixed upon her, and bewailing, in the loudest tone of voice, the Countess's perplexities. "Not to be able to get horses!" she said, "and to have all those diamonds sewed into the carriage cushions! What a prize it will be for the French when they come!— the carriage and the diamonds, I mean; not the lady!" She gave this information to the landlord, to the servants, to the guests, and the innumerable stragglers about the courtyard (VF 394).

When Becky enjoys her greatest triumphs many years later in London, she again meets Lady Bareacres. Not only has Lady Bareacres been forced by Lord Steyne to invite Becky into her own home only to be outshone by the upstart, she also has to endure Becky's public reminder of the lady's past humiliation:

> "I had the pleasure of making your Ladyship's acquaintance at Brussels, ten years ago," Becky said in the most winning manner. "I had the good fortune to meet Lady Bareacres at the Duchess of Richmond's ball, the night before the Battle of Waterloo. And I recollect your Ladyship, and my Lady Blanche, your daughter, sitting in the carriage in the *porte-cochère* at the Inn, waiting for horses. I hope your Ladyship's diamonds are safe." (VF 617)

Becky is eating off golden plates in the company of the king while Lady Bareacres and her ilk are left to fume at their defeat and eat off inferior silver plates. This, it appears, is Becky's greatest accomplishment: her enemies have been defeated and she has reached the top of the power pyramid. The narrator claims that "the world of female fashion and its customs" is full of mysteries impenetrable to a man who can at best glean a little information "by inquiry and perseverance" (VF 468). He wonders at the "meannesses" to which women are willing to submit to enter into the highest circles of society and adds that "the pursuit of fashion under difficulties would be a fine theme for any very great person who had the wit, the leisure, and the knowledge of the English language necessary for the compiling of such a history" (VF 469). The "difficulties" in this witty humblebrag (*Vanity Fair* is exactly the kind of history the narrator hints at) refer to the already mentioned "meannesses," the majority of which are both perpetrated and suffered by women. While the London society men are celebrating Becky, these same men's wives cut her and make sure she is never invited into their homes.

Becky's most critical spectators are other women, particularly the ones who also want to eat off golden plates. Our readerly admiration for Becky the protagonist contrasts with the envy and hostility she inspires in the female population of VF. While we enjoy seeing Becky rise, her rivals in VF naturally resent her success. It is of course not hard to guess why we as readers are in a better position to appreciate Becky than are her fictional counterparts. Becky is a direct threat to the women around her while we are spectators at a comfortable distance. However, the fact that we are safe from the threats posed by a fictional character does not explain why we *like* Becky and want her to succeed. We know she is a Siren and we know what lies beneath the waterline, yet we enjoy her victories and even appreciate the wit and cleverness with which she exacts revenge. "It is agreeable to sympathize with joy;" Smith writes, "and wherever envy does not oppose it, our heart abandons itself with satisfaction to the highest transports of that delightful sentiment" (TMS 96). Envy does not oppose our sympathy with Becky because we have no skin in the game – we are mere spectators, unaffected by a character's exploits in a work of fiction. Yet the joy Becky typically experiences is different from the "delightful sentiment" Smith has in mind. Becky's joy more often than not accompanies a victory over others, a successful act of revenge, or a spontaneous act of cruelty. According to Smith, revenge is "the excess of resentment" and "the most detestable of all the passions," "the object of the horror and indignation of every body" (TMS 362). So why are Becky's acts of revenge enjoyable to the reader of VF?

It appears that we enter into Becky's resentments as we enter into the more praiseworthy sentiments of the heroes of tragedy and romance mentioned in TMS. Perhaps our appreciation of Becky is related to our tendency to despise a defect in resentment, which is indicative of "too little spirit." Resentment, Smith explains, aims "not so much to make our enemy feel pain in his turn, as to make him conscious that he feels it upon account of his past conduct." We want to make our enemy "repent of that conduct" and make him understand "that the person whom he injured did not deserve to be treated in that manner" (TMS 137). Considering Becky's actions, we must conclude that she exemplifies the first but not the second part of Smith's description of resentment. She wants her enemy to feel pain and she wants him or her to know that they are feeling it on her account. But her goal is never repentance on the part of her enemy; rather, the pay off for Becky appears to lie primarily in the joy of having bested someone – usually by making them look ridiculous.

Our enjoyment of Becky's joy at the embarrassment of others is more than a simple case of Schadenfreude. As the case of the Lady Bareacres cited above shows, Becky rather has too much than too little spirit and we like her the better for it. Amelia, by contrast is uninteresting in large part because she has little to no spirit and rather resembles the picture of the simpering doll Dobbin carries around with him (VF 549). We share Becky's attitude toward Amelia, regarding her as she does with "a sort of contemptuous kindness" (VF 865). Amelia does not know how to look out for herself and is a passive victim of circumstance. She is always in need of rescuing and when she finally lets Becky convince her to marry Dobbin, the narrator bids her farewell, adding: "Grow green again, tender little parasite, round the rugged old oak to which you cling!" (VF 871) Amelia's passivity and lack of spirit are less innocent than they may at first appear (to us, the readers, as to men like Dobbin) and make her resemble a vine which needs the old oak to survive but is apt to smother it in time. Becky regards Amelia's parasitic nature with a mixture of scorn and condescension. There is much to pity but nothing to admire in Amelia and she evokes in us nothing like the esteem we have for Becky – even if that esteem is mixed with apprehension and even indignation at her ruthless ambition.

It has become clear that if we admire Becky, we do so not because we can "enter into" the sympathy she feels for, or evokes in, others. In some respects we may be more like Lord Steyne, the only person who appears to really "get" Becky and to both recognize her ambition and appreciate her (often cruel) wit. He is one of the few men smart enough to see through Becky's performance, but to enjoy it nonetheless (unlike Dobbin, who sees through Becky's act but fears rather than enjoys it). But Lord Steyne, too, is vain like all other men on Becky's long list of conquests. After Rawdon violently interrupts the romance between his wife and Steyne, the wealthy peer never allows Becky into his company again. Becky regrets not the loss of his affection and sympathy but the loss of her position in society. Our appreciation is not of the kind one might experience toward a fictional character who, we imagine, would be our friend if we were to encounter them in real life. A real-life Becky would likely just frighten us. But we can appreciate her on the page – not despite her ambition and resentment, but because of it. Becky's ambition is never heavy handed or surly and her resentment almost always has a cheerful quality to it. And, very importantly, she is not vain and hence not open to the ridicule invited by the other inhabitants of Vanity Fair. She is a deeply ambiguous role model and attractive to us because of her ambiguity. Driven by ambition, she is never "duped by integrity" the way a truly moral heroine would be. Becky has her own coherent set of principles and is consistent in her conduct. Her conscience is clear and perfectly aligned with her actions.

Boredom at the Top

We readily enter into Becky's joy but do not have opportunity to go along with her grief for the simple reason that Becky never seems to experience it. On the few occasions in VF when somebody feels genuine sorrow, the narrator steps back out of respect, like when Amelia mourns the loss of her son to the Osbornes. Vanity Fair is "not a happy place" by the narrator's own admission, and its inhabitants' unhappiness is largely the effect of hurt vanity and pride. Envy and resentment are common, especially among Becky's rivals, and keep people busy. Vanity drives industry, and so do the sentiments related to it. The toil and bustle characteristic of the struggle for rank and position may be mistaken for a means to an end (as they are by the poor man's son) but Becky comes to realize that she enjoys nothing more than the practice of her art to dominate and control.

Becky wants to perform and find ever-new stages to display her act, winning over new audiences and scoring victories with her craft. Dealing with Rawdon's creditors in London, Becky brings them "unanimously to accept her proposals," purchasing "with fifteen hundred pounds of ready money more than ten times that amount of debts." The narrator describes her negotiation prowess:

> Mrs. Crawley employed no lawyer in the transaction. The matter was so simple, to have or to leave, as she justly observed, that she made the lawyers of the creditors themselves do the business. And Mr. Lewis representing Mr. Davids, of Red Lion Square, and Mr. Moss acting for Mr. Manasseh of Cursitor Street (chief creditors of the Colonel's), complimented his lady upon the brilliant way in which she did business, and declared that there was no professional man who could beat her (VF 462-3).

When Sir Pitt later appoints Becky "general-in-chief" "to sell, barter, confiscate, or purchase furniture," she enjoys herself "not a little in an occupation which gave full scope to her taste and ingenuity" (VF 556). When she and Rawdon are in need of money, it is "Becky's habit to levy contributions on all her husband's friends: going to this one in tears with an account that there was an execution in the house; falling on her knees to that one and declaring that the whole family must go to gaol or commit suicide unless such and such a bill could be paid" (VF 556). Her ingenuity and play-acting allow her to throw "much-talked-of parties, which cost this lady very little more than the wax candles which lighted the walls" (VF 556). Of all the inhabitants of Vanity Fair she appears to have the most fun, relishing her ability to manipulate and control others with her skill as a consummate actress.

During the time of her biggest triumphs, Becky is "admitted to be among the 'best' people." But the narrator cautions us not to "envy poor Becky prematurely – glory like this is said to be fugitive." It is reported, the Manager of the Performance continues, that "even in the very inmost circles, they are no happier than the poor wanderers outside the zone; and Becky, who penetrated into the very centre of fashion and saw the great George IV face to face, has owned since that there too was Vanity" (VF 637). As Smith was quoted to observe in Chap. 5, tranquility is perhaps more easily obtained by those living a humble life. Rose Dawson, who married Sir Pitt and so became the second Lady Crawley, traded a quiet life of humble contentment with Peter Butt for "a coach and four" only to end up unhappy and as useless as an unplayed piano. As for Becky, her success during "this season of her life, when she moved among the very greatest circles of the London fashion" first "excited, elated, and then bored her." Though her "former acquaintances hated and envied her," Becky herself "was yawning in spirit." She tells Lord Steyne: "how much gayer it would be to wear spangles and trousers and dance before a booth at a fair" (VF 638). Now that she has won and gained the highest position in society, she is prone to ennui and boredom. She has fulfilled her ambition but finds that life without "bustle" and novelty is tedious. Her intelligence, skills and self-command have brought her here but now what? To simply continue to meet the same people in the same contexts talking about the same things is tedious to Becky. She is shocked to fall from grace and to lose her status but when the reader meets her again in Pumpernickel after several years of living in the "unnarrated depths," she appears quite as spirited and ambitious as she ever was.

Becky comes to realize that she loves her "art" more than anything: after Jos's death, Becky is wealthy but continues her "bustle:" "She busies herself in works of piety. She goes to church, and never without a footman. Her name is in all the Charity Lists. The destitute orange-girl, the neglected washerwoman, the distressed muffin-man find in her a fast and generous friend. She is always having stalls at Fancy Fairs for the benefit of these hapless beings" (VF 877). She is still performing, artfully crafting an image of herself that wins her admiration and respectability. Her past does not haunt her and she appears to have no regrets. She knows that satisfaction does not lie in achieving a static position but in self-aware and continuous performance. Becky enjoys operating what Smith calls the "operose machinery" of industry and society, exercising her power and mastery. Satisfaction does not come with the fulfillment of desire but lies in the toil and bustle on the way there. As the narrator of VF remarks on the final page: "Ah! Vanitas Vanitatum! which of us is happy in this world? Which of us has his desire? or, having it, is satisfied?" (VF 878).

The Advantages of Being an Unnatural Woman

Once Becky has made it to the top she neglects both her husband Rawdon Senior and her son Rawdon Junior. Lady Bareacres and other women in the aristocracy resent her success, but Lady Jane takes issue with Becky for other reasons as well. To be sure, Lady Jane is envious of her husband's admiration for Becky, but she also (and perhaps primarily) judges Becky for failing to be a good mother and wife. Becky is not interested in "being all things to all people" (Armstrong 1990). Lady Jane recognizes this, as did Amelia before her. Most women dislike Becky because she eclipses them with her art, but a few find fault with her for apparently less vain reasons: Becky does not love her husband and her child the way a woman should. This makes her appear monstrous and unnatural, a view confirmed by the suggestion at the close of *Vanity Fair* that Becky has slowly poisoned her husband Jos

Sedley to collect his life insurance. As readers we are made deeply uncomfortable by this husband murder, the final step Becky takes to better her condition. And yet her crime does not take away our appreciation for Becky.

Though the impartial spectator is not, for Smith, the highest tribunal before which we may appear, it is the most important one because it is (to a degree) under our control. Though our childhood circumstances are out of our control, we may in later life choose to strengthen the "man within" by exercising our self-command and habitually adopting a third person perspective on our actions and motives. A recurring issue throughout this book has been the partial perspective this imaginary third person tends to represent, in particular the nature of this partiality when the actor the spectator observes (and judges) is a woman. Even if we live among strangers, as Smith recommends, our spectators are likely to not only humble our self-love but also make us regard ourselves not in a "candid" but in a partial and biased light. Their biases and partiality may not be the same as ours, but they are not impartial either. The conduct literature of the late 18th and early 19th Century requires that women playact and perform – be a humbug, as the Manager of the Performance would have it. To succeed in any career, she must observe the "sacred" rules and be first and foremost a woman. But a good woman, again in the words of the narrator of VF, is a hypocrite and a manager. She must be sympathetic and, on Smith's account, possess the virtue of humanity, and she must show these traits in her love for her husband and children especially. But can she be trusted in her displays of affection? If she is a good actress, and we have come to suspect that a successful woman must be, then we will never know; or not until it is too late – as the victims of Becky's success find out.

Society holds up a mirror and reflects an image of the person looking into it but this image is warped, or colored, or blemished according to the prevailing rules. These rules and terms are not impartial (what rules or terms could be?) but pass for common sense nonetheless. They may even pass for moral standards, as clearly Smith regards the rules for proper masculine and feminine behavior to be no mere habits. The highest moral standards are exemplified by the impartial spectator, the manly man within the breast and highest arbiter of our conduct while we are among the living. Becky Sharp is dangerous because she combines some of the traits (self-command, courage) this entity most values with high self-esteem and the ability to dissimulate. They are the fictional examples of what happens when a woman who likes to win defines success on her own terms.

As discussed, our admiration for the great is based in part on the common human desire to contribute to the near perfect "system of happiness" we imagine the great are building for themselves. We sympathize with this happiness, wish to emulate it, and our imagination allows us to "change places in fancy" with the rich, famous, and powerful. But we also admire Becky Sharp, be it perhaps in a guarded way because we are aware of the moral complications and ambiguities (to say the least) of her actions. More importantly, as readers of fiction we have the chance to learn about Becky's intentions. Because we know what drives her, we are aware not only of her ambition but also of her hypocrisy and humbuggery. She shows us the darker side of ambition and self-command yet this makes the "system of happiness" she is building for herself more, not less attractive to us. Safe from the threats of a fictional character, we both root for Becky's particular brand of success and cannot help but imagine how we might emulate her ambitious ways. Success is of course mere vanity. But as the Manager of the Performance remarks, comparing the transitory nature of vanity to the temporary pleasure of roast-beef: "It is all vanity to be sure: but who will not own to liking a little of it?" (VF 634)

References

Armstrong, Nancy. 1990. *Desire and domestic fiction: A political history of the novel*. Cary: Oxford University Press.

Smith, Adam. 1981. An inquiry into the nature and causes of the wealth of nations. In *Vol. 2 of the Glasgow Edition of the Works and Correspondence of Adam Smith*, ed. R.H. Campbell and A.S. Skinner. Indianapolis: Liberty Fund.

———. 1982a. The theory of moral sentiments. In *Vol. 1 of the Glasgow Edition of the Works and Correspondence of Adam Smith*, ed. D.D. Raphael and A.L. Macfie. Indianapolis: Liberty Fund.

———. 1982b. Lectures on Jurisprudence. In *Vol. 5 of the Glasgow Edition of the Works and Correspondence of Adam Smith*, ed. R.L. Meek, D.D. Raphael, and P.G. Stein. Indianapolis: Liberty Fund.

Thackeray, William Makepeace. 1983. *Vanity Fair: A novel without a hero*, ed. John Sutherland. New York: Oxford UP.

The manufacturer's authorised representative in the EU is Springer Nature Customer Service Centre GmbH, Europaplatz 3, 69115 Heidelberg, Germany. If you have any concerns regarding our products, please contact ProductSafety@springernature.com

Printed and bound by CPI Group (UK) Ltd, Croydon, CR0 4YY
30/09/2026
02225234-0003